£ 8·95

# FIRST ASSEMBLIES

Rowland Purton
and
Caroline Storey

# FIRST
# ASSEMBLIES

Basil Blackwell

Reprinted 1981, 1982, 1983, 1986, 1987, 1989

ISBN 0 631 15168 0

British Library Cataloguing in Publication Data

Purton, Rowland
    First assemblies.
    1. Schools – Exercises and recreations
    I. Title   II. Storey, Caroline
    377'.1   LB3015

Photoset in VIP Times by
Belmont Press, Northampton
Reproduced from copy supplied,
printed and bound in Great Britain

# Contents

# Introduction

FIRST ASSEMBLIES is not a book of assemblies: it is a book of resources which can be used in various ways to make a large number of assemblies tailored to meet the individual requirements of the school. The authors, both of whom have many years' experience in preparing and taking school assemblies, recognize the importance of assemblies which arise out of the children's everyday activities. These will clearly differ from year to year and from school to school. It is also anticipated that the material offered here will not be used in isolation but will be supplemented by other stories, poems, songs and contributions by the children themselves, to make lively and meaningful, rather than stereotyped, assemblies.

With this in mind, the book has been planned particularly to meet the needs of those with responsibility for assembly in Infant or First Schools or with lower juniors, though, with a little adaptation much of the material could be useful throughout the Junior School. Its value will be recognized by those with responsibility for children's worship out of school too.

The comprehensive indexing of subjects and prayers add to the general usefulness of the book, which can prove a very useful addition to the staff reference library.

The themes which have been chosen are those which are very close to the hearts and needs of young children. Most of the sections include eight 'stories' to which Head Teachers may like to add others of their own choosing that are of particular relevance to their schools. A lot of supplementary material can also be found in DAY BY DAY and ASSEMBLIES, both by Rowland Purton (*Blackwell*). Whilst intended mainly for older children, many of the stories in these books are easily adaptable.

This book has been written with the multi-racial, multi-cultural community in mind. Whilst many of the themes are obviously of a very general nature, there are some in which it has been possible to include stories and activities which involve children of parents from overseas. It may be that the names of some of these will need to be changed to make them relevant to the children for whom the assemblies are being planned. Some aspects of the food, festivals, customs and culture of ethnic minority groups have been included.

It is the experience of the authors that a good selection of prayers is always welcome. Each general theme has twelve prayers, most of them especially written for this book. They are printed together after the stories so that the most appropriate can be chosen for use.

There is at least one which links directly with each story within the theme.

In addition there is a prayer supplement (pages 347–60), containing prayers for the opening and closing of assembly if desired and others for special occasions.

Hymns are also suggested for use with each theme. Some are related specifically to the theme: others are of a more general nature. In some instances one verse only may be particularly appropriate. These hymns have been collated from a number of hymn books commonly used by infant and lower junior children or as source books by their teachers. The books in which they may be found are indicated in the reference list on pages 361–6.

A few Bible readings have been included in many of the themes. It is not suggested that these should be read to the children but they could supplement the stories.

The Interest Work and Activity section at the end of each theme is of a very general nature and intended to give a few ideas to augment those which undoubtedly the teachers will already have. Although this section is printed after the stories, it is not envisaged that the activities would come after the assemblies. In fact the opposite is more likely to be the case, with the children having embarked upon some, at least, of the activities before the subjects arise in assemblies. Many of the most meaningful assemblies are those which arise out of the children's activities and in which they are able to make their own special contributions.

It is important that the assembly should be well planned and devised so that it becomes much more than a daily duty or get-together and has its own special atmosphere. Music and flowers will help to ensure that the assembly is an activity associated with, yet a little different from, the ordinary work of the day. It goes without saying that much thought and care is needed if it is also to become a special offering of the day to God.

CAROLINE STOREY
ROWLAND PURTON

# Acknowledgements

The authors and publisher would like to thank those who have given permission to reproduce copyright material.

The verse on page 3 is from Hymn No. 17 from *The Morning Cockerel* by Rose and Cook, Granada Publishing Ltd.

The quotations on page 137 are from the *Good News Bible—New Testament* © American Bible Society 1966, 1971, 1976; published by the Bible Societies/Collins.

In addition to actual quotations, reference has been made to many source books and this is readily acknowledged. Some of the stories have been used by the authors for many years and the original sources are not remembered. Should any copyright have been unwittingly infringed, the authors extend their sincere apologies and, if notified, will gladly correct any such omission in future editions.

The authors also wish to express their appreciation to Mrs. Sylvia Purton for much practical assistance in the preparation of the book.

# Everyday themes

*The themes chosen are concerned with people and things which form a part of the children's everyday experience. We begin with those which are at the very centre of the children's lives—home, family, friends and school, moving on to daily living, attitudes, activities and those vital necessities, food and drink.*

*People play an important role in the children's lives. Some of these feature in the earlier themes but there are sections dealing specifically with people who help and those who care. Through these sections we may be able to show how much we depend upon other people. The themes on the natural world are an obvious sequel. The animal and plant themes touch on the familiar, but also introduce the important aspects of interdependence, caring and responsibility.*

*Seasonal themes are important, since they draw so naturally upon everyday experiences and observation. Autumn, winter, spring and summer are followed by the festivals of harvest, Christmas and Easter.*

# 1 Home

*At half past three we go home to tea,*
*Or maybe a quarter to four;*
*And ten pairs of feet go running up the street*
*And in at their own front door:*
*And it's rough and tumble, rattle and noise,*
*Mothers and fathers, girls and boys;*
*Baby in the carry-cot, cat by the stove;*
*A little bit of quarrelling, A lot of love.*

*This would conjure up a picture of the normal happy home of most children—plenty of bustle, business and noise. It isn't always like that. Children need to have times when they can be quiet to read, play with toys or watch television; times to talk to parents and brothers and sisters; and times to play with pets—feeding, cleaning and caring for them.*

*Home means many things. It is a place to head for at the end of the day to be among familiar things with people known and loved. Home is the place where everyone knows all about us, the good things and the naughtiness, and yet still loves us. Outside the home a different kind of face has to be maintained. Children may find this difficult but at home can really be themselves, feeling able to give way to frustrations, temper and anger—and at times being loving too.*

*The home is the very centre of a child's life, so important that even in adulthood the childhood home is remembered because it set a pattern to be followed. Yet because home is there waiting for the family with love and caring, it is easily taken for granted.*

*In this section an attempt is made to bring the children close to the particular facets of home life which play an important part in their lives. We would like to help them to understand and appreciate all that is needed to create the right kind of home, to remind them to be aware of their blessings and to say 'Thank you.'*

## 1 MY ROOM

*My* room. That really means something special. Of course, it may be that we do not exactly have a room all to ourselves, we may share with a brother or sister, but it is still our *own* room. This is where we

3

may feel independent of our family. Here we keep our personal belongings, our clothes, our 'treasures'. Probably mother and father allow us to put up pictures—perhaps the pictures we paint at school, or posters—all kinds of things which may not mean much to anyone else, but are things we like.

This is where we may take our friends to play, where older ones amongst us may play records or cassettes, talk to friends, share books and toys. Perhaps it is the quiet place where we can draw or read or work quietly without interruption.

Your room can show the kind of person you are. If you are untidy your room is likely to be untidy. If you like things to be neat and tidy your room will be tidy with everything in its place, because you will make sure it is kept this way. However small we may be we can all take a pride in our rooms and share in keeping them pleasant places; putting things away, and keeping books and pictures carefully, preventing them from getting torn and tattered; taking care not to cause damage.

I wonder if any of you have your name-plate on the door? Some people do. Whether it is named or not, it is *your* room. Be grateful and show how happy you are by taking care of it.

## 2 MY BED

Where is the place you most like to be when you are tired, or cold, or unhappy? I'm sure you will immediately think of your bed—warm, cosy, just the right place to snuggle down at the end of a busy day, put your head on the pillow and sleep. Bed is especially nice, I think you will agree, when the sheets are all fresh and clean and smooth.

Can you remember a time when you were not feeling very well? You felt hot, aching and very uncomfortable. Then mother came along and re-made the bed, smoothing the sheets and shaking the pillows. Soon you were able to slide back again into a bed all smooth and comfy.

Bed is a special place. It is where we rest and sleep, or stay when we are unwell. But it is also somewhere to be quiet and think about all kinds of things without having to tell anyone else, or where we remember happy, exciting times and picture them all over again. It is a place where we can cry when we feel unhappy, and don't want anyone else to know!

We remember all kinds of bed we have slept in. On holiday, it may have been a strange bed in a strange house, a camp bed, or a sleeping-bag on the ground. Perhaps at grandma's, the bed was high and soft and old—maybe mummy's or daddy's bed when they were small. It is exciting to go away from home and sleep in strange beds, but how lovely to come back to your own bed in your own room, safe and secure again.

Some children do not have beds as we have. In many parts of the world children have no comfortable place to sleep. Even in our own country, about 100 years ago, Dr. Barnardo was shocked to find children curling up in barrels and gutters to sleep out in the cold. He was able to help some of them and care for them.

Remember to be glad for your home and especially your bed. You could show how glad you are by helping to make your bed and so help mother.

## 3 MY TOYS

Think about your toys at home—all kinds of toys, large, small, some costing a lot of money, some not so expensive. Sometimes we find that the toys we like best are those we have made or helped to make ourselves. We all have favourite toys which are used far more than others.

As birthdays and Christmas draw near, children begin to think of the kind of presents they would like and almost always think of toys. Perhaps something seen in a shop window or on television has caught our interest and we feel that is just what we want. I wonder what your favourite toy is? Think about it. Why is it the favourite? Was it given to you by someone special? Did father or mother or auntie make it for you? Or did you make it yourself?

When we are very small, people give us soft, cuddly toys, the kind that babies and very small children like to hug and take to bed with them. Quite often these are the toys that are kept the longest, and are the most tattered and worn out.

Do you know, there are grown up people who still have their specially favourite toys from when they were very little? Dolls and teddies are the toys that seem to be most cherished, and loved and cared for. Even quite big children, when staying away from home, will take their own old favourites with them, usually a soft warm and cuddly toy, to help them feel they have not left *everything* behind at home. It is like taking a little part of home with them. When little children first start school, they often like to take a toy along with them, to help them through the rather frightening time of being separated from home and mother. Their toys are a comfort to them. Our toys are like friends to us. They are very important. Be happy to share your toys with others, and show you care for them by taking care of them. And remember again those important words . . . 'Thank you.'

### 4   HOME—MADE BY PARENTS

Before we were born our parents began to make a home. At first, there were just the two and they prepared a home for themselves. It may have been quite small, just big enough for two people and they probably worked hard and spent a lot of time thinking about the kind of home they would like, the colour of walls, the curtains and carpets. What else would they put into their home? Chairs, table, beds, blankets, towels, sheets?

Then, when we came into the family, our parents had to think of more things to provide—things *we* would need. They would need room for us to eat, and sleep and play. When children come into a home, good parents think of them first, and make sure the home is safe and warm and a happy place.

As the family grows, mother and father need to find a larger house or flat and provide more furniture to go into it. Some of the nicest parts of our home are the things our parents, our father or mother or other members of the family have made, perhaps the places to put our books and toys.

Just think what it would be like if everyone had exactly the same kind of home, exactly the same furniture, curtains, pictures, ornaments. How dull it would be! There would be no fun in making a home that was especially ours. Our parents put into the home the kind of things *they* like, choosing carefully, choosing together. All kinds of presents, too, help to make our home our own especial place. In school we may be able to make small articles to take home to be used. At Christmastime we make special presents that can be displayed in the home. Older brothers and sisters add their gifts and make it a place created by everyone. The best kind of home is that created by parents who love us and care in a very special way.

## 5  HOME—A PLACE TO SHARE

Do you ever wish you could have a home all to yourself, so that you could do just as you like and when you like? No one to tell you to clear the table, put away your toys, wipe your shoes, take your feet off the furniture, be quiet, eat up your dinner? Then, of course, there would be no one to cook the dinner, clean the house, wash up after a meal, wash the clothes. There would be no one to tell us a story, tuck us up in bed and give a good-night kiss or look after us when we feel unwell, sad or worried.

We are glad that we share our home with our family. It is good to share, to learn to give-and-take and be thoughtful for others. Think of the fun we can have through being with a family and sharing the home, sharing happy times and sad times, helping each other when help is needed. There is great happiness to be found in doing things together for the home and for everyone in it, helping with shopping, helping in the garden, helping wash the car.

Some families share with other members of the wider family, with grandparents, aunts and uncles, who have made their home with the family. Grandparents can be good fun to share a home with. They may have more time to talk and play with us. They can tell us wonderful stories about days gone by, and about our parents when they were children. Sometimes they may find us rather noisy and we need to remember that they get a little tired. But if grandparents also remember that children like to be active and sometimes make a noise, then the family can be very happy together.

With other members of the family sharing the home there are more adults to learn from and talk to, to tell of our ideas, our hopes and our fears.

In some countries in the world it is the custom for all the family to live with the grandparents as one large family. It is not so here in Britain, but sometimes it is necessary and then we have the chance to learn how to care for each other in yet another special way.

6 ALL SORTS OF HOMES

The kind of home we have depends partly upon where we live. In large towns and cities there is not much room for building homes, so many people live in flats or maisonettes. Others live in houses built in rows with back yards or gardens joining on to those of houses in the next street or road.

In country villages or small towns people may live in small houses or in larger houses or on farms, but there is more space, with gardens and fields in which to play.

Children in the cities have to learn to live close to other people and it is sometimes difficult to play without disturbing other families. Usually there are parks and playgrounds where children can run and jump and shout and have fun with their friends. Homes in the cities and large towns are often close to busy roads with large lorries, buses, and endless lines of cars always filling the roads, so that extra care has to be taken when outside the home. Town children may lack the open space and the trees and fields of the country, but they can find many different interests. Zoos, parks, play spaces and museums all help to provide interests.

City children often envy those living in the country. Country children can see animals and birds close at hand, enjoy the green fields, climb trees or look into the ponds for all kinds of creatures. They can watch the changing scenes throughout the year, help in gardens and on farms and feel the wonderful freedom of space all around them.

Some children have no family home. Through some misfortune they have to live in a home specially provided for children lacking the closeness of a family. Perhaps parents are ill or unable to care for them. These children have a different kind of home. They share, perhaps with a larger group than the usual family, but usually there are people who really care for them and try to provide the kind of home their own parents would give them.

Wherever our home may be, in town or country; in a flat, a house, a caravan—it is a home where we are part of a loving and caring group. However much we may think we would like our home to be elsewhere or different, we know our real home is where our mother and father and family are, and that is where we want to be.

## 7   ANIMAL HOMES

Human parents work to prepare homes for their children. Animal parents, too, know when it is time to make a home for their families. Have you seen a bird's nest close to? Did you notice how very carefully it was made?

Before the baby birds are hatched, before the eggs are laid, mother and father bird are busy preparing the home. They collect twigs, grasses, feathers, tiny pieces of wool and material, anything they think would help make a home warm, dry and safe. Back and forth they go, carrying their findings in their beaks. When it is firmly made and the inside made smooth, the eggs are laid.

Rabbits make their homes under the ground with lots of tunnels leading down from the surface of the ground. Animal parents work hard and busily to make their homes in trees, in hedges, in the banks of rivers and streams. They make sure the place they choose is safe, protected from the cold winds and from other animals that would harm them.

Even our own pets, our cats and dogs prepare a place for their young if they know they will soon have babies of their own. How do you think they know what to do, where to look for a home, how to build and prepare for their young? Isn't it wonderful that God has made sure that all His creatures know about these things and know what is best for their families, especially their young. He has ensured that they know where to look for a suitable place and exactly how to prepare and build.

It gives us a safe and happy feeling to know that God cares for *all* his creatures, and for us, in this world that he has made for us.

## 8   OTHER PEOPLE'S HOMES

We have been thinking a lot about our own homes and the homes of people and animals we know and understand. Let us now think about people who live far away from our own country, because they, too, have families and homes as we have. Because they live in different kinds of places with different climates, their homes cannot all be just like ours.

In hot countries they will not need the same kind of protection as we need in our houses. Children living in warm climates are able to spend more time out of doors; they don't need fires and heating in their homes. Many of them see the meal being cooked on an open fire out of doors and they sit on the floor to eat their dinner. This is sometimes served in a big dish and is eaten with their hands. Bed is sometimes a bed roll—a long roll of material which is rolled up during the day and put down at night to make a bed.

In very cold climates, of course, much more protection is needed. Homes have stout walls and fires or other heating to protect against the cold winds and the snow.

In other parts of Europe, in Spain, Italy, Germany, Holland, people live in houses built as ours are, in towns, cities, and in the country. It is very sad that many children in poorer parts of the world have no real home as we have. Many children, due to wars, famine, and other hardships, have no family home as we know it. They sleep where they can, and eat whatever food they can find.

It is most important that we remember children in such places and try to help in some way to make life much happier and more comfortable for them. As we grow up with our homes and families around us, with people caring for us and showing us how to provide homes for our children, we need to think more and more of people in other parts of the world. There should be sufficient in the world for everyone to be able to enjoy a home and its protection. We must make sure that everyone knows this and tries to arrange for the good things of the world to be shared.


RELATED THEMES

*How pleasant, after work and play*
*To head for home and those I love;*
*And, when I reach the end of day,*
*To thank my God in heaven above.*                    R.P.

PRAYERS

1. As we remember the comfort of our own homes, we think of those people in many parts of the world who have no home. Bless them and help them we pray. *Amen*

2. Dear God, you know each one of us; you know all about us; and you love us every one. May we be loving too. *Amen*

3. For health and strength; for food and clothes; and for all the good things that are ours today; we thank you, Lord. *Amen*

4. God bless our homes and our families today and always. Show us how to be helpful in our homes and kind towards all the members of our families. *Amen*

5. O God, when I go home at night I go to my own home, to my special room and my comfortable bed. I have lots of things that are mine and I have people to love me. Thank you for all these things. *Amen*

6. Thank you, Father, for all the joys of our homes.
For all that our homes mean to us,
          *We thank you, Father;*
For a comfortable place to live,
          *We thank you, Father;*
For parents and family to help us,
          *We thank you, Father;*
For good food and plenty of it,
          *We thank you, Father;*
For books and toys and games,
          *We thank you, Father;*
For our special room,
          *We thank you, Father;*
Keep us thankful for all we enjoy. *Amen*

7. Thank you, God, for all the love and care which our parents have put into our homes to make them the kind of place where we can enjoy love and care. Help us to live in such a way that we will help to keep our homes happy. *Amen*

11

8. Thank you, God, for our homes
   For the comfort and warmth that we find there;
   For the love of our parents and our family;
   For all the things that we can call 'ours'.
   Help us to show how much we enjoy our homes by being kind
   and helpful. *Amen*

9. Thank you, God our Father, for all the people who share our
   home. We enjoy living with them but we know that we are not
   always as nice to them or as helpful as we ought to be. Teach us
   not to be selfish, bad-tempered or unpleasant in any way so that
   others will enjoy living with us. *Amen*

10. Thank you, God our Father, for those people who share our
    homes or who come to stay with us sometimes. May our homes
    always be places where friends and visitors can feel 'at home'.
    *Amen*

11. We know, dear God, that there are many kinds of home. Some
    people live in bungalows, houses, flats, tower blocks and even
    in palaces. If sometimes we wish that we lived in a bigger or
    better house, help us to be thankful for what we have and to try
    to make it the best and happiest home we can. *Amen*

12. We thank you, O God, for our own rooms at home, for our
    books and toys, and for all those things which we enjoy. Teach
    us how to share our special enjoyments with others. *Amen*

[*Perhaps the children can be encouraged to write their own simple
prayers about home and family for use in the morning assembly.*]

HYMNS SUGGESTED

A tiny little bird
At half past three
For all the things which we enjoy
God takes good care of me
I'm very glad of God
When Jesus was a little boy

# 1 HOME

INTEREST WORK AND ACTIVITIES

*Books*

Have available a few simple books about homes. A few suggested books are:

HOW WE LIVE (Picture book), Kestrel
HOME *(Young ideas)*, Macmillan
HOMES *(Starters)*, Macdonald
HOMES *(Leaders)*, Ladybird
THE STORY OF HOMES *(Blackwell's Learning Library)*, Blackwell
MY HOME/OUR HOUSE/ME *(Terraced House Books)*, Methuen
HOMES/PROTECTION *(Living and Growing)*, Macmillan
AT HOME/WHO LIVES HERE? *(Headstart)*, Burke
AT HOME WITH THE FAMILY *(Our World)*, Burke
SLEEP IS FOR EVERYONE *(Let's Read and Find Out)*, Black
BOBBI'S NEW YEAR (Sikh New Year Festival), Hamilton

*Other people's homes*

Find pictures of other people's homes. There are plenty to be found in newspapers and magazines. How are they different from the homes of the children? Comparisons with homes of children in other countries if pictures can be found. Discussion—What advantages do children have? Which do they prefer? How would they improve own home? Lead on to writing simple prayers of thanks for home blessings and for others less fortunate.

# 1 HOME

## Animals' Homes

Encourage children to look for and observe the homes of animals and birds. Country children may be aware of homes of animals in hedges, banks of rivers and streams, of rabbits in the fields, foxes and other mammals and to bring news of their findings. Keep diary notes, draw or paint pictures or tell of their findings so that teachers may make the notes.

Town children, if unable to observe animals in their natural surroundings, may be able to observe their own pets, or those of their friends, when kittens, puppies, rabbits, hamsters, etc., are born. There may be birds' nests in trees nearby or nesting boxes in gardens. Help children to be aware of the preparations made by mother animals to ensure their newly born have a suitable place.

Show how even domestic animals look for a suitable place—it may be one provided by humans, but sometimes is found and prepared by themselves.

## Simple craft activities

Construct a simple dolls' house—just a floor and four walls—from a large cardboard box. Cut out door; decorate walls; and paint in windows, fireplaces, etc. Make furniture from oddments—pieces of cardboard, matchboxes, cotton reels. Use scraps of material to make curtains and rugs. Small dolls may be made from pipe cleaners and dressed in scraps to represent mother, father and children.

A cradle, large enough to hold a doll, can be made from a shoe box or any other suitable box. The lid is placed upright and the base glued into it at the bottom. It may be painted or decorated, with material glued to cover the entire cradle. Covers can be made from pieces of material. In the same way a carry-cot can be made with handles of strong tape or string through two holes pierced in each long side of the box. Decorate in the same way as the cradle.

These toys could be used for play in the classroom where they are made, or could be passed on to the nursery class or reception classes.

Make something for the child's *own* home—a simple clay pot, painted and varnished; a woven paper mat; a picture or calendar; or some other small item to be presented to Mum or kept in own room.

# 1  HOME

*Visitors*

Invite mothers from various kinds of home and culture to come and talk to small groups about their homes. Mothers from other countries may like to tell of the kind of home people have in their native country. (If language permits—older children may sometimes act as interpreters.) Such mothers may be prevailed upon to show how to make special dishes of food or sweet-meats which are peculiar to their culture or country of origin, to bring in trinkets, embroidery, articles of clothing, and other things which give their own particular home its character.

*Visits*

Find out about residential homes for children, or homes for handicapped people—children and adults. If there is one close to the school, try and arrange a visit, but, if this is not possible, obtain information which can be adapted for the children to understand how people are able to make their homes in these situations—through the caring of others.

*Practical help*

In large cities there is a great deal of work being done to help the homeless. In the Third World there are many children who are homeless and obliged to beg in the streets—sleeping rough. Seek information about organizations which help these people and organize a practical way of helping.

A liaison between the school and a home or organization may be possible. Write notes and paint pictures to send. Fund-raising to help the work of the organizations also encourages feelings for the needs of others.

[A school in the East End of London was able to help a local Mission and to take an interest in the work being done among the homeless—the drop-outs of society. These men and women are fed by the mission and clothed. On occasions the children collected money to ensure that at Christmas time the homeless folk were able to have an extra treat. They also made up packets of sweets, nuts, and made Christmas cards, so that each visitor to the Mission received a small gift from the children of the school. It must be stressed that no contact was made by the children, but they were aware of the need and willingly helped in this small way.]

Tell stories of people who have helped to make homes for others, e.g. Dr. Barnardo (Children's Homes), George Muller (Children's Homes), Thomas Stephenson (National Children's Home), Arthur Pearson (St. Dunstan's for the blind), Leonard Cheshire (Homes for the incurable). These and others can be found in assembly books for older children—DAY BY DAY and ASSEMBLIES— Blackwell.

# 2 Family

*A small child's whole world is firstly home and family. With the widening of his experience—starting school, meeting people outside of the family—his world grows, the boundaries extend, but at the centre is the family. His earliest experience of life is bound up with the contact, the closeness of mother, the source of his being. Gradually father becomes a part of the world, then brothers, sisters, grandparents. The family unit is the greatest social arrangement providing a suitable environment for the developing child emotionally and socially. The security of family is very necessary to a child's well being.*

*Because the family is so much a part of the child's life, the inclusion of this may seem superfluous, but, just because it is an integral part of life, it is important that we encourage the child to take a look at those closest to him to help him appreciate how necessary and desirable it is to be part of a loving, caring unit, each member of that unit making his or her own special contribution.*

## 1 MOTHER

Caroline was painting a picture of her mother. Other children in the group were doing the same, they were making a kind of picture gallery of all the members of their families.

As Caroline painted, she thought about her mother—the colour of her hair, how it was soft and rather curly. She thought of her mother's eyes as she looked at Caroline, usually happy, twinkling as she smiled, sometimes a little sad, but always loving. She remembered her mother's hands as she did things for Caroline. Think about *your* mother and you will see her face, remember her voice, her smile and her eyes.

But that is just one side of mother, isn't it? She is much more than that. Right from the beginning of life, mother has always been there. In fact, even *before* you were born your mother was thinking about you, although she didn't know what you would look like. She was planning and taking care that you would be born healthy and strong, preparing a home for you.

When you were a tiny baby it was mother's hands that you were first conscious of—the hands that held you safely and securely. You

17

were dependent upon her for your food, for being washed and dressed. She was always very close. As you grow bigger and stronger and able to do things for yourself you still know that Mother is always ready to help. When hurt, or afraid, it is Mother we want most of all.

Mother is always interested in us and whatever we are doing, and she wants us to do well, to be healthy and happy.

Mother is really our first teacher. Long before we go to school she teaches us so many things. She plays with us, takes us shopping and visiting. Perhaps she teaches us to count, sings to us, shows us books, shows how to do up buttons or put on coats and gloves. Mother knows us very well, knows what we like and dislike, knows how good we can be, and how naughty—and still loves us.

How can you say thank you for all the many things Mother means to you? Think about this—it could be a different way for each one of us.

## 2 FATHER

Caroline began painting her picture of her father. She thought about him as she saw him. He was big and strong. He had strong arms, which picked her up and lifted her on to his shoulders. She remembered a time when she was so very tired and how glad she was that her father was able to carry her. She was very thankful for his strong arms. He was very clever. He could drive the car and repair it, too.

He had a very jolly laugh. She liked to hear her father laugh. He could use a firm voice, too, when he thought they were all getting too excited or out of hand. He was rather a special friend to her brothers as he could show them how to do things that boys liked doing—to play games and talk about football and fishing and cycles and cars, how to make models and use tools. Think about your own father. What are the things he does? Let us tell each other how our father helps us.

Father is the other person in the partnership that is the important centre of our family. He is the person we are next aware of as little babies, because he is usually there, with Mother. He works to provide a home for Mother and children. He is interested in seeing us grow up and learn many things.

A father is a very special person in a family. Sometimes he is called the head of a family. This is because he takes responsibility for us. He cares for us.

We talk about God as our Father because he cares for his whole family throughout the world.

### 3 BROTHERS AND SISTERS

It was the turn of brothers and sisters to be included in the family picture gallery and Caroline was thinking of her two brothers. Mostly she liked them and was glad they were in the family, but sometimes she wished they would go away! They seemed so big and noisy with their football and football boots, their cricket bats, their skates and cycles. And they were so particular about the things they were making, especially their models. They often wanted to watch different programmes on television. To them Caroline sometimes seemed too silly for words! When they wanted to play tricks on her and joke with her, she didn't seem to understand.

Of course, usually they were all quite happy in each other's company and there were all kinds of things they enjoyed doing together. They played games and helped in the garden and went out or on holiday as a family. They shared their home and their parents in their own special way, learning to understand and respect each other. Not everyone liked the same things or had the same way of doing them. Their family life helped them to understand that everyone is an individual.

Uncles and aunts came to visit and the children learned, as they grew older, that these same uncles and aunts were brothers and sisters of their mother and father. It seemed strange to think of them all living together as Caroline and the boys were now. Caroline began to understand that some day in the future she and her brothers would be grown up with their own families and probably visiting each other as the uncles and aunts were.

Caroline was glad that she had brothers and they were glad to have a sister to look after and protect if necessary.

It was such a good idea of God that we should live in families. Let us say thank you for families, and be glad we have them around us.

## 4 NEW BABY

One day when Caroline and her brothers came in from school, Mother looked as she did when there was something special about to happen. She looked specially nice and cosy and warm. Afterwards, as they were getting ready for bed, Mother said she had something special to tell them. They were going to have a new baby in the family! This meant there would be lots to do to prepare for the baby.

Mother began getting things ready for the baby as the time came nearer. She was making tiny baby clothes, and other members of the family and friends helped, too, knitting and sewing. They had to get a pram and a cot. What else would they have to get? [*Children's suggestions.*]

The time came when Mother went to hospital and stayed there. Father took some of his holiday so that he could stay at home and look after the home and the children. He came back from the hospital each day to tell them the news of the baby and their mother. It was a little girl, a sister for them all. Caroline was glad about that. Then came the great day when Father brought Mother and the new baby home from hospital. She was so very tiny, so helpless. 'Look at her tiny fingers and toes,' said Mother. They were, indeed, very tiny, with such weeny fingernails.

The baby made a big difference to the family. They loved her, of course, but sometimes she cried, and there were so many things Mother and Father had to do for her. Mother and Father explained that each of them as a baby had to have most of their parents' attention. The needs of the baby must come first in a family as she is so dependent on them. Each of the children had special jobs to do for the baby and this helped them to understand that she was *their* baby, and they had to look after her. So whenever they felt a little resentful at the attention the baby had from Mother and Father they remembered that she was theirs, too, and this helped.

Caroline was so thrilled that she told her teacher and friends all about her baby sister. Then the very next day, Rashida, her friend, came along to tell them that she, too, had a little new baby, a brother, who was to be called Abdul. Her parents were very happy with their new son. The children's mothers promised that when the babies were a little older they would bring them into school to show the children in the group. Rashida and Caroline each painted a picture of the new baby to put in their family picture gallery.

## 5 GRANDPARENTS

The picture gallery was growing. All the family was included—even the new baby. Now Caroline's grandparents were to be added. There were two sets of grandparents, so four people to think about, and how they looked. One set of Caroline's grandparents lived very near. These were her mother's parents, and she was able to see them quite often. Grandma came regularly to visit the family, sometimes with Grandpa. They were usually great fun; they had time to talk and play; and they told lovely stories about long ago when they were young. They told the children how times had changed and places had changed. To visit their home was even better, as they had so many interesting things to see and touch and hold. There were photographs of the family long ago and little presents mother had given them when a little girl.

Their other grandparents lived quite a long way away, and the visits were not as frequent, but they wrote letters, sent cards and sometimes spoke on the telephone. Both grandmothers and grandfathers were loved very much by the children. Grandmothers have a way of producing all kinds of goodies from bags; grandfathers produce them from pockets. 'You spoil them,' Mother would say, and then Gran or Grandad and the children would look at each other in the kind of way that made them feel conspirators.

Caroline's friend, Rashida, had her grandparents with her always. This was the way the family had lived in Bangladesh and they did so in this country. They lived as one big family, having their meals together and always being together. Other children in the group rarely saw their grandparents. Some of the children had come from Cyprus, some from Jamaica, Nigeria, Malaysia and other places too far away to visit. But how lovely it was to receive letters and what a great occasion if grandparents were able to come on a long visit! Then, all the family would go to the airport to meet and welcome them. Yes, grandparents are very special people in a family.

## 6 FAMILY AND ME

Looking at the pictures she had made—Mother, Father, brothers and sisters, grandparents—Caroline felt that there was something or someone missing. The family group was not complete—of

21

course, she herself was not there. How did one paint a picture of oneself?

She would like to show herself as being very pretty, and think herself always good, kind, obedient and of course very clever, but deep down in her heart she knew she wasn't always nice and there were some things she couldn't do very well. She was not as clever as some. Then she cheered up. She did try hard most days and she *knew* there were some things she could do fairly well. She had her own place in the family. We all have our own special place in the family, a place that could not be filled by anyone else. Each of us has our own personality and special contribution to make. Older members of the family may be more capable but as we grow and develop we shall learn to do things and take our share of responsibility in the family.

The important thing for us to remember is that, although each one is different, our parents love us all. It is also important to be ourselves in the best possible way, not try to be someone else: we can't because we are just ourselves. As our parents love us, every one, so God loves us, too.

All those children in the group, Caroline, Rashida, Winston and their friends, are each one a member of a family, different kinds of family. What a good idea of God to make sure we were born into families.

## 7  FAMILY FAR AWAY

Winston's parents had come from Jamaica. They often told Winston and his brothers and sisters about their home in that sunny island—how the sun shone and it was warm all the time. They came to this country to make their home and to make a future for themselves and their family. As Winston was born in England, he did not know what it was like in Jamaica, and he loved to hear his parents talk of their childhood. They promised the children that they would save hard so that one day they could all go for a holiday to see their grandparents and aunts and uncles they had never met. There were so many cousins too, all waiting for them to visit as soon as they could.

Meryem had come to England from the island of Cyprus with her parents, leaving her grandparents behind. She was just a baby when she came, so she did not remember very much about it, but she knew her parents were so happy to receive letters and cards from their families in Cyprus. They, too, were working hard to save for a visit.

Caroline's aunt, uncle and cousins lived far away, too. They had gone to live in Australia and they sent pictures of themselves living in a different kind of house with a huge garden. It seemed so strange to Caroline to hear that, in Australia, it was summer time at Christmas and winter time in June, almost as though the world was upside down, but as father explained, it was right across the other side of the world.

Rashida's family came from Bangladesh. She was a very tiny girl when they left their home in the country, travelled miles through the forests to the city, then to the airport where they had the excitement of seeing an aeroplane for the first time, and actually getting on one to travel to England. They were overwhelmed at everything they found in England and sometimes wished they were back with their family in Sylet.

Many families are separated and know they will not see each other for a long long time. It is good, then, to remember, that God watches over all our family, wherever they may be. The same God, looks after us all at the same time.


8 GOD'S FAMILY

As God showed us how to live in families and made it possible for us to be born into families, we can begin to understand that we are, in our families, just small parts of God's big family. This family is so large we cannot possibly know everyone in it—it spreads all over the world.

Just try to imagine all the millions of people in all parts of the world—people with brown skins, yellow, black or white. We look different on the outside, but inside we are all people made by God and part of his family.

Sometimes in families people get cross with each other and quarrel. They get envious and jealous and selfish, but with love and understanding they learn to forgive, to forget and to be friends again. In the large family of the world, people of different nations also quarrel sometimes. They, too, become envious, jealous and selfish. It becomes serious and unhappy when people of different nations become angry and do not trust each other.

It is not easy. We are all very different and we naturally like most the people who are like ourselves. Our best friends are usually the ones who like the same kind of things as we like. There are some people that we find it very hard to like because they are so different from ourselves.

Take a look at the person sitting on your left. Do you like him or her? And what about the one on the other side? If you do not like either of them it means that you need to try extra hard to do so. We have to spend a lot of time together in school.

The whole world family is made up of individual people, like Rashida, Meryem, Winston and Caroline, and like all those children near you now. If all children can learn to live happily together in the family of the school, they will help to make God's family a happy family. Just as in our own family, each one of us has to make sure that we care for all the others, not just ourselves.

RELATED THEMES

*My Mum, and Dad, and brother*
*All mean so much to me:*
*We live at home together—*
*A happy family.*

*We love and help each other . . .*
*It's what we like to do:*
*If only all God's children*
*Would love each other too!*                    R.P.

PRAYERS

1. Dear Father God, bless us and bless all your children everywhere. Help us to know that whether we are black or white,
   brown or yellow, we are all your great family. *Amen*

2. Dear Father God, you have made the world and all the people
   in it. Help us to love all your children. *Amen*

3. Dear God, please help me.
   I know that I am important to my parents;
   And I know that I am important to you.
   But please help me to know that I am not the
   only one:
   Other people are important too.
   Teach me not to be selfish . . . or big-headed . . .
   or unpleasant . . .
   But a helpful member of my family. *Amen*

4. For mothers and fathers, brothers and sisters, grandparents,
   aunts and uncles and all those people who make up our family
   we give you thanks, O God. *Amen*

5. God, our Father,
   We are your children,
   All the people in the world are your children,
   We are one big family,
   Help us to love one another. *Amen*

6. Help me to remember, O God, that I am part of
   a family. Teach me
   To be kind and helpful in all I do;
   To do what my parents would wish me to do;
   To remember that I cannot always please myself.
   Help me to love and care for all my family and
   be the kind of person that they can always love. *Amen*

7. Sometimes, God our Father, we are not very nice to our brothers and sisters or to other boys and girls and sometimes they are not very nice to us. Help us to be nice to one another because we know we are all your children. *Amen*

8. Thank you for fathers, O God. They are so big and strong and can do so many interesting things. It is very nice to know that Father is there when we need help and that we can always ask him to help us. We thank you, too, that you are our Father in heaven and that we can ask for your help too. Be with us and help us, we pray. *Amen*

9. Thank you, God, for Mummy. She looks after me in lots of ways. She cooks me some lovely food. She sees that I have clothes to wear. She keeps my room clean and makes my bed. She cares for me when I am not well. She takes me to lots of different places. I am so pleased that she is 'My Mum'. Thank you, God. *Amen*

10. Thank you, God, for parents who look after us;
Thank you for brothers and sisters to play with;
Thank you for others who live with us;
Thank you for Grandma and Grandpa who visit us;
Thank you for aunts, uncles and cousins,
Thank you for our whole family, which means
so much to us. *Amen*

11. Today, Dear God, we want to say thank you for babies. They are so small and helpless and we like to help to look after them. We say thank you especially for any that belong to our family. Help us to be kind to them always. *Amen*

12. We often think, O God, about people in our family who live a long way away. We cannot see them as often as we would like so we ask that you will look after them until we can see them again. *Amen*

*Use any prayers about families that have been written by the children*

HYMNS SUGGESTED

A little child may know
A tiny little bird
Father, now we thank thee
Father, we thank you
For the beauty of the earth
Jesus was born in Bethlehem
Mummy does the shopping
Thank you
Think of a world

FAMILIES IN THE BIBLE

| | |
|---|---|
| Abram and Lot | Genesis 13; 1–13 |
| Joseph and his brothers | Genesis 37; 1–11 |
| The Prodigal Son | Luke 15; 11–32 |
| Obedience to parents | Ephesians 6; 1–4 |

INTEREST WORK AND ACTIVITIES

*Books*

There are lots of simple books about families and relations. Some
are picture books with but a caption or a few lines to read. Others
give more information that the children may find helpful when
thinking about families. The books suggested here deal mainly with
human families but no doubt others can be put in the book corner
which inform about animal and bird families too.

ME/MY MUM/MY DAD/MY AUNTIE/THE NEW BABY
   *(Terraced House Books)*, Methuen
BIG SISTER, LITTLE BROTHER/A NEW BABY *(Feelings)*,
   Macdonald
BABIES/GROWING UP *(Living and Growing)*, Macmillan
AT HOME WITH THE FAMILY *(Our World)*, Burke
ONE OF THE FAMILY/THE LOVING FATHER/JOSEPH
   AND HIS BROTHERS *(Little Lions)*, Lion

WHO MADE MOTHERS AND FATHERS *(Lion Board Books)*, Lion
MY NEW SISTER, Black
A BABY IN THE FAMILY, Dinosaur
LET'S FIND OUT ABOUT BABIES *(Let's find out)*, Watts
NEWS FOR DAD (A Sikh family), Hamilton

*News*

Ask children to bring news of their families. This will no doubt arise incidentally in the children's news time as it is a topic close to the children's hearts and everyday experience.

Encourage children to bring in news of members of the family far away. Such news could be enlarged upon by teacher.

*Family album*

Perhaps children could bring in photographs of members of the family or group photographs. If these are to be handled ensure that they are suitably protected, e.g. in plastic envelopes or folders, so that they can be returned in good condition. Wedding photographs often include a wide coverage of the family.

*New baby*

A new baby is always a centre of interest to young and old alike. Mother of a new baby might be persuaded to come to school to show baby to the children and perhaps say something about the baby as regards feeding, caring and any differences baby makes to family life.

*Family portraits (Art)*

Make a picture gallery of members of the family as described in the stories. Children may like to have their own family folder to contain these and any other materials about their families.

*Animal families*

The general topic could be extended to include animal families. This may be particularly relevant if there are pets in school which are reproducing. Children may also have pets at home which could be observed.

Note any preparations made by the mother, e.g. building a nest or gathering materials in the bed space.

Observe any young that may be produced. How are they different from the parents? How do parents care for them? Keep a diary of their development. How do baby animals resemble human babies in terms of development, attention of parents, etc?

*Mothers' Day/Fathers' Day*

Make suitable cards, greetings or small gifts which can be taken home on these or other 'family' occasions.

*Happy families*

Older children might like to make their own version of the game, using imaginary families which they invent for themselves. They can make their own cards, drawing and colouring the pictures. If each child makes one family there will be enough cards to play the game.

*Families around the world*

Collect pictures of families from other lands, especially any with children. Display so that children can see similarities and differences.

*Stories about families*

Whilst working on this assembly theme use 'family' stories in the normal story-time.

## 2  FAMILY

*God's Family*

Learn a new hymn or song about God's family, the family of man throughout the world. In what sense are people all one family when we all look so different? What does this tell us about how we should think of others and behave towards others. We are all brothers and sisters, children of God.

Extend the thought to the world of nature. St. Francis referred to the animals and birds as 'little brothers and sisters'.

*All things which live below the sky,*
  *Or move within the sea,*
*Are creatures of the Lord most high,*
  *And brothers unto me.*                    *Edward J. Brailsford*

# 3   Friends

From the world of Home and Family a child extends his world to that
including friends and neighbours. People living close by, people in
the shops, the tradesmen who may come to the house, all help to make
up his world.

The most significant group is that made up of personal friends.
This first experience of social contact with others independent of
parents is a big step in the child's life. At school, without the props of
home, learning to be part of a community with most members in his
own age group, the child is taking his first steps in forming personal
relationships.

Starting school is the first big break away from home and has to be
faced largely alone. So friends become very important. In this
situation he is again learning to give-and-take, this time outside the
family and home. He learns to share with others, to make allowances
for others and to live in the world as seen in the immediate community
outside the home.

The two additional stories in this theme extend the scope if desired.


## 1   FRIENDS AT HOME

Jason first became aware of children able to play with him when he
was taken by his mother to the Infant Welfare Clinic and there he
saw other children with their mothers. As he grew old enough to
notice others he realized that there were people apart from his
mother and father and grans and grandads. There were people in
the shops, the butcher and the lady at the supermarket. The
milkman came to the house and usually had a smile and something
to say to Jason.

One day he was very interested to see some men busy making a
hole in the pavement outside his home and he asked his mother if he
could stay out and watch them. 'As long as you stay close to the wall
and don't go near the road,' she said. Jason really felt he had made
friends for the few days the men worked there. He watched them
work and when they stopped to drink a cup of tea he sat with them
and talked to them. He felt very grown up.

He made friends with other children nearby. Friends of his
parents came to call with children of their own. One of these,

George, became a great friend of Jason. They spent a lot of time together, visiting each other's homes and playing in the park. Some of these friends went to the same school as Jason and he could see them there, too, but others attended other schools. When they met they were able to talk about their schools and what they were doing in school.

Why do we like to have some people as our friends? Usually, it is because they are of the same age as ourselves, like the same kind of things and have the same interests. Friends are important to us – we are so made that we need the company of others. It is important to *be* a good friend as well as to *have* friends, and we have to learn to be loyal to our friends. This is one of the good characteristics that God has put into each one of us, that we may be better people.

2 FRIENDS AT SCHOOL

Do you remember when you first started school? Perhaps it was so long ago you have forgotten, or perhaps you were first in a Nursery class, or a Nursery school or a play group before going to school and so had already made friends.

Jason remembered his first day at school—it was the first time his mother had left him with other people for very long. His mother went with him and settled him into school but after a while she left and he was alone. He was not really alone with so many other children around, but until then mother had always been within calling distance, to come if he needed her.

He was so busy, doing so many things for a time that he didn't miss her, but as the morning went on he felt he wanted to talk to her and make sure she was near, and he felt a little unhappy.

This feeling passed after a while, because he found that there were grown-ups in the school taking care of him and there were so many other children near and so much to see and do. What a lot he would have to tell mother and father when he was home again! As he grew older, Jason thought how nice it was to have so many friends here at school. Most of them he only saw at school as they didn't live near him. They had so much to tell each other, and things to show each other every day. They were invited to each other's homes to play and to parties.

---

In school it was possible to play and work with a larger number of friends and to learn to do exciting things in a group. He learned to be a member of a team, playing in games. Among all these friends he found that there were one or two who became special friends, and he was happy in their company.

Most people are like Jason. We have a lot of friends in school and one or two or three special friends. Try to be a good friend, to be close at hand when your friends need you. There is so much you can give to each other, just by being loyal friends.

### 3 MAKING FRIENDS

Noorul was excited, but a little anxious. Today he was going to school. He had been to school before—in Bangladesh—but this would be different. He felt cold and shivery. In Bangladesh it was warm and sunny and he did not have to wear all these clothes to keep warm. He had come to Britain just a few weeks ago, with his parents and brothers and sisters, and his grandparents. They travelled to the city from their home and then on a 'plane which had brought them all the way to Britain.

It was all so strange: so many people with white faces speaking in a strange language. Now he was to go to school and he wondered how he would like it. His father took him to the school, where he was taken to a large room and met his teacher. It was a lady: the teacher in Bangladesh was a man. There were children everywhere, not in rows, as in his other school: they were moving about the room, all very busy. Most of them stopped what they were doing to look at Noorul and he moved closer to his father.

Then came the time when his father was to leave. The teacher was talking to other children in the class. Noorul could not understand what was being said, but a cheerful looking boy came forward and grinned at him, and made him understand that he was to follow. Noorul was taken to a lobby, where coats were hanging on pegs, and was shown where to put his jacket.

Back in the classroom the teacher settled him on a chair at a table with some pictures and some soft stuff he later learned was plasticine. Jason, his new ·friend, stayed with him. It was all very confusing to Noorul. He went through the morning as though in a dream. So many things to do and try to remember! A big yard with children running and playing, but always close at hand was Jason, helping, smiling, and being kind.

Noorul suddenly looked all around – at his teacher, at all the other children, then at Jason and smiled. He had made a friend.

## 4 BEING A FRIEND

Jason liked school. He had no brothers and sisters and so he enjoyed being with other children in school. Sometimes if the work seemed difficult or rather boring he wished he could be at home or playing out with his friends, but mostly he was very happy. His classroom was bright with pictures and some work displayed. There were Interest and Nature tables, which always had something of interest to look at and touch and hold. Jason had many friends, and one or two special friends so there was always someone to share in work and play.

One day a new boy came to the class. He was with his father. He had dark skin and dark eyes and he looked a little frightened. When he saw the children all looking at him he drew closer to his father as though that made him feel safe. Their teacher spoke to the father for a while and then he said good-bye and went off.

Their teacher introduced the boy 'This is Noorul,' she said. 'He has come from Bangladesh and is to be in our group. He doesn't know or understand English. Who will look after him this morning?'

Jason didn't hesitate, he liked to have friends. 'I'll look after him.'

'Thank you,' said Miss Andrews. 'Show him where to put his coat and then we'll settle him in the class.'

Jason showed Noorul where to put his coat and, back in the classroom, he made a place for him at the table. Noorul could not speak to Jason but he quickly understood when Jason showed him what to do. All the morning the boys stayed together. In the classroom and outside Noorul stayed close to Jason.

At the end of the morning Jason looked round at the friends in his class. His teacher, Matthew and Lisa, Meryem and Andreas from Cyprus, Winston, whose parents came from Jamaica, and now Noorul from Bangladesh. Noorul looked at Jason and a big smile spread over his face. 'I'm glad I have another friend,' thought Jason.

## 5  BEFRIENDING

Although Jason was such a friendly boy, there were some people he didn't like very much, and probably there were some people who didn't like him very much. We are all like that. There was one particular boy in the school whom nobody seemed to like. Perhaps it was not that they disliked him as that they did not understand him. He seemed to have no interest in anything or anyone. Once or twice some children had played with him but found that he was rather spiteful. He liked to pinch and poke, especially when he thought nobody was looking! So, he was left alone most of the time and, of course, he never looked very happy.

When Jason's birthday came near, he was thinking of the friends he would ask to his party. There seemed to be so many and his mother said he must choose carefully as she had to limit the number. He made the list and there was room for one more, but several names came to mind and he could not decide which to include.

'Why not ask that quiet little boy,' said his mother, naming the child nobody liked very much. Jason didn't like that idea at all: he thought the party would be spoilt. But his mother explained that they could all help the boy by showing him how to play with others without being mean.

In the Bible we can read a story about someone whom everyone disliked because he was so mean. Jesus knew all about this man, who was called Zacchaeus. He knew that Zacchaeus was disliked, but he knew that Zacchaeus wanted to see Jesus so much that he was hiding up in a tree to see him go by. The other people hated Zacchaeus so much that they wouldn't let him stand in the crowd to see Jesus. So they were very surprised when Jesus called Zacchaeus to come down as he wanted to have dinner with him that day.

That day Zacchaeus was changed, because of the friendship of Jesus and he promised to be a much nicer person in future. We can help people to want to be better, by showing them that we would like to have them as friends.

## 6  SHARING

It is sometimes quite hard to share with others. Very small children like to keep things all to themselves, especially their toys, because they have not yet become used to being with and playing with others. As we grow older we learn to play together and work together: we learn to share, perhaps sweets, or cards or stamps we are collecting, 'swopping' or exchanging.

Sharing, though, is much more than just giving out our sweets, although that is important. It may be difficult to understand at first, but there is a way in which we have to learn to share ourselves with others. We share our families and homes with our friends. They visit us and get to know our families. We visit them and become familiar with their homes and families. In our world as it is today, with people coming to our country from all parts of the world and people from this country going out into the world, we learn to share on a much larger scale. Language is shared, as we learn to speak a language different from our own. Customs and traditions are shared: we see how other people live and dress and sometimes we begin to copy their ways.

Many grown-ups and children too, of course, like to visit restaurants where food from other countries is cooked and served. In this way we share the eating habits of others. Mothers experiment with new dishes and make the kind of meals people in other countries cook for their families. There is so much we can learn from others and share with them, and we must learn to do this as we grow up into adults.

The world is brought much nearer to us than in the days when our great-grandparents were small. There should be sufficient food and space in the world for everyone to have a fair share. This is not always possible at present, but as we grow up learning to share, it is to be hoped that in time there will be enough for everyone to live healthily and happily.

With your own friends it is good to share in all ways—possessions, toys, sweets, friendship. In time we learn to share ourselves, as we share our thoughts and ideas. We each have something to give to the world. There is no other person just like you. *You* can do for your friends and the world things which no one else can do. God has made *you* just as you are.

7  HELPING

Jason's mother was a very helpful kind of person. She was a good friend to so many people living nearby. When they went to the shops his mother usually brought back some shopping she had got for elderly people they knew. Or, if people were not well enough to go out, she would help them, too, and perhaps go along to their house to see if there was anything she could do for them. So Jason learned very quickly that there was more to being friends than just playing together.

He was playing with George and Lisa one day when they found a kitten that had hurt itself. Its paw was injured. After mother had bathed the sore paw they took the kitten along to the address they had found on a collar the kitten wore. Its owner was so pleased to have her pet back again. Afterwards the children sometimes went along to see the kitten and his owner.

There is such a lot each one of us can do to help others, and by helping we are being a friend to them. Look for all the ways you can help others. You can hold doors of shops open for people with heavy bags, or for mothers with prams trying to get in or out. You can pick up things for older people who find it rather difficult to bend, or play with a baby while its mother is busy. Quite often we can be a great help just by keeping quiet! This may be the most difficult way of all.

Can you think of ways you can help others? Think about it. By helping others, however old or young they may be, you are being a good friend to them.

## 8   GANGS

'Do you want to be in our gang?' Jason was asked. He was rather flattered because the boys who asked him were quite popular in the school. They played together all the time and seemed to organize such good games. So he was made a member of the gang and was very proud: he always had people to play with.

But the gang, while having very good times themselves, forgot that other children like to play, too, and they expected everyone in the school playground to give way to them. *Their* game was most important, they were not concerned with others. Soon the gang was in trouble and it was not pleasant.

It is a good thing to be a member of a group who all enjoy doing certain things together and share the same kind of interest. In such a group we can share and help and learn from each other: but it is wrong when such a group becomes so selfish and only concerned with what *they* want that they ignore the needs and rights of others.

Organizations such as Cub Scouts, Brownies, Brigades, Clubs, Choirs, Bands and other interest groups all give opportunities for us to join with others; and they are led by people who know how to plan and organize so that we may enjoy the best kind of activity. In this way, the idea of a gang is still there. We can be with people who like the things we like, remembering to do things together without making others unhappy. People who lead and organize groups for children work hard to help them. Remember to say thank you to them by being loyal and helpful.

### 9  A FRIEND IN NEED

'I like being Christina's friend,' said Helen to her mum. 'She's always giving children sweets and sometimes she gives them money as well.'

Mum stopped preparing the tea and turned to Helen. 'Is that the only reason why you like being Christina's friend?' she asked. 'Would you like her just as much if she didn't have any sweets or money to give away?'

Helen wasn't sure. She didn't think she would because Christina could sometimes be spiteful and she did always like to have things her own way. So mother explained that it was probably because of those things that Christina was giving things away. She wanted to buy friendship that she could not otherwise have. If only she could be a nicer kind of girl, Mum explained, she would not need to keep giving people things. She would have friends who wanted *her* and not her sweets or money.

Jesus once told a story about a young man who had plenty of money to spend and plenty of friends to help him spend it. One day all his money had gone and so had his so-called friends. When he no longer had anything to give them they soon left him. True friends are those who will stick by you always, even if you have nothing. There is an old saying, 'A friend in need is a friend indeed'.

It was not long before Helen was remembering those words of her mother's. She was on her way home from school when she found

Maria lying on the pavement crying her eyes out. 'What's the matter?' she asked.

Between loud sobs Maria told her that some older boys had jumped on her and snatched the box of pencils she was carrying. As she fell she had cut her knee and torn her dress. 'Come home with me,' said Helen. 'My mum will wash that blood off and put something on your knee.'

While Mum was doing what she could to patch up Maria's knee and put a few stitches in her dress, Helen disappeared into her room. She came back with a few of her coloured pencils. 'You can have these,' she said.

It was a much happier Maria who walked home with Helen for company. 'There you are!' said Mother later. 'You have been a friend in need—a proper little Good Samaritan.'

'What is that?' asked Helen. So mother explained that Jesus had told a story of a man who had been robbed and left bleeding by the roadside. Two men passed by but the third, a Samaritan, helped him, took him to an inn and offered to pay any costs to get him well. The Good Samaritan had proved to be a good friend in need.

And Jesus told his listeners to do the same sort of thing.

## 10   FRIEND OF THE FRIENDLESS

From time to time you have probably seen a tramp walking beside the road. His clothes are probably old and tattered, his shoes well worn and uncleaned. He probably looks as though he has not had a wash, a shave or a haircut for a very long time. In his hand there may be a plastic bag containing everything he owns—and that is precious little! Day after day he walks the streets in hot sunshine, pouring rain or in the snow. At night he looks for some kind of shelter where he can sleep, covered perhaps by nothing but newspaper, because he has no home.

There are lots of men and some women, like this. They have nothing they can call their own. They spend much of their time begging for food or for money to buy food. Sometimes they spend any money on cheap drink or on drugs which make them ill. Sometimes we call them 'down-and-outs'. There are lots of them to be seen in the big cities.

Usually the down-and-outs are very lonely people. They have no real friends. Perhaps that is their own fault. Who would want to make friends with dirty, smelly people who are often rude or bad-tempered?

Well! Strange as it may seem, there are lots of people who like to help in any way they can, to be friends to the friendless. And many of the down-and-outs know where to go to find people who will give some kind of help.

In the East End of London, for example, is the Whitechapel Methodist Mission. Every Sunday night a hundred or more men gather there. After the evening service they are given a meal—food that has been sent to the Mission by people who want to help. At the Mission there is a clothing store where they can be fitted out free of charge with clothes—sent to the Mission by people who think of the down-and-outs.

Also in the Mission are a few beds for those who urgently need a 'home' for a night or two. A doctor treats those who are ill—free of charge as his way of befriending—with medicine and dressings also given by friends. But most important are the friendly help, the kind words and the caring shown by the people who work at the Mission. And there are many missions like this in many parts of Britain. The people who run them, and those who help in any way, know that Jesus was always a friend of the friendless and they want to be the same.

RELATED THEMES

*We like to play . . . and quarrel, too;*
*We like to laugh and sing:*
*When we are happy with our friends*
*We like just **everything**.*
*Thank you for our friends, dear God,*
*And pleasures that we share;*
*And thank you that you are the friend*
*Of children everywhere.*                                    C.S.

## 3 FRIENDS

1. Dear Father God, we enjoy having friends at school and some we play with out of school. Help us to remember that we have 'friends' in our home as well and that we should be at least as nice to them as we are to the friends we choose. *Amen*

2. Dear God,
   I enjoy playing with other people
   So that we can do lots of things together;
   And I like working with them too.
   Help me not to be selfish
   But to try to think of the needs of others. *Amen*

3. Help me today, O God, to be a good friend to someone.
   Help me to look for someone in need.
   Help me to love.
   Help me to care.
   Help me to be like Jesus
   Who always cared more for others than for himself. *Amen*

4. How nice it is, O God, to have friends! I enjoy working with them and playing with them and they seem to enjoy being with me. Help me always to be a good friend. *Amen*

5. Lord, make me kind and unselfish, thinking more of others than I do of myself and trying always to be a good friend to everyone. *Amen.*

6. May we make this a happy day for each other, O Lord: help us to work hard and to do our best in everything. *Amen*

7. O God, I am thinking about the children in
   my class;
   Some of them I like more than others;
   And some I don't like very much.
   Help me to learn how to be a good friend
   to them all. *Amen.*

8. O God,
   I like to be able to do things by myself
   But I also like to do things with other children.
   I like to be part of a team or a gang
   So that we can do things together.
   Teach me to be a good member
   Always working as part of the team
   And not just for myself. *Amen*

9. O Lord, I feel sorry for people who have no friends.
   They seem so lonely at times.
   Perhaps I can do something to help.
   Teach me how to be a friend to others
   And especially those who seem to need a friend. *Amen*

10. Sometimes, dear God, I like to tell people about *me*;
    Sometimes I want to tell them of happy things;
    Sometimes I want to talk about sad things.
    It is nice to have someone to listen to me.
    I am glad they like listening.
    Sometimes people like to talk to me about
    themselves:
    Please make me a good listener. *Amen*

11. Teach me, O God,
    What it means to be a true friend;
    To like people for what they are
    And not just because of what they give me;
    To be ready to share the things that are mine,
    And to help others who may have less than I have.
    Help me to know that the best way of giving
    Is to give of myself. *Amen*

12. Today, O God, I shall meet lots of people.
    Some may be feeling lonely;
    Some may be a little sad;
    Some may need a kind word;
    Some may need a helping hand;
    And some may be looking for a friend:
    Help me to *be* a friend to these. *Amen*

## 3  FRIENDS

At work beside his father's bench
Hands to work and feet to run
Jesus, friend of little children
Jesus is the best friend
Look out for loneliness
Thank you
Think of a world
Think on these things
'Tis good to see our father's world
When Jesus was a little boy
When the world is dark and dreary

SOME BIBLE READINGS

| | |
|---|---|
| David's friendship with Jonathan | 1 Samuel 18; 1–3: 20; 42 |
| Jesus, friend of sinners | Luke 5; 27–32 |
| Jesus chooses his close friends | Luke 6; 12–16 |
| The Good Samaritan | Luke 10; 25–37 |
| Friends in the Church | Acts 4; 32–35 |

INTEREST WORK AND ACTIVITIES

*Books*

Provide for the book corner a selection of books which the children can enjoy looking at and reading. Here are a few that could be included.

BEING ALONE, BEING TOGETHER *(Feelings)*, Macdonald
A FRIEND CAN HELP *(Feelings)*, Macdonald
WHO MADE FRIENDS? *(Lion Board book)*, Lion
THE FRIEND, John Burningham, Bodley Head
MY SCHOOL *(Terraced House Books)*, Methuen
KATE'S PARTY/SPUD COMES TO PLAY, J. Soloman and
    R. Harvey, Hamilton.

YOUR SKIN AND MINE *(Let's Read and Find Out)*, Black
THE GOOD SAMARITAN *(Little Lions)*, Lion

## Portraits of friends

Draw or paint pictures of friends or write descriptions. See how many can be recognized by others in the class.

## Animal friends

There are many people who have an animal which is regarded very much as a friend or companion. There could be some discussion on aspects of this theme. A few suggestions are:

Guide dog for a blind person.
Dog or cat companion for an elderly person.
A budgerigar, parrot or mynah which 'talks' to owner.
Care for a horse or pony which develops into 'friendship'.
Unusual friendships—e.g. with lions (Joy Adamson *Born Free*).

Such a discussion could illustrate the two-way relationship showing how the animals may regard people as friends and come to trust or depend upon them.

Do such friendships sometimes have more depth than many human friendships?

# 4    Work and play

*These two are very much interwoven in the experience of young children. With present day teaching methods it is not always easy to see where one ends and the other begins: they are complementary to each other. The child's day needs to be enjoyable, creative and productive: the balance is important. It is good that children learn from each experience, developing their own powers and skills and helping each other to develop too.*

*Few young children can appreciate the principle of competitive team games, but they can learn the technique of playing in a group and of depending on each other. In this theme we concentrate on work and play, individually and with each other, so that these things may be regarded not merely as enjoyable to oneself but also when being with and working with others. All our skills can be used for the benefit of others.*

## 1 BOOKS

Do you know what we call a collection of books? A library. We have libraries in our towns, cities and villages, where we may go to borrow books to read and study. We have our own school libraries, as well as reading areas in classrooms and other parts of the school. We may have books on the shelves at home, perhaps in our own bedroom. In all these places we find books we can enjoy, to read stories or to find out things. There are so many lovely books for us to enjoy. It may seem hard to learn to read—we read first one book and then another, learning more and more words and enjoying the stories. Most people have their favourite books. Have you?

Very small children, not yet able to read also have books—with pictures and perhaps just one word on each page. The pictures are of things which the babies can recognize. After a while little children will point and perhaps try to say what is in the picture. So they learn to use books. As we grow older, if we have worked hard and learned to enjoy reading, we want to read more and more. There is a way in which books become our friends and we like to spend time with them, reading and learning from them.

There are so many books all around us. Long ago there were very few books. Not many people were able to read and all the books

45

were written by hand, mostly by holy men living in monasteries. They did beautiful writing and sometimes decorated the letters with pictures. Then a clever man invented a machine to print words and it became possible for more books to be made. This was the beginning of the kind of book we know today.

There are books written about every subject under the sun, more than we can ever think of, and they have been the work of people who worked hard to learn and think about what they were learning so that they could put it all down for others to read. This is a wonderful way of helping others and is the way in which all knowledge can be passed on. Books are very precious and it is important that we take care of them and use them in the right way.

Some most important books are those used by people to learn about God and their religion—The Bible, the Qur'an, The Granth and others. These are very special books for people who try to learn more about their God and follow Him in the way they feel is best. We must learn to read and understand these as we grow up, for they teach us a lot about God and how he wants us to live.

## 2  PICTURES

Looking around our schools we see many different pictures—mostly pictures painted by children, perhaps, but some specially printed to help us to learn about things. Long before we can read we can enjoy looking at pictures—such as the pictures in our 'baby' books.

Sometimes, when something very special has happened and we are feeling really happy, we like to draw or paint a picture about it. We may find this much easier than writing about it. This is a special gift that God has given us—that we can make pictures. *All* of us can make pictures, no matter how clever or not-so-clever we may be in other things. We can put our thoughts and ideas into pictures. Thousands of years ago, long before people could read or write, they painted hunting pictures on the walls of caves.

In some big city halls and buildings called art galleries, we can find collections of famous pictures painted by clever people, some of them a long time ago. People stand and look at these pictures and think about them. They look at the colours and the figures and shapes. They enjoy seeing the work done by people we call artists, who were very clever at painting.

Think of a world with no pictures. The world is a nicer place because we can see pictures made by others who have brought to us the lovely things they have seen or imagined. Before cameras were invented people could only rely upon paintings to know what people and places looked like.

Pictures were painted of people's faces, so that others could know what they looked like. This took a long time. Now, with cameras, we can make pictures very quickly—pictures of people and very lovely places we see. But people still like to paint pictures as well.

God has shown man how to use his skills to produce pictures for his own pleasure as well as to help and give pleasure to others.


3  USING OUR HANDS,

Look at your hands. What do you see? Four fingers and a thumb on each hand. Spread out your fingers, wide: curl them up tightly: make a fist. How strong our hands can be! We use them all day without even thinking about them. Think about the ways you use your hands throughout the day. To hold, to lift, to make things. You use them to write, to hold the pencil or pen, to draw or paint, to sew or hammer, to cut out shapes or to pick up things. Our hands are very important to us.

We can show people how we care for them by holding their hands. We hold the hand of a smaller child who needs comforting, or an older person we love. Can you remember how you needed to hold Mummy's or Daddy's hands when you were a little afraid or unhappy?

Sometimes, alas, we use our hands to hurt . . .

Almost the first feeling we had as tiny babies was of the hands of our Mum doing so many things for us—washing, and feeding, and comforting us when we felt uncomfortable or sick. And Dad's hands, too, the strong hands we need to help us and show us how to do things, often help to give us confidence.

There are so many things for which we need our hands, to steer our bikes, to use tools or play instruments, to knit or sew. The games we play as we grow older, tennis, cricket, netball, need the skill of our hands as well as skill of our feet and minds. As grown-ups our hands are important to us when we need to operate machinery, or drive a car or tractor. Think of some of the work people do which needs skilled and careful hands.

As folk get older they sometimes find that it is not so easy to hold things or to pick them up. Sometimes we can use our hands to help them. This is one way in which we can show them a little kindness and caring.

Our hands are part of the wonderful body God has given us, and like all the good things we have, our hands are best used in the right way—to give, to help and to work. In this way we make the best use of the good things we have as a gift from God.

### 4 OUR EARS AND EYES

'I spy, with my little eye, something beginning with . . .' This is a game which has been played for many years by children and adults, too. When you play this game, have you noticed that very often it is quite difficult to guess the right answer? People try so hard to choose something which they think the others in the game will not see.

We have our ears and our eyes, but so often we seem not to be using them. We look at things without really seeing them, and we hear so much noise in the world we miss some very important sounds. Perhaps because we are so used to having ears and eyes we take them for granted and do not use them properly.

Just think what it would be like if you couldn't see or hear lots of the things you are able to enjoy.

Think of the sounds you hear every day . . .

Voices of the people at home.

The knock of the postman and the 'plop' of the letter through the door.

The sounds of telephone, radio, television, record player, people singing.

The patter of raindrops and the splash of puddles when you stamp in them.

Water gurgling down the drain.

Sausages sizzling in the frying pan.

And what do you see . . .?

Faces of family and friends.

Bright colours in the world—buses, flowers, birds, clothes.

Things other people have made, beautiful pictures.

Books to read.

All these things are there for us to enjoy if we use our ears and eyes. Not only are these things important to us but we need also our ears and eyes if we are to work as well as we are able and to play properly, too.

When we think of all these things we are very glad that we have ears and eyes with which to hear and see the world and people around us. Sometimes we need to stop and think about those people who cannot enjoy what we enjoy—deaf people who cannot hear and blind people who cannot see. They learn to be very clever and to do all kinds of things, but, of course, they miss a lot of what we take for granted every day. Try to help these people when you can. You will probably learn as much from them as you are able to give, perhaps more.

Thank God for the wonderful gifts of sight and hearing, and remember that the best way to say thank you is to use these gifts properly so that you can learn and understand more of God's world.

## 5  USING OUR MINDS

On a television programme especially for children there was a strange little character. He was really just two big eyes with hands and feet. He probably had a whole body but the artist had created him so that all we saw or thought we saw, were his eyes, his hands and feet. This character did all kinds of thing. He did everything his mind told him to do. 'My mind tells me to pick up the pen.' 'My mind is telling me to walk . . . to run . . . to jump.' He was a cheerful character and watching him everyone knew exactly what he was going to do, because he was repeating whatever his mind told him to. We are like that, you know. At the very centre of each one of us is a kind of 'radio' which tells us what to do. We call it our brain or our mind.

Our mind sends us messages . . . 'Walk' . . . 'Sit down' . . . 'Open your eyes' . . . 'Scratch your nose'. Everything we do is directed from our mind to the part of our body which has to be used. What a wonderful idea this was, for God to make us so that we have a nerve centre which tells us what to do, and how to do things.

Because we have such a wonderful 'radio' we must learn to use it in the right way. This is the part of our body which helps us learn to read and write and speak. A most important part of its work is to help us to *think*. If we do not use any part of our body it gets weak and stops being of much use. It is the same with our mind, so we have to use it properly, to think, and to explore the ways by which we can learn.

By thinking about what we are doing, and how to do things as best we can, we keep our minds in good use. Sometimes competitions or riddles or puzzles are called 'brain teasers', which means that we have to use this part of our 'radio' quite a lot so that we can think things out. Most of us enjoy puzzles and competitions. We work at them as long as possible, trying to find the correct answer.

An important function or work of our mind is thinking about other people and other things than those which are special to ourselves. It is also because many people, right from the beginning of the world, have used their minds, their brains that they have been able to learn many new things,—the things which are important to us today. Every one of us has a special way of making the world a better place if we use our minds in the best possible way.

It is sad that very clever brains have been used to hurt and destroy. This is a big temptation, so it is very important that we use *our* minds in the right way, as God would have us use all his gifts.


6  WORKING WITH OTHERS

How would you like always to be by yourself and never in a class or group? It would not be very pleasant, would it, to have no other companion to share your work or play? It is good sometimes to work alone and not depend on others, to work at our own speed and discover things for ourselves.

It is usually much more fun to work together with another boy or girl or in a group. God has made us so that we enjoy the company of others and doing things together. In working with others we can share our ideas, try them out and help each other to find even better ways of doing things. This is especially helpful when we are starting something new, when we need to plan and work things out. Then we can help each other such a lot. Quite often when another person in the group does something or makes a suggestion of what to do, we can see how good it is, and we ask ourselves, 'Why didn't I think of that?' Each one of the group working alone may do quite well but when all the group work together and share their ideas they can arrive at much better results.

We have to take care, though, that we do *work* together so that everyone takes a share of the work and does not leave it to the others. Working together can sometimes be so much fun that we have to be strong to turn away from the temptation to forget the work and just play around.

To have shared in something special, or perhaps have made something together helps make us good friends. We learn the art of working together, being patient when others seem rather slow, helping those who find the work difficult and discovering that we do not know all the answers. All through our lives we need other people and they need us.

## 7   PLAYING TOGETHER

What kind of games do you like to play with your friends? Very small children like to play alone and keep their toys to themselves most of the time. As we grow a little older we learn to share our toys with our friends, exchange our toys for a time and learn something which grown-ups call 'give and take'. This means that we share and don't take more than we give, whether it is our toys, our other possessions or ourselves.

As we grow, we like to play with others in a group. Think about the games you play together . . . Mothers and Fathers . . . Play in the house . . . Shops . . . Cops and Robbers . . . School. Some people always like to have the leading part, they like to be the father or mother, or the shopkeeper, or the teacher in school. Why do you think they like to do this? Others are happy to be just part of the group, and it seems that we are made in that way. Some will always be the leaders to show the others the way to go: the others are quite happy to 'follow my leader'. It is important that we have the right kind of leaders.

Older boys and girls prefer to play in games which are played by teams—football, cricket, and netball. In tennis and other games we sometimes play with others. In any team game we have to learn that the important part of the game is playing as a member of a team, not as just ourselves, however good we may be at the game. The members of the team play as one, because they know that, however good the rest of the team may be, if just one person thinks only of himself, the team will not play so well, and the game may be lost.

Members of the team look to the captain to lead them and they follow their leader even when they may not agree with him. This is a very difficult lesson to learn and we cannot understand it fully until we are old enough to play together as a team. We have to learn to share in this way, to share our abilities and the things we can do well, to help others.

Our world consists of a great team of people who all need to work and play together according to the rules given by the greatest leader of all—God himself.

## 8   SCHOOL

Do you remember when you first started school? It must seem a very long time ago, now that you are settled down and have made friends with children and teachers.

Before you began school, you probably looked forward to being with lots of other children and learning to do exciting things, but you may also have felt a sinking feeling in your tummy when you thought of this big place you would go to without Mother. While you were very small at home, Mum was always there, and you knew she was there when you wanted her, or even just wanted to see her. Then came the day to leave Mum and the family for however short a time in the day, to go to school. You met your teacher and lots of strange children. It was a very big day in your life. Probably you felt rather lost and lonely at first, but then as you came to know your teacher and the other children you learned to settle down and be happy. There were so many interesting things to do and see, and working and playing together made a new sort of life.

This is our first step into the big world outside our family. We learn at school to be part of a different kind of world from home. We learn to obey rules, and work with others. In school we learn to share in so many ways and to think about others. As we grow up in school life we learn other things too. We learn to do things for others, to be trusted to do some jobs for children and teachers, and to care for others.

Most of all we learn how to *learn*. We are shown ways of making and doing things and are taught how to use our special gifts—to use our hands, and ears and eyes, and most of all the part of us that thinks—our own special radio—so that we may grow and develop in every way. Our time in school is a very important part of our lives for it is here that we learn the way of life that will be best for us as we grow up to be adults.

There are lots of people who work for us so that we can do well in school—teachers, helpers, dinner ladies, the Lollipop lady or gentleman—all of whom want to help us. Together with our parents, they show us how to grow up well so that we can live, work and play in the best possible ways.

School days are very important days. We are very fortunate to have a school like ours where we can learn and we must not waste all the opportunities that are given to us.

RELATED THEMES:

OUR SCHOOL

The last part of this theme could easily arise from or lead into a brief 'Story of our School'. Most children take school for granted. It is there: and they have to attend it.

Perhaps a little of the history of the school can be told—how it happens to be there and who was responsible for building it, any interesting facts unearthed from the records or log books and well-known people who were once pupils there.

One could give a simple outline of the large number of people responsible for the school today—including many at the Committee or Office level whom the children will never see.

Inculcate simply some awareness of the corporate body we call 'the school'. It is not just buildings, furniture and equipment: it is a body of people having to learn to work and play together, helping each other.

1. All through today, in our work and our play, help us to remember that you, our Father, are near us. *Amen*

2. Be with us, dear Father, all through this day. Do not forget us, even though because we shall be very busy we may forget you. Keep us in your care and bring us safely to our beds tonight. *Amen*

3. Bless our school, dear Lord. May we learn to work together and play together, to serve one another and to serve you. *Amen*

4. Dear Father God, be with us today. Help us to know that even when we are very busy you do not forget us. *Amen*

5. Dear Father God,
   I am thinking about all sorts of pictures:
   Drawings made by people who are clever with their hands;
   Beautiful paintings with lovely colours;
   Pictures made from bits of paper or odds and ends.
   Thank you for these pictures and the people who
   made them.
   I like making pictures myself:
   Help me to learn how to do them well. *Amen*

6. Dear God,
   Thank you for all my books,
   I like to sit and look at the pictures
   And I like hearing or reading the stories.
   Thank you for the people who wrote them
   And for those who bought them for me.
   Thank you for people who taught me to read
   So that I can really enjoy my books.
   For all these people and so many books
   Thank you, God. *Amen*

7. Father God; show me how to help others. Give me helping hands and a loving heart so that I may do so gladly because you, my Father, would like me to. *Amen*

8. Help me, my God, to use my mind to learn and to understand as much as I can about the world around me, and about you, who made everything in the world. *Amen*

9. Help me, O God, to learn all I can in school, to work hard at my lessons and to play fairly with others, so that I may grow up able to live a happy and useful life. *Amen*

10. In our work and in our play, please God be always near to help and guide us so that we may be kind and good. *Amen*

11. Teach me, my God,
    To use my eyes to see everything around me,
    To use my ears to enjoy all sorts of sounds,
    To use my mind to think things out;
    And teach me to be thankful to you. *Amen*

12. Thank you God our Father for making us as we are:
    For bringing us as babies into your lovely world,
          *Thank you, God our Father;*
    For giving us eyes to see all the beauty around us,
          *Thank you, God our Father;*
    For ears to hear all lovely sounds,
          *Thank you, God our Father;*
    For noses that smell and tongues that taste,
          *Thank you, God our Father;*
    For hands that do so many things
          *Thank you, God our Father;*
    For feet and legs to walk or run,
          *Thank you, God our Father;*
    For minds that think and work things out,
          *Thank you, God our Father;*
    And for hearts that can be loving and kind,
          *Thank you, God our Father. Amen*

## 4 WORK AND PLAY

At work beside his father's bench
Father, we thank thee for the night
God whose name is love
Hands to work and feet to run
I love to play among the flowers
In our work and in our play
I've two little hands to work for Jesus
Jesu's hands were kind hands
Jesus, child of Mary
Standing in the market place
Thank you
Two little eyes to look to God

RELATED BIBLE PASSAGES

| | |
|---|---|
| Job, helper of the needy | Job 29; 11–17 |
| In search of wisdom | Proverbs 2; 1–6 |
| Jesus growing in wisdom | Luke 2; 39–52 |

INTEREST WORK AND ACTIVITIES

*Books for the book corner*

BOOKS/TOYS/EYES *(Starters)*, Macdonald
BOOKS *(First Look)*, Watts
FINDING OUT BY TOUCHING/LOOK AT YOUR EYES
    *(Let's Read and Find Out)*, Black
PLAYING *(Head-Start)*, Burke
CHILDREN'S GAMES *(Blackwell's Learning Library)*,
    Blackwell
TOYS AND GAMES/LISTENING/SCHOOL *(Our World)*,
    Burke
YOU AND YOUR BODY *(Look it up)*, Macmillan
LISTEN AND HEAR/LOOK AND SEE/TOUCH AND FEEL
    *(Use your senses)*, Burke
AT SCHOOL *(First Time books)*, Macdonald

GOING TO SCHOOL *(Starters Facts)*, Macdonald
DANNY'S CLASS *(Starters Stories)*, Macdonald

## Book week

A special 'book week' could be held in connection with the first aspect of this theme. Talk to children about books. There may be a local author, illustrator, publisher or bookseller who would come in to talk to the children.

## Book Club

This might be an opportunity to introduce the older children to one of the book clubs through which children can purchase books for themselves, such as CHIP CLUB (Scholastic Publications Ltd).

## Pictures

Draw attention to any especially interesting pictures that may be available. Have a school picture or art exhibition to include many aspects of art. Perhaps children from one class could paint pictures for other classes to see.

## Craft activities

Lots of things can be done by way of simple craft work, illustrating use of hands and eyes. Easy to make things like carry-cots from shoe boxes can be made. Covered with paper, they look quite effective. Girls can make simple covers and pillows.

Peg and pipe-cleaner dolls are easy to make and can be dressed using odd bits and pieces.

It may be that some of the older children could make things to be played with by children in nursery or reception classes.

Get the children to draw round their hands and cut out the resulting shapes. If done on coloured paper or painted they can be mounted in interesting arrangements.

*Co-operative working*

Since part of the thought, within this theme is that of working together, any opportunities should be found to work, not just as groups within a class but in collaboration with other classes.

The making of things for others has already been suggested. Perhaps classes could produce activities to which others could be invited. There is also the possibility of some form of entertainment which could be performed to other classes.

The obvious thought is that of producing something which will be used in assembly.

It may be possible to form a school percussion group, the children being drawn from various classes. This could accompany some of the hymns or songs used in assembly.

*Use of senses*

Some introduction can be given to the human body and how it works. Think especially of use of senses.

*Eyes:* Observation in various ways.
Games like 'I spy with my little eye'.
*Ears:* Close eyes: Recognize sounds.
Recognize voices of other children.
*Hands:* Feeling things with eyes closed. What is this?
What is this made of?
*Minds:* Various activities to show how minds work.
Simple mental sums and exercises.
Reactions to noises, pictures, a pet, books.
Mind-teasers of various kinds relative to age level.

# 5 Attitudes

*This section is a little different from most of the others in so far as it does not lend itself in the same way to follow-up activities. In fact it may well be that the stories could be used individually rather than as a group, arising out of some incident which has occurred in school or affecting one or more of the children.*

*It may be argued that some of the attitudes dealt with in this section are irrelevant to younger children—they may not appreciate the finer points, for example, of lying, cheating, dishonesty or being a good loser.*

*Taking something they want at that moment can hardly be called stealing. Nevertheless, such actions are motivated by an attitude of mind and it is perhaps as well to make some attempt to help the children understand and develop a regard for the possessions and rights of others, not merely to satisfy their personal desires.*

*If they can appreciate a little of these attitudes early in life, it is hoped this will lay foundations for standards of behaviour later in life.*


## 1 'I WANT IT!'

Dean and his small brother were preparing for bed. They had been playing with Dad for a while after tea, and had enjoyed the romp and the fun. Now it was time for bed. Dean was old enough to get himself undressed and into the bath, but Mum helped Paul, his young brother. Paul was not yet five years old, and he attended Nursery class at the same school as Dean.

Mum helped Paul to take off his clothes and, as she always did, made sure nothing was left in the pockets as the clothing was put into the basket ready to be washed. Something hard caught her hand as she felt in the pockets of Paul's trousers. It was a tiny 'plane, a red plastic 'plane, which Mum knew did not belong to Paul. 'Has one of your friends given this to you, Paul?' she asked.

Paul made a grab at the 'plane. 'It's mine, I want it!' he said and tried to hide it.

Dean came to see what the fuss was about. He recognized the small 'plane. 'That belongs to school,' he said. 'They have all kinds of toys in the Nursery which they sort into boxes; 'planes, cars, shapes, all kinds of things in different colours. I've seen them.'

Mum looked at Paul. 'Did you forget to put this one back in the box, Paul?'

'No! I want it,' said Paul, 'and now it's mine.'

Mum explained that however much we want things, we just do not take them. 'This is not yours. It belongs to school, and tomorrow you must take it back.' Mum went on to explain that we share things and we use things which belong to others. We have our own toys and possessions, and those which do not belong to us belong to others and are not *ours* to take. It was a difficult thing for Paul to understand but he had to learn that we cannot have everything we want, and we must sometimes see things we would like but cannot have for ourselves.

Mum explained to both boys that sometimes things which are the property of others are left lying around, but they are still the property of others and to take them would be stealing.

'What about something I may find in the street?' asked Dean. 'Could I keep that?'

'Why, no!' said Dad who had come along to join in the discussion. 'Finding's keeping's is not a good idea. Just think how you would feel if you lost something you treasured very much and it was found by someone who decided to keep it. When we find things in the street the best thing to do is to take them to the Police Station.'

Next day after school Dad took Dean and Paul along to the police station and asked the policeman on duty to explain what happens to things found and handed in. The policeman showed them the big book where details would be written and explained that if, after a time, the article found was not claimed, it would be given to the finder.

'Ooh!' said Dean. 'I shall keep looking, just in case I find something valuable and it is not claimed.'

'Good idea,' said Dad, 'but remember, if it is valuable, it will probably be claimed.'


2 'I DIDN'T DO IT!'

Sarah felt dreadful, deep down inside herself. She was playing with her pet cat Barney. As she chased him round the room she knocked against a small table and the vase standing on the table fell to the floor. The carpet on the floor would have protected the vase but it hit the edge of the table and Sarah looked with horror at the vase lying on the floor with a broken piece lying beside it. She knew that her mother was very fond of that vase, it had been in the family a long time. It probably was not very valuable, but Mum liked it—she remembered it being in *her* home when she was small. Sarah picked up the pieces. She put the vase back in place and tried to balance the piece, which was broken, back into its place, but it just toppled off.

Sarah sat down and thought about it. When Mum came in she saw at once that the vase had been damaged and asked how it had happened. 'I don't know,' said Sarah. 'It probably fell down.'

'Perhaps Barney knocked it down,' said Mum. She wasn't cross but Sarah knew that she was unhappy about it.

When she went to bed Sarah found that she could not sleep. She felt very unhappy—every part of her—as she thought about the vase. It was not so much the fact that the vase had been broken as that she had not told her mother the truth and had allowed her mother to think that Barney had been responsible. She tossed and turned and tears welled up in her eyes.

After a while Mum came into the room, she had heard Sarah moving about and came in to make sure all was well. Perhaps she thought Sarah was not feeling well. She saw a troubled unhappy face looking up at her. 'What ever is wrong?' asked Mum.

It was all too much for Sarah. She told her Mum the truth about the vase and said how sorry she was, not only for breaking the vase, but for pretending that Barney had knocked it down. Mum explained to her that it was not a good thing to do—especially the lie she had told in saying that she didn't know how it came to be broken. Mum explained to her that things happen in life, and we do things we cannot always help, but they hurt others. The important thing is to be honest about them, to tell the truth and be prepared to take any punishment. As Mum explained, usually, when we are quite honest and know we have done wrong, it is thought that we have been punished enough.

Sarah and Mum had a long chat that night before Sarah settled down to sleep. Sarah was telling her mother about people copying each other's work in school, and Mum explained to her that in that way they were cheating, but they were cheating themselves as much as anyone else, because they were not really learning how to do their work. 'Always be quite honest; don't be afraid to tell the truth; and especially don't be afraid to say in school if you cannot understand the work,' said Mum. People can help you if you are quite honest with them.

This is a good thing for us all to remember.


### 3 'I'M SORRY!'

'Now say you are sorry . . .'

'Sorry,' said Mark. But he wasn't. He wasn't a bit sorry that he had pushed Matthew so that he stumbled and fell. After all, Matthew had pushed him, and so Mark felt he was only giving Matthew what he deserved. Their teacher had said he was to apologize, and if that pleased her—well he would say he was sorry, but he wasn't really!

There is much more to being sorry than just saying, 'sorry'. It is a very hard thing to do—to feel sorry for something we think we were right to do, but if we can stop for a moment, put ourselves in the other person's place and try to understand how he feels, we will learn to be a much better person.

It is not only by hurting each other physically that we do harm to others. We can hurt by saying nasty things or by just ignoring people so that they feel unhappy and left out.

Being really sorry means that we know that we have done wrong by making another person hurt or unhappy and we want to make them feel better. It helps make us better too, when we know we have tried to put things right. It is very easy to say 'sorry' because we have been told we must, or because we know something not very nice will happen if we don't, but that doesn't make the wrong right again.

Something much bigger than ourselves is at work when we are truly sorry for anything wrong we have committed. Probably it is the little bit of God which is inside everyone, the very best part of us, that is also hurt when we do wrong. We all have a good side to ourselves and, when we are put out in any way, the best side of us is not seen. Think about this. Think about Mark, when he apologized just because he was told to do so. He didn't really feel any better for having said he was sorry, but if he really *was* sorry that he hurt someone, whether or not he actually said sorry, that is what really matters. It must make God happy when we know that we have done wrong and are truly sorry for having done so.

4 'I WISH I COULD . . .'

Katy looked at the watch Sharon was showing to her friends. Sharon was always showing new things to her friends—she had all the latest toys and clothes and it seemed that she never, ever, wanted for anything. Katy wished so often that she could have a watch and more toys or new clothes and shoes whenever she wanted them, but she knew this was not possible. Mum and Dad had promised that she would have a watch for a special present as soon as they could afford to buy one for her, but so often she wished she could have things when she wanted them.

Katy saw that Sharon always seemed to have a lot of friends, too. She wished she could be the kind of person everyone wanted to be with and share their games. She had friends, of course, and they were very good friends, they played together in school and did lots of interesting things together out of school. They visited each other's homes, shared their toys and pets and really were very happy together. Katy looked at Sharon again—she did so wish she could be the centre of attention in that way.

That evening, after tea, Katy was telling her mother all about the lovely watch Sharon had shown them in school and about the clothes and toys—so many things that Katy would have liked for herself. Mum tried to explain a very important point to Katy and it was rather difficult for her to understand, but she began to see what her mother was trying to show her.

We all wish, from time to time, that we could have something we cannot have. We see people being the kind of person we would like to be, to have the kind of friends we think we would like to have; but if we were to stop wishing for things we cannot have and think about all the things we have, we would be very surprised to see how much we really do have.

The important things of life are not the possessions which are bought or given to us, so much as the thoughts, the feelings, and the people who make our lives what they are. To have people who love and care for us, friends, kindness shown to us, a helping hand when we need it—these are the precious things. These things are important to everyone, and so we have to take our share in passing on the kindness and friendliness and love to others.

We each have our own personality—the kind of person we are—and no one else is quite like us. God loves each and every one of us in a very special way, so why should we want to be like someone else? You are just you, and a very special person. It is very important we should be the very best kind of 'us' that we can be. Each one of us has his or her own place in the world and in life.

## 5  A HAPPY FACE

Glenville had such a happy face. His white teeth and his twinkling eyes lit up his brown happy face, and when he grinned, or chuckled, it seemed as though his cheerfulness was infectious, because others wanted to laugh, or smile, too. Glen's parents had come from the sunny island of Jamaica, and although he had not been outside this country, it seemed as though some of the sunshine was trapped inside him and had to come out through his happy face.

People liked being with Glen. He seldom quarrelled, or complained, because he was such a cheerful person. Even when things seemed to be going wrong, such as the times when the sums just wouldn't come out right, or he was not feeling too well, Glen could be counted on to keep a cheerful outlook and get over his feelings of frustration or disappointment. These times come to all of us and make us feel despondent, or even angry, and it is just at such times that we need to have the kind of feelings that we know as cheerfulness.

Many people all through the ages have been able to overcome really serious and anxious times by keeping cheerful and helping to cheer others. During the last war when people were in great danger it was having a cheerful manner which helped them. Not only soldiers, sailors and airmen were exposed to danger. People living in their homes were in danger of being hurt, too, and it was decided that children should be sent away from the big cities to stay in villages and other places in the country until the danger was past. So it was that a number of children from London were taken by some of their teachers to a tiny village in Wales. It was a sad day for them all, as they had to leave their mothers and fathers behind. They went off with their clothes in suitcases, and with a gas mask, and a ticket showing their name and address fastened to their coats.

The teachers were anxious about the children and did as much as they could to see they were happy. At the village hall the children were to meet the people they would stay with. In twos and threes they were collected by the kind people who offered to look after them in their homes. Many of the children were already missing their homes and they were tired and a little tearful. As the teachers saw them all off they were anxious for the children, they knew how sad they might be feeling. So it was with heavy hearts that the teachers went to their own new homes that night.

Next morning, the teachers set off for the village hall where they were going to make a temporary school for the children and as they walked along the street in the centre of the village they felt so happy. On all sides doors were being opened and cheerful, smiling children were coming out from the cottages of the people they were staying with. They had rested and been fed and, although there would be times when they would want their own parents, the cheerful spirit which is in most of us was helping them to be happy in the situation they were in, with people helping them to be safe from the dangers of war.

6 WHO CARES?

Richard and Diane were feeling rather lost and lonely. Their mother had to go to hospital and stay there for a while. It would not be for long and Mum had let them help her get things together to take with her. While Mum was away, they were to stay with Gran and Grandpa. They always enjoyed staying there. It was a nice comfortable home to be in, and they had always looked forward to going. This time it would be different, because they were going without Mum and Dad, but it would be all right.

So much had happened in a short space of time. When Mum had been taken ill and had to stay in bed for a while people had been so helpful. Dad did as much as he could, of course, but Richard and Diane had been very glad that friends and neighbours had helped, too. The next-door neighbour had made sure they had meals prepared and gave them their breakfast and tea; another friend had been in to help with housework. People had invited the children in to play with their own children and, although they felt anxious about Mum, Diane and Richard knew that other people cared.

The doctors and nurses cared, too, and it seemed that the sun was shining particularly brightly on the day Mum was brought from hospital by Dad and they were a family together again. Of course, for a while Mum could not do all the work about the house that she usually did, but the children were glad to help Dad so that Mum could get well soon.

They were happy, too, that the cards and pictures they made to send to hospital had helped Mum. She said they helped her as much as the care of the doctors and nurses so that she felt much better by receiving them.

Another word for caring is thoughtfulness. It helps people in so many ways to know that others are caring and being thoughtful for them. We feel safe in knowing that we are being cared for.

God loves and cares for each and every one of us. In the Bible we read of the time that Jesus told the people how much God *did* care. Jesus told them that God knows all about every one of us, so much that 'every hair of our head is counted'. That is a rather funny way of telling us, but we understand what it means. He told the people that even a sparrow cannot fall to the ground without God knowing about it.

How wonderful it is to know that we are cared for in such a way. It makes us feel safe and secure. We can help, too, by caring and being thoughtful for others, so that in a very small way we can help God in his work.


## 7 'IT'S NOT FAIR!'

The boys were having a very good game. They had tossed for sides and were playing football in the playground. It was a nice day. After days of rain the skies were now blue and the playground had dried so it was just right for a good game. They were enjoying it, and suddenly everything changed. One side scored a goal, and they were very excited . . . Then 'Foul! . . .' 'It's not fair!' was a cry taken up by someone on the losing side. The game was spoiled, because by the time the boys had argued about the goal it was end of break and everyone had to return to lessons.

Later that day a group of children were playing some games indoors—table games. As the dice was passed round and thrown and the chips were moved along the board it became quite exciting. At last someone finished the game – the winner. They should have been happy, having played a game together, but they were not *all* happy. One of the losers was sure he should have won. 'You cheated!' he told the winner. 'It wasn't fair!'

It is so difficult sometimes to be the loser and see others winning, but this is a lesson everyone has to learn. In games and in competitions of all kinds there has to be a winner and so there must be losers. Not everyone can win. If that were possible there would not be a game or a competition and it would not be so exciting or enjoyable.

The most important thing is the game and how it is played. Games are some of the ways in which we learn to give and take with each other. Some people will always be good at some games: others will not be quite so good, but that doesn't matter. In playing together we are giving each other enjoyment, companionship and the feeling of taking part with others in a special way. Of course, we would all like to be the winners, but that is not possible.

Later, in life, we shall find that in many different ways we will have to learn sometimes to be the losers and accept the fact without being unkind or bitter. When grown up people want to do a certain kind of work and they apply for a position, there will be other people who also want the position, so that even in this case there will be a winner and some losers. This is a part of life that we have to try to understand.

It is a good thing to prepare ourselves for any kind of game, learning to know more about it, how to play the game well and practise, so that we get good at it. Then, in the game, we can do our very best, and if it means, in the end, that someone else has been even better, or managed to play a more skilful game than ourselves, we must accept this and be good losers, thinking what a good game it has been in spite of this.

## 8  PLAYING 'THE GLAD GAME'

In a story written many years ago, there was a girl with the kind of name we don't hear very often. She was called Pollyanna. Her mother had died when she was very small and Pollyanna lived with her father who was a Minister. They were very poor, and there were many things that Pollyanna would have liked. She would often think of the lovely things she would like—toys to play with, especially. Each year they received a parcel from some kind people, and each year Pollyanna looked forward to the parcel coming and seeing what it contained. One year, she did so hope that there would be something especially nice for her, and when the parcel arrived she could hardly wait to get it opened. There were all kinds of things in the package, but no specially nice toy for her. But there was a pair of crutches—the kind of sticks to help someone walk if they are injured or crippled. Pollyanna just wept with disappointment! Her father tried to comfort her. 'Just think,' he said, 'that you are so fortunate that you do not need these to help you to walk. Be glad that you have strong legs and are fit and healthy.'

So began the playing of 'The Glad Game' which Pollyanna taught many other people to play. Whatever happens, good or bad, you have to look for something to be glad about.

It is amazing, that if you begin playing this game you find that there really is something to be glad about always. It may be just a very small thing, but it helps to fight the disappointment or unhappiness. It is not very easy to play. In fact there are many times when it is very hard . . . but it is worth trying.

There is a little bit of good in everything and everybody. So often the good part is covered up by the bad and we think only about the unhappy or bad things. It would be a good thing to try playing the 'Glad Game' yourself when things seem to be against you, or even when they are not. We have so many good things in life and so often forget them because we are looking for something we cannot have. Give the game a try!

RELATED THEMES

*I sometimes think it isn't fair*
*That others have a bigger share:*
*Perhaps, instead, I should ask why*
*So many have much less than I.*                      R.P.

1.  As we go through this day, dear Father God, may we see ways
    in which we can help you by helping others. *Amen*

2.  Dear Father God, help us to grow in your love so that others
    may see something of you in us. *Amen*

3.  Forgive us, O Lord, when we do things which are not very nice
    and may hurt others.
    For words we say which are unkind,
    > *Forgive us, O Lord;*
    For anything we do that is hurtful,
    > *Forgive us, O Lord;*
    For any times when we are selfish,
    > *Forgive us, O Lord;*
    For sometimes being thoughtless or unfriendly,
    > *Forgive us, O Lord;*
    For any times when we are sulky or bad-tempered,
    > *Forgive us, O Lord;*
    Forgive us that sometimes we are not ready to admit we are
    wrong or to say that we are sorry; and help us to grow to be
    better children of yours and nicer friends to others. *Amen*

4.  Help me, O God to do only what is right but, when I do make
    mistakes or do wrong things, help me to admit that I have been
    wrong and to say I am sorry. *Amen*

5.  Help me to remember, dear God, that I cannot
    always do the things *I* want to do.
    Sometimes these things would not be good for me
    And I have to be told so.
    Sometimes it is the turn of other people
    To do things *their* way.
    Teach me not to be greedy or selfish
    And not to sulk or be spiteful.
    Show me how to be a friend to others
    And to think more of them than I do of myself. *Amen*

6. Help us, dear Lord, to please you today by being helpful to others, especially those who are weaker than ourselves, or who need us to be their friends. *Amen*

7. Help us, O Father God, not to think too much of ourselves but to remember the needs and the cares of other people. *Amen*

8. Help us, O God,
   To be kind to others;
   To be helpful and loving;
   To be honest and true;
   Because we are your children. *Amen*

9. Help us, O God, to understand what is right and then to do nothing else. *Amen*

10. O God, sometimes I lose my temper and do things that are not very nice. Forgive me and teach me to control myself. *Amen*

11. Sometimes we get upset by other children, O God.
    They say things that are not very nice;
    They do things that upset us;
    Sometimes they are spiteful or bad-tempered;
    They get sulky if they do not get their own way;
    They don't seem to care about us or what we think.
    Help us not to be upset by children who do
    these things
    And to make sure that we are not like this
    ourselves. *Amen*

12. Teach me, O God
    To be honest in everything I do;
    To avoid cheating or telling lies;
    [*Add here any other prayers that may be
    particularly relevant to the assembly theme*]
    And to do nothing else that would hurt others. *Amen*

## 5  ATTITUDES

Father, we thank thee for the night
For the things that I've done wrong
God whose name is love
In our work and in our play
Jesus, friend of little children
Jesus, good above all other
Little drops of water
Long ago when Jesus walked in Galilee
Stand up, clap hands
Teach me to love
Tell me
Two little eyes to look to God
When the world is dark and dreary


SOME BIBLE STORIES

| | |
|---|---|
| Dishonesty—Ananias and Sapphira (part) | Acts 4; 32–5; 4 |
| Ahab's covetousness | 1 Kings 21; 1–16 |
| Zacchaeus is sorry | Luke 19; 1–8 |
| Cain envies his brother | Genesis 4; 1–8 |
| Joseph's jealous brothers | Genesis 37; 3–11 |
| Jesus cares | Matthew 20; 29–34 |


ACTIVITIES

Behind all the stories there is the question of attitudes and relationships. These are subjects that do not lend themselves greatly to
practical work—rather to discussion and play about the attitude in
question.

Discussion with the children on how *they* would react if someone
were to adopt an unpleasant attitude towards them might present
opportunity to suggest that the children should think about their
own attitudes.

Encourage the children to play out the particular problem in their
play groups, e.g. Someone has taken something belonging to
another member of the group; or someone keeps saying, 'I want

71

that!' See how the children respond in their play world to real life situations.

Paint pictures of faces—sad faces and happy faces. When would you expect to see faces like these?

Have a 'Smile' campaign in class/school.

Perhaps the following prayer, found in Chester Cathedral, whilst being beyond the children's comprehension, may give food for thought.

Give me a good digestion, Lord,
    And also something to digest;
Give me a healthy body, Lord,
    With sense to keep it at its best.
Give me a healthy mind, good Lord,
    To keep the good and pure in sight,
Which seeing sin is not appalled
    But finds a way to set it right;
Give me a mind that is not bored,
    That does not whimper, whine or sigh;
Don't let me worry overmuch
    About the fussy thing called I,
Give me a sense of humour, Lord,
    Give me the grace to see a joke,
To get some happiness from life
    And pass it on to other folk.

*Anonymous*

# 6  Making and growing

*It is good that we use the skill of hand, eye and brain to create, and to make full use of our abilities and knowledge. We must also come to appreciate that there are areas in which we alone cannot create or produce. Man can achieve many objectives but he has his limitations.*

*In the following we attempt to introduce to the children the idea of our being able to do many things, but there are still areas in which our own skill or experience is not sufficient and the power of more important forces than ourselves are needed.*

## 1  MAKING PICTURES

Do you know that you could draw before you could write? The very first attempt we make to form a shape or a letter is a way in which we are expressing, or 'telling' something we want to say. Baby scribble is the beginning of drawing, the first attempt at making a shape. We gradually learn to hold and control the crayon or pencil so that we can make more shapes and so eventually learn to make those shapes which form letters and words. Then we are writing!

Making pictures is something we can *all* do. Of course, other people do not always see our pictures as we do, and may not understand what we are trying to 'tell' in the pictures, but the important thing is that we have put what we want to say or what we are thinking or feeling into some shape. To make pictures, to use colour, or to make shapes is an enjoyable thing and something everyone must be allowed to do.

Pictures, in a way, are a means of speaking to others, even if we come from another land where a different language is spoken. We may not be able to speak to people in their own language, but we can help them understand us, and in our turn understand what they are trying to tell us, by using pictures. In comics, magazines and newspapers, the artists sometimes use this way of telling a story. It is a way of helping everyone to understand the story, even if they cannot read very well.

For many hundreds of years, people have drawn pictures to tell others about themselves and about their lives. Very clever people, who have travelled to far distant lands and tried to learn about people of long ago, have found some most interesting things. They have discovered very old buildings, perhaps buried for hundreds of years by sand or by volcano dust, and when they brushed away the dust and dirt covering the walls, what did they find?

Often they found pictures painted all those hundreds, even thousands of years ago, showing the kind of things people did in those days, how they lived, and the games they played. From the pictures we have learned that they kept animals as pets and also to work for them. They hunted and fished, and they built homes where they looked after their families, just as people do today.

The pictures may seem strange compared with our present day ones. The clothes and the kind of animals they show are different but the main ideas are just like those in our own pictures. In fact, some of the pictures some children paint today look very much like the kind of pictures men have discovered!

Our pictures or drawings may not be actual *pictures*. They may be shapes or forms that we find pleasant to make and look at. They may also be pleasant for other people to look at. It is not important that they should look 'real', but that they help us to say something other than by speaking.

There is another sort of picture too. I wonder what kind of picture people see when they look at us. Is it a pleasant picture, showing a pleasant person? Think about this. We are 'telling' people about ourselves.

## 2  MAKING MODELS

When you want to make a model, how do you start? Do you think about what you want to make and then start collecting the things you need? Or do you just get ideas from the things you have at hand? At different times we find we do both. Sometimes, if we are wanting to make a model of a particular thing, we have to collect the necessary bits and pieces.

Some of the best models are those we make in the company of others. Have you looked at a pile of junk—cardboard boxes, reels, paper, cotton wool, rubber bands, paper clips—and suddenly got an idea of what you could make out of it? Sometimes you may have started working on one idea and then seen something else even better that could be made.

What a lot of fun, enjoyment and satisfaction we find in making all kinds of thing. We sometimes call this by another word—'creating'. There are small models of the kind which need the very careful use of our hands and scissors. There are especially fine models made by a group working together to build something really big, using large boxes and making it all on a large scale. Sometimes we make model trains or cars that we can actually sit in and pretend to drive. A group of children, with a teacher at hand to help, once made a huge robot. He was quite a favourite with everyone and had his place in the school hall for a time.

Older children like to make models that are much harder to make—'planes, motors, ships and figures of people. This takes quite a lot of skill, and nimble fingers. It needs careful measuring, cutting, sticking and painting to produce a worthwhile model of this kind.

In so many ways, then, we 'create', produce something which is a model. God is our Creator, and has made us, each a special model of our own kind. We sometimes hear of people being models in a way that makes us feel they are so good, they are almost perfect. We cannot be perfect very often, or for very long, and perhaps it is just as well! But we should try to be the best person we can be, as near a 'model' as we are able, for our Creator—God, who made us in his own likeness.

3  MAKING FIGURES

Some of the most popular models that people like to make and to look at are figures which represent people. There are figures which look like small statues, carefully made so that the faces and clothing are copied to make us think of the person they resemble. Features, like mouths, noses, hands and fingers, are very carefully fashioned. You can see these figures in shops and in people's homes. They are very lovely to look at—made by craftsmen.

The kind of figures most familiar to children are dolls and puppets. Dolls have been the favourite toy of little girls for many years. If we can take a look at dolls which have been kept by people for a long time we find that they are often very fragile, easily broken. It would not be possible to play with them as we are able to play with our dolls in these days. But they are carefully and beautifully made. Little girls who played with such dolls so long ago would be so surprised to see the kinds of doll we have today. All the time people are learning new ways to make toys look more like the real thing. Dolls are now made to be like real babies—they cry and speak and drink and wet.

We have dolls dressed in clothing of long ago to show figures of people in history, and dolls dressed in clothing worn in other lands. There has even been a doll made for boys, with the clothing and uniform of an action man, to be dressed and undressed and made to act like the real person.

Those which give a lot of satisfaction to many children are the dolls they can make themselves, perhaps from pegs or pipe cleaners and then dress with scraps of material. It is good to make toys for ourselves and not just have them made for us.

Puppets, too, give a great deal of pleasure, both when we make them and when we use them. Think of all the different kinds of puppet there are. Some are very cleverly made and skilfully used by people in a puppet theatre to tell us stories. There are hand puppets which fit over the whole hand, finger puppets to fit on a single finger and string puppets which are worked from above by moving strings. We can make our own very simple puppets or more difficult ones if we are shown the way to make them.

Sometimes people make puppets that look a little like themselves. It is as though we put a little of ourselves into whatever we make and, when making a face, we may use our own as a pattern. Look at some of the puppets made by your friends and see if this is so. This is quite possible, for God made us and there is a little bit of God in everyone. In making our toys—whether they be dolls, or puppets, or any others, we must put into them the best skill we have, so that they last, and can be used to give pleasure both in the making and the using.

### 4 MAKING MUSIC

One thing we can all do is to make music—whether we make music alone or together with others. It does not always sound very musical when some people sing, and it is not always very easy for very young children to sing in tune, but music can be made in many ways.

The important thing is that we use our ears and *listen* to the sounds and the music of the world around us. What can we hear if we stay very still and very quiet for a few seconds . . .? Birds sing to us. We hear the music of the voices of others, the ticking of the clock, the hum of a bee, the swish of cars through puddles, a stream splashing over stones, someone singing or humming, the clopping of horses' hooves. We hear all kinds of sounds which can be used when we make our own music.

Clap hands to make a rhythm . . . clap . . . clap . . . clap-clap-clap, one . . . two . . . one-two-three. Even the smallest among us can make up simple rhythms and tunes. When we work with others to make music it is even better. In this way we can make music to enjoy together and for others to listen to.

When older people and grown-ups play instruments to form an orchestra or a band they have to learn first of all to play the instrument by themselves, where to place their fingers, how to control their breath and how to recognize notes. This needs some hard work and a lot of time for practice—time when they may perhaps prefer to be playing, but as they are interested they are prepared to give their time to learn to play the instrument and make music.

It is enjoyable to listen to one instrument playing or one voice singing, but when a group plays together or sings together it needs extra care and practice so that all the notes fit together to give enjoyment to people listening. The singers or musicians enjoy it very much too. For thousands of years people have made music. They have listened to sounds and put these sounds together to make something lovely to hear.

This is one of the ways in school that we may work together to make something good for people to listen to. Even very young children may learn to play percussion instruments, the bells, tri-angles, cymbals and drums. Try to make music whenever you can, tapping one hand with the fingers of the other, clapping hands, or beating time and making rhythm with two sticks.

Make happy sounds together.


5   PLANTING SEEDS

Take a few seeds. They may be small or large, wrinkled, brown, not beautiful, perhaps rather ugly and hardly worth bothering with. If we leave them out in the open, or allow them to shrivel without nourishment, they will die. But if we do something with those seeds and care for them properly, something will happen. So many of the things we need and enjoy in our lives begin with a seed. Much of our food, flowers, green grass and trees, begin as seeds.

To make it grow properly, the seed has to be used in the right way. It needs to be fed and nourished. It is planted in the ground or in a pot, and kept warm and moist. When it has been fed by the soil, refreshed by water and kept warm and snug in the darkness, something wonderful happens. The seed's outside covering bursts. It is coming to life. Soon, it begins pushing out in two ways: its roots reach down, down into the dark soil, and, at the other end, a shoot begins to feel its way upwards reaching for the light. Properly cared for, it grows and grows, with the shoot getting longer and stronger until it breaks through the surface of the ground. Then we have our grass, or our lovely flowers, or our food growing and developing. This is one of the wonderful ways in which we are provided for. We have to do our part in helping feed and nourish the seeds, but God has provided for us in this way and we could not do it without His help.

The story of The Sower in the Bible tells us what happens to seeds. Jesus used this way of telling a story to people so that they could understand and learn even greater truths. The Sower scattered the seeds and some fell on the path where they were eaten by the birds; some fell on rocky ground and when the sun shone they dried up and perished. Some of the seeds, though, fell into good soil and the sun, wind and rain helped them to grow, strong and healthy.

Sometimes we hear and see things which make us think and use our minds. These can help us to be better or make us not so good. They are different kinds of seeds, that Jesus was trying to help the people understand. The good seeds which settle into the good soil and grow properly are the healthy, happy, kindly things, and the words of God which help us to live our lives in the best possible way.

## 6  GROWING BULBS

When spring is here we feel so happy because we know that winter is behind and summer is on its way. We know it is really spring when we see the green blades coming through the ground and the daffodils, crocuses, tulips, narcissi and all the lovely flowers of spring are there before us. Even if we live in big cities, in flats or maisonettes and have no gardens of our own, we can grow spring flowers in our window boxes or see them in the parks. They make us think about the sunshine, and green buds and baby birds and lots of other wonderful things.

Preparation for the spring flowers starts in the autumn when the bulbs are prepared. They are not seeds, but bulbs which are not very pretty to look at. Some look just like onions but would not taste as good if they were used as our mothers use onions. They have a different kind of part to play.

Like the seeds, the bulbs need to be planted in the right way, sometimes with their tips showing through the soil. They may even be grown in a special way, perched at the top of a glass vase with water inside the vase.

Bulbs need to be kept in the dark for a time, and fed and nourished. If they are kept too long in the dark after they have begun to grow, the shoots will not grow strong or green: they will be very pale and sickly. So it is necessary to bring the bowls out into the light at the proper time. The leaves of bulbs planted in the ground find their way to the top and the daylight is there to help them to develop and become a lovely fresh green colour. Who would think, when looking at a dull bulb, what loveliness would grow from it in time?

Perhaps some people think we are dull ordinary people, but like the bulbs, it is possible for us to grow and develop into interesting, thoughtful and helpful people. All around us we see good things and bad things in the world and in the lives of people. We need to see the way we should go so that we may grow into the kind of person who does good things and thinks the right kind of thoughts.


7   GROWING FOOD

Spring, summer, autumn and winter. The four seasons come each year. In planning the world and thinking about the people and creatures who would live on the earth, it was a wonderful idea God had, to split the year up into seasons. Each season has its own kind of weather and atmosphere to produce things from the land and from the sea. In this way we have been provided for, so that man and animals can eat and drink and live.

The farmers, and all the other people who work so that we may have the food we need, have to do their share of the planning and working too so that each year the crops grow and are harvested. Wheat, vegetables, fruit, fish and animals all fit into the plan so that throughout the year there will be sufficient to feed us all.

It is not only on the farms that food is grown. Our fathers, uncles and other members of our families work in their gardens to dig and sow and tend the plants which will feed the family. Does your father grow vegetables in his garden? What kind of vegetables and fruit do we grow in our gardens?

In many towns where people haven't gardens large enough to grow food, they may be able to rent pieces of land which are called allotments. They are used by people to do just what they would if they had more garden space at home. People plan their allotments and decide just what they will grow. They must think what kind of seed they will need and how to train the plants which grow and trail—the peas, beans and marrows. They dig the ground and sow the seed, then work on the allotment regularly and take great pride in the food they produce, just as other people do in their gardens.

Working on the land and growing food is one way in which we always work with God. We can do quite a lot to make sure that food is grown, but without the help of the rain and sun, the food will not grow and ripen.

## 8 WE GROW UP

We have been thinking about all the things we are able to make with our hands, and use our brains, thinking out ideas and planning. We have also thought about the things that only God can make. We cannot make a seed or a bulb, or a tree or bush.

We read in the Bible that when God made the first man he made him like himself. God was the pattern for us to copy.

We have also thought about the growing seeds and plants, and how they need to be fed and nourished in the right way if they are to grow and develop to be healthy and strong. We, too, have to be fed and nourished in the right way in order to grow strong, healthy bodies. A tiny baby depends on mother and father to see he is fed. Then all through our lives we depend on each other.

As we grow older we take more responsibility for ourselves and so we must always make sure that we take care of our bodies, to keep them clean and to feed them in the right way. While growing up in our bodies we also have to remember the part of us that thinks. Our thoughts and feelings must also develop and grow as our bodies grow.

As the body is cared for and fed, so our minds need to be cared for and fed by reading books, listening to people, hearing music, talking about important things which mean a lot to us and using our hands and eyes and ears in the right way. In these ways we are helping to give the right kind of food to our minds, so that they grow, too.

Another part of our being is our character—the kind of person we are. We all know people we like and others we do not like very much. It is the character of the person we like or dislike, perhaps more than how he looks! Kind thoughts, being helpful, thinking of others before ourselves, considering others, trying to control ourselves when we feel angry or want to hurt someone: these are the things that help make us the people we are, the kind of person that others see.

We are born to be tall, short, fat, thin perhaps and there is not much we can do to change that, but there is a lot we can do to make our characters as we grow up. Life is sometimes unhappy or hard, and characters that have grown and developed in the right way help us face the times in life when we may be unhappy or uncertain. These are difficult things to understand when we are young, but it is important to remember that they are a part of life, and we can try to help each other at such times to be strong.

RELATED THEMES

*I can plant and I can sow*
*But only God can make it grow.*                      C.S.

PRAYERS

1. As I grow up, please God, help me to be the kind of person you would like me to be. *Amen*

2. As I watch the seeds grow, dear Father God, help me to remember that you have made them and put life into them. *Amen*

3. Dear Father God, I like to make things with my hands but I am not very good at it yet. Teach me how to do things well so that I can be pleased with what I make. *Amen*

4. Dear God, we say thank you for all the kinds of music that we can enjoy and for all the instruments on which we can play it. *Amen*

5. Dear God, when I think how ordinary-looking seeds and rather ugly bulbs can grow up to have lovely flowers which people enjoy, let me remember that you can help me to grow up to give pleasure to other people. *Amen*

6. For hands to work and minds that think things out, so that we can make and do so many interesting things, thank you, God. *Amen*

7. Help us today, dear Lord, to learn how to use our hands to create lovely things and our minds to think lovely thoughts. *Amen*

8. Sometimes, dear God, I feel very happy
   And then I like to sing:
   I like to hum and make other music too:
   I enjoy tapping out the rhythm of a tune,
   Or listening to music with a good beat:
   Sometimes I like to make music with other children:
   So thank you, dear God, for music. *Amen*

9. Sometimes, O God, I like to grow things
And I know that some grown-up people like to do so
as well.
Thank you for food and flowers,
And for places where they can be grown;
And thank you for sending the sun and rain
That help to make them grow. *Amen*

10. Thank you, O God, for things to do and make:
For pictures we can draw and paint,
                    *Thank you, O God;*
For things to make with paper and card,
                    *Thank you, O God;*
For different kinds of model to make,
                    *Thank you, O God;*
For dolls and figures to make and dress,
                    *Thank you, O God;*
For seeds to plant and bulbs to grow,
                    *Thank you, O God;*
For these, and for every way to use our minds and our hands for
making or growing, we thank you, O God. *Amen*

11. Thank you, O Lord, for all the fun of growing things: and thank
you for all the things, like the sun and rain, which you send to make
them grow. *Amen*

12. We remember, O God, that all we have comes from you. Help
us to use those gifts you have given us to help others for your sake.
*Amen*

SUGGESTED HYMNS

At work beside his father's bench
Clap, clap, clap, clap
Dinner, breakfast
Glad that I live am I
In our work and in our play
Jesus, friend of little children
Look up! look up!
Lord I love to stamp and shout

# 6 MAKING AND GROWING

*Books*

This is a fairly wide subject and there are lots of simple books which
may be useful, especially those giving simple instructions as to how
to do things. Here are just a few:

SEE HOW IT GROWS series, Macmillan
SEE HOW IT'S MADE series, Macmillan
PAPER/PRINTS AND PATTERNS/CLAY/SCULPTURE/
   PUPPET PEOPLE/GROWING THINGS INDOORS/
   MAKING MUSIC *(Starters Activities)*, Macdonald
TOYS AND TOYMAKING/STORY OF PUPPETS/YOUR
   BODY AT WORK *(Blackwell's Learning Library)*, Blackwell
TOYS AND GAMES *(Our World)*, Burke
HOW A SEED GROWS/WHERE DOES YOUR GARDEN
   GROW? *(Let's Read and Find Out)*, Black
THINGS TO DO WITH PLANTS *(Things to do)*, Macdonald
MUSIC *(Starters)*, Macdonald
SOUNDS AND MUSIC *(First Library)*, Macdonald
THANK YOU FOR A BOOK TO READ *(Thank you books)*,
   Lion
YOUR BODY *(Ladybird Nature)*, Ladybird.
THE SEED/THE BULB *(See how it grows)*, Macmillan
PLANTS IN A HOUSE *(First Interest)*, Ginn
WHAT CAN I DO TODAY?, Purnell.
MAKE YOUR OWN DOLLS, PUPPETS AND HOUSES,
   Purnell

*Making pictures*

Not an activity especially associated with this series but a familiar
one with pictures made using any media.

*Puppets*

A simple puppet can be made with a paper bag, preferably white.
Draw or paint a face on the bag, fill the bag with crumpled paper,

insert a lolly stick and tie the open end of the bag tightly round the stick, or fasten it with a strip of Sellotape. This method is particularly useful when making animal puppets, the points of the bag can be screwed to form ears.

### Finger puppets

On thick paper 7.6×5 cm (3″×2″) draw a figure, making the body wider than your finger. Colour the figure with crayons and cut it out. Cut a piece of paper 3.8×6.3 cm (1½″×2½″) roll it to make a tube to fit the finger and glue it. Glue the figure to the front of the tube. Bend the arms forward.

### Dolls

Dolly pegs can be used. Paint or draw a face on the rounded top part of the peg. Twist a pipe cleaner to form arms. Dress with scraps of material.

### Paper bag dolls

You will need two small sweet bags. Crumple soft toilet paper and half fill one bag with it. Twist a pipe cleaner round the neck. Fill the second bag with crumpled tissues and tie the top with cotton. Glue the head on to the body. Draw a face with felt tip pens and glue wool or paper strips to the top of the head to make hair.

A cat may be made in the same way, but use a piece of narrow ribbon or wool to tie round the neck. Bags could be painted in the colours of the cat. Glue on a piece of string to make a tail.

### Planting

Bulbs could be planted in the usual manner. Those grown over water make it possible for the roots to be observed. Mustard and cress seeds on damp cloth or cotton wool soon grow.

*Fruit pips*

Soak for a day or two before planting. Keep well watered and warm. To watch seeds sprout quickly, you will need a drinking glass, a strong tissue, water, some seeds.

Wet the tissue slightly and line the inside of the drinking glass with it. Put about an inch of water into the bottom of the glass, so as to keep the tissue wet. Put the seeds carefully between the wet paper and the glass, so that you can see them from the outside. To make the seeds sprout fast, soak them first overnight. Try several kinds of seeds.

Some seeds will sprout faster than others. A diary could be kept or drawings made of how each seed is growing.

*Making music*

Make up a simple 'school song' to be sung at assembly.
Percussion to accompany singing at assembly.
Make simple instruments such as maraccas, using plastic containers containing beans, beads or other 'rattling' material.

*Measuring growth of children*

Measuring stick or other measure fastened to a wall. Children keep a note of their height. Measure from time to time to see rate of growth.

# 7   Food

*There are few things that can be of greater importance to children than food. It is something with which they are very familiar, superficially at least; it is something with which they come into contact several times a day; and even at an early age they know that it is vital to life itself.*

*In this theme we begin with the familiar and proceed from there to introduce various facets; the shops and the people who serve in them; the farmers, the fishermen and many others who work in difficult circumstances and sometimes in danger to produce it; the people of many other lands who grow our food and those who transport it. Other aspects of the subject will be found in different sections, notably 8, 9 and 23.*

*It is hoped that the children will become aware of so many things that have been done to give them their food and be thankful for these things.*


1   GROCERY AND FOODSTORES

What did you have for breakfast this morning? Cornflakes? Porridge? Bread and jam or marmalade? Bacon and eggs? Or something else? When you go home from school you will probably have another meal and maybe a chocolate drink and some biscuits when you go to bed.

Most of the things we have mentioned will have come from one kind of shop. Where does your mother do most of her shopping? If you live in a village it may be in the village shop or store where lots of different things are sold. If you live in town it may be the local grocer's shop with rows and rows of packets and tins on the shelves, a counter for bacon and other cooked meats, and racks for bread and perhaps some fruit and vegetables.

Lots of people now do their shopping in a large food-store or supermarket. Perhaps you have been shopping with your parents in a supermarket and have watched them take all sorts of things from the shelves and put them in the wire basket until they have all they need. Then they go to the check-out to pay for all they have in the basket.

What a lot of things there are in the supermarket! There are tins of fruit, meat, fish, soup, baked beans and vegetables; there are packets of sugar, tea, rice, flour and dried fruit; there are eggs, cheeses, milk foods, drinks, sweets, frozen foods and lots and lots of other things.

If someone were to ask you where your food came from, you might say, 'the shop' or 'the supermarket' and you would be quite right. But where did the shopkeeper get it from? And who put it in the tins or the packets? And who grew the things that went into the tins? Where were these things grown and how did they get to us? There are lots and lots of people in many parts of the world who have produced our food.

When you eat your food, remember to say thank you for all these people, and to God who made the food grow.

## 2   MILK

Do you have bottles of milk brought to your house every day? The milkman, or dairyman, who brought it got it from a bottling factory; the people at the bottling factory got it from the farmer; and the farmer got it from the cows. Your milk may have travelled a long, long way before you drink it.

In many parts of the country there are dairy farms with herds of cows that are kept just to give milk. The cows do not make milk for people to drink. They make it for their babies—the calves. Cows do not make milk until they have had a calf. Calves, like other baby animals, cannot eat solid food but need the milk which they take from their mothers.

The farmer leaves the calf with its mother at first but then takes it away and gives it a different kind of milk to drink. The creamy milk from the cow can then be used for feeding people. The dairy farmer milks the cows to get this milk. Most farmers milk their cows twice a day, early in the morning and again in the afternoon. The milk is put into large churns or a tank, to be collected and taken to the bottling factory.

The dairy farmer has a busy life. He is up in the morning, long before you are, for the first milking. Apart from milking he has to spend a lot of time in looking after the cows, preparing their food and perhaps growing some of it in his fields, cleaning their sheds and doing all sorts of other things, including sending for the vet (animal doctor) if they are ill.

The farmer has a busy life with very few holidays. Remember all he does to give you milk.

### 3 MEAT

If you look in your butcher's shop, you will see lots of different kinds of meat. There will be joints of meat—beef, pork and lamb. No doubt, too, there will be chickens and perhaps turkeys, ducks or other birds. How many other meats can you think of that you might see there? Sausages, chops, liver, bacon, kidneys, tripe, black-pudding, and rabbits are just a few. Which of these do you like? All of them have come from animals which have been killed to give us food.

If you take a closer look at the labels on the meat, you will see that it has come from lots of different places. Joints of beef may be marked 'English' or 'Scottish'. They have come from animals which were kept on English or Scottish farms. But you will also find joints of beef which have come from Argentina, in South America.

Joints of lamb and lamb chops may be English but they may have come from New Zealand, which is right on the other side of the world. A lot of our bacon comes from pigs which were bred in Denmark. We may even have rabbits from China. We have to get meat from other countries because we cannot breed enough animals to feed all the people who live in Britain. Our islands are too small.

In some parts of the world there is much more room for breeding animals. On the plains of South America there are huge ranches on which thousands of cattle are bred for beef. In New Zealand there are millions of sheep, many of which will end up in our butchers' shops as joints of 'New Zealand Lamb'. The animals are killed in these far-off lands and the meat is frozen to keep it fresh. Then it is sent to us in ships. We have many people to thank for our food.

### 4 FISH

When we see all the fish in the fishmonger's shop, we probably do not give any thought to the people who caught it. It is there for us to buy and we often take for granted that it will be there—just as we do so much of our food.

Yet some of the fish comes from far away seas and the fishermen who catch it have a hard and uncomfortable life at sea. A lot of our fish is caught in cold seas off the north of Europe—cold even in the summer months but much colder in winter, when fishermen often work with their ships coated with thick ice.

Some of the trawlers, the large fishing boats, will be at sea for many days at a time until their holds are filled with fish. Nets, like large bags, are pulled along behind the trawler, scooping up the fish as they move through the water. Then the heavy net of fish has to be pulled on to the ship and the end opened so that the fish fall on to the decks. There they have to be sorted out—and that is very hard on the hands when handling cold, scaly fish.

During the time they are on the fishing grounds, the fishermen have very little sleep. Once the net has been emptied it is let out again for more fish. Then, when the holds are full, it is full-steam-ahead for the home port and a brief rest ashore. But before going home, all the fish has to be unloaded and put into boxes for sale.

Some smaller fishing boats do not sail so far away. They fish in the North Sea or around the coast of Britain. But it is still a hard life for the fishermen, especially in bad weather.

## 5   VEGETABLES AND FRUIT

If someone were to ask you what is your favourite food, or which food in the shops you find most exciting, what would you say? Cakes? Jellies? Chocolate biscuits? Baked beans? Sausages?

How many of you would say potatoes? Or cabbage? Carrots, peas, beans or onions? They all belong to that rather uninteresting group of foods that we call vegetables. None of them seems particularly exciting, yet it is difficult to imagine what our meals would be like if we did not have them.

Fancy eating fish without any chips, or a roast dinner without any roast potatoes! Many people like some 'mash' with a pie or with sausages, or maybe potatoes baked in their jackets as a special treat. Most people, too, would think a meal very strange if there were no green vegetables—cabbage, brussels sprouts, peas or beans—or cauliflower, carrots or onions.

These vegetables can all be grown in this country and there are lots of farmers who do grow them so that we can buy plenty in the shops. There are others who grow what we call salad crops—lettuce, cucumber, tomatoes, radishes, spring onions and beetroot, which many people like to eat in the summer.

All these vegetables and salad crops are sold by a man whom we call a greengrocer. He may sell lots of other interesting vegetables too. There are many shops in towns and cities where people who once lived overseas, in places like India, Pakistan or the West Indies, can buy the kind of vegetables they like. These are vegetables such as yams, sweet potatoes, aubergines and bread-fruit.

The greengrocer who sells vegetables probably sells fruit as well, so his correct title is Fruiterer and Greengrocer. The fruits make his shop look much brighter than if he sold only vegetables. Bright juicy oranges, apples, pears, bananas and grapes are much more mouth-watering than vegetables. He may also sell fruits for people from overseas, such as guavas, mangoes or plantains.

Some foods seem much more exciting than others but we need them all if we are to grow up healthy and strong. Remember that your body needs these foods; and remember to thank God for so many different kinds of food to eat.

### 6 FOOD FROM OVERSEAS

Many of the foods which we enjoy have come to us from other countries. The butcher may sell beef from South America, lamb from New Zealand and bacon from Denmark. We get this meat from overseas because we cannot rear enough animals ourselves.

But there are lots of things that we cannot grow in our country because we do not have enough sun or rain. Think of all the fruits in the shops. We can grow apples or pears, though not as many as we need. We cannot grow oranges, bananas or pineapples which need a lot of sunshine. We get oranges from places such as Israel, Cyprus, South Africa or Spain. Do you know where bananas come from? Or pineapples?

Think of other foods we eat, too. Do you like bread and jam? Most of our wheat for making bread comes from Canada. The butter you spread on the bread may also have come from another country and so may the fruit and the sugar used to make the jam.

Look at the labels on the tins and packets that Mummy buys in the shops. Ask her which ones have come from another country. There may be tomatoes from Italy, peaches from Australia or a box of dates from Iraq. Even some foods which were put into tins in this country, such as baked beans, were grown overseas.

Do you eat curry and rice? Lots of people, especially those from India and Pakistan, enjoy hot, spicy foods. In an Indian shop you will find lots of foods such as rice, flour for making chapatti, rooti, parhata, singhara and other things, as well as spices such as garlic, ginger, paprika, chilli, black pepper and cloves—all of which came from another country.

It is nice now and then to eat different kinds of food. People sometimes enjoy going for a meal in a Chinese restaurant or a Tandoori Indian restaurant, or perhaps for special meals cooked by Greek or Italian chefs. Maybe with their meal they have a glass of wine from France, Spain or Italy.

Those other things that we drink have also come a long way. Tea, coffee and chocolate are all grown overseas—and so is the fruit to make your orange or lemon drink.

So many different kinds of food from so many different places, and they are all ours to enjoy! We would have fewer things to eat if it were not for lots and lots of people in many countries all over the world.

There are lots of people who remember to say a little 'Thank you' prayer to God before they eat their meals. Do you remember to say thank you for good food . . . and enough of it?

## 7 BRINGING OUR FOOD

When you need some food, Mummy goes to the shop to buy it. There is always plenty there and, as long as there is some money to pay for it, you need never go hungry. But have you ever thought how many people have helped to get that food to the shop?

Let's just think of one thing you might buy—a tin of peaches maybe. If you look on the label wrapped round the tin, you may find that it came from Australia. There, on the other side of the world, somebody had a large number of peach trees on which the fruit was grown. When it was ripe, the people who worked for him picked the peaches from the trees and packed them carefully so that they could be taken by lorry to the place where they would be peeled, cut and put into cans.

Remember, too, that there were other people who had made the cans; there were people who made the paper for the labels; and there were others who printed the labels. The cans were all packed in cardboard cartons made by yet other people.

Australia is a long way away across the sea. Those cans of peaches had to be taken on a big lorry to the docks, where they were loaded on to a big ship. Then, for several weeks, sailors sailed that ship many thousands of miles to the port in this country where it was unloaded.

Once again the cans of peaches were taken by road, this time to a large store or warehouse, where they were kept until another lorry took them to the shop where Mummy bought one. What a lot of people were needed just to get you one tin of fruit! And that tin of peaches was only one of the things that Mummy might have bought in the shop. Think of all the other foods in the shopping basket and of the lots and lots of people who helped to grow them, get them ready for you to eat, or carry them in their ships, lorries or trains from far-away places.

When you eat your food, remember all those people and especially any whose work may be difficult or dangerous.

Remember, too, to say a big thank you to God, not only for sending the sun and rain to make the food grow, but for all those people too.

## 8 SPECIAL FOODS AND CUSTOMS

There are some foods that we enjoy eating very much. What are your favourite foods? [*Children's response*] There are other foods that you do not like. Which are these? [*Children's response*]

Foods that some people like are the same as those which other people do not like. Have you every watched somebody eating and thought to yourself, 'Fancy eating that!'? But, of course, we are all different in so many ways. Our liking for certain foods may depend upon what is eaten in our homes. John enjoys his fish and chips but does not like curry. It is too hot for him. Tariq, whose parents once lived in Pakistan, would sooner have the curry.

Who likes a nice rasher of bacon? Or some nice sizzling pork sausages? Lots of people do. But Hussein has never eaten bacon or pork sausages or anything else which has come from a pig. He is a

Muslim and his religion says that he must not eat meat from pigs. Rachael never eats pork either. She belongs to a Jewish family and they remember that the Jewish laws say that there are some animals which should never be eaten.

The food that Jewish people are allowed to eat is called Kosher food. You will sometimes find this word printed on tins or packets so that Jewish people know that the contents are fit for them to eat. Muslim people usually eat meat only if it is Halal meat—that is meat from animals that have been killed in a particular way and the name of Allah (God) mentioned when the animal is killed. So what we eat depends upon our religion too.

Then there are certain foods which are eaten at special times of the year. When would you eat Christmas pudding? Pancakes? Chocolate eggs? These are all connected with special Christian days. Jewish people have their special foods, too, such as dry biscuits or *Matzoth,* eaten during the Passover festival. There are certain times too when people may *not* eat. Muslim people keep a month called Ramadan, when they eat nothing during the day. This is called fasting.

Fasting helps to remind people of others who have no food. It also helps them to remember that they do it in the name of God—and so they remember God. There are lots of people of many religions who always remember God when they eat and say a prayer to thank him for all his goodness in providing us with food.

# 7 FOOD

People of most religions have prayers or 'graces' which may be offered at meal times. Children will probably be familiar with simple verses or prayers that they may have used themselves, perhaps the most familiar being 'For what we are about to receive, may the Lord make us truly thankful. *Amen*'

Christian prayers may thank God or be offered in the name of Jesus Christ. Sikhs offer prayers similar to these (but not in the name of Jesus Christ), or to the Hindu prayer below.

*A Hindu grace before evening meal:*

'O God, let us stay together, eat together, do good deeds together.'

*A Jewish blessing before meals:*

'Blessed are you, O Lord God, King of the Universe, who brings forth bread from the earth. *Amen*'

Muslim prayers:

Before a meal: 'Bismillah' (*In the name of God*)
After a meal: 'Alhamdulillah' (*Praise be to God*)

*The example of Jesus:*

| | |
|---|---|
| When feeding the multitude | Matthew 14; 19 |
| On the road to Emmaus | Luke 24; 30 |

PRAYERS

1. As we eat our food, dear God, help us to remember those children who will not have a good meal today. Make us thankful for all our blessings and mindful of the needs of others. *Amen*

2. As we say thank you, Heavenly Father, for those who bring us our food, we recall that all good gifts come from you and ask that we may always remember this. *Amen*

3. Dear God, fill our stomachs with food, our hearts with love and our minds with thankfulness. *Amen*

4. Dear Heavenly Father, thank you for farmers and all people who work very hard so that we can have our daily food. *Amen*

5. For food to eat
   And those who prepare it;
   For health to enjoy it
   And friends to share it;
   Thank you, Heavenly Father. *Amen*          *Source not known*

6. O God, there are so many people who help to
   give us our food.
   We think of farmers who grow it and gather the harvest,
   And farmers in lands across the sea;
   We remember the fishermen who catch our fish,
   And sailors who bring us food from overseas;
   We think of shopkeepers who sell us our food
   And our parents who earn the money to pay for it.
       Thank you for them all. *Amen*

7. Thank you, God, for the farmers in many lands who work to give us our food; thank you for the sailors who bring it to us; and thank you for people who sell it in the markets and shops so that we have plenty to eat. *Amen*

8. Thank you, God our Father,
   For filling the seas with fish for us to eat;
   For fishermen who work hard to catch them;
   And for those who sell them in the shops.
   Give us thankful hearts. *Amen*

9. Thank you, God our Father,
   For our wonderful world and all its people;
   For so many different kinds of food
   And so many ways of preparing it.
   Teach us to share it more fairly. *Amen*

10. Today we think of all sorts of mouth-watering fruits and lots of
    not-so-interesting vegetables. We know we need them to help
    us to grow big and strong and so we say thank you for all these
    things you have given us. *Amen*

11. We say Thank you, God:
    For all the food that is ours to enjoy,
    *Thank you, God;*
    For people in many lands who grow the food,
    *Thank you, God;*
    For those who work hard to gather the harvest,
    *Thank you, God;*
    For those who carry the food in trucks, trains
    and ships,
    *Thank you, God;*
    For market workers and shopkeepers who sell it,
    *Thank you, God;*
    Thank you for so many people who help us get
    our food. *Amen*

12. We thank you, God our Father, that there are cows to give us
    milk and people to look after them. Keep us thankful for all
    who help provide our food. *Amen*

[For other prayers, see the section on Harvest—pages 319–20.]

*For golden wheat to make our bread;*
*For juicy apples, green and red;*
*For milk and eggs, and fish and meat;*
*For all the foods we like to eat;*
*We thank you, God, and praise you, too,*
*For all these good things come from you.*                    R.P.


SUGGESTED HYMNS

Father, bless our bread and meat
Father, we thank thee
Find a trolley, push it straight
See here are red apples
Thank you for the world so sweet
We thank you, heavenly Father
When lamps are lighted


BIBLE READINGS

| | |
|---|---|
| Famine in Egypt | Genesis 41; 46–57 |
| Unclean foods | Deuteronomy 14; 3–21 |
| Forgetfulness of God | Deuteronomy 32; 13–15 |
| Feeding the five thousand | Matthew 14; 13–21 |
| Parable of the rich farmer | Luke 12; 16–21 |
| The disciples go fishing | John 21; 1–13 |


INTEREST WORK AND ACTIVITIES

*Books*

Make available in the book corner a selection of books about food.
Some suggestions are:

SHOPS/MILK *(Starters)*, Macdonald
MARKETS AND SHOPS/FOOD AND COOKING/FRUIT
    AND FRUIT GROWING *(Blackwell's Learning Library)*,
    Blackwell

IN THE SHOPS *(Zero)*, Macdonald
THINGS WE EAT AND DRINK (6 books in slip-case), Chambers
THE SUPERMARKET/THE MARKET *(Terraced House Books)*, Methuen
THE SHOPKEEPER/THE TRAWLER CAPTAIN/THE DAIRY FARMER *(What do they do?)*, Macmillan
THINGS TO DO WITH FOOD *(Things to do)*, Macdonald
EATING AND DRINKING *(Our World)*, Burke
GOOD FOOD *(Young Ideas)*, Macmillan
FOOD AND DRINK *(First Library)*, Macdonald
WHERE DOES FOOD COME FROM?/THE FARMER, Dinosaur
THE FARMER/THE FISHERMAN *(Easy Reading)*, Ladybird
WE DISCOVER FARMING FAR AND WIDE, Arnold

## Collections

Collect pictures of different types of food and mount in books or make friezes—one for each type of food, e.g. 'Meat', 'Fish', 'Fruit'. There are plenty of suitable and attractive coloured pictures to be found in magazines.

A variation on this theme is to make a large composite picture or collage on the general subject of 'Food'.

Make a collection of labels. Older children will be able to bring labels and wrappers to school. These can be mounted in a scrapbook type magazine with a few lines written about the produce and the country from which it came. Try to get as varied a collection as possible.

## Class shops

Make good use of class shops. Encourage the children to bring in any packets which could be used in a grocery or general shop.

'Shopkeepers' could also sell food that has been made by the children themselves.

*Food from overseas*

In a multi-cultural community it may be possible to persuade parents from the various ethnic groups to make a batch of biscuits, cakes or other sweetmeats for the children to eat, giving a little indication of the various tastes.

*Special foods*

Some introduction could be given to the various customs and taboos of certain religions concerning foods and to the foods eaten on special occasions. Samples could be seen and tasted if appropriate.

*Project work*

Older children could undertake simple projects on various aspects of food, working individually, in groups or as a class.

Milk and dairy farming is a popular theme with younger junior-age children. It can incorporate some study of the people and processes involved in bringing the milk to our tables. Production of butter, cheese and other milk products will form a part of the study.

How do we get our food? Such a study could include details of food growing, preparation, transport, markets and shops. Again this can be tackled at a fairly simple level by the lower junior age groups.

# 8　Bakers and bread

*Bread is a basic, necessary food. It is also one that is very familiar to children. It may differ in form and vary according to the taste or tradition of differing lands and cultures, but the basic structure is that of a food essential to man.*

*In this section we deal with the provision of bread as a necessary food and extend the theme to include the other foods in this group which are familiar and popular with children.*

*Underlying this theme is the need for us to be constantly aware of the needs of others. Food is available for all if properly and correctly shared. Our children on the whole are well fed—compared with children in other parts of the world who really know what it means to be hungry.*

## 1　YOUR LOAF OF BREAD

For many people, bread is the food that is most often eaten. What sort of bread do you like? Brown bread or white bread? Crusty or soft? Do you like bread rolls? Where does mother buy your bread? A supermarket? A grocer's shop? Or a baker's shop? The baker makes loaves in different shapes and sizes. Some have funny-sounding names. We may ask for a Tin, a Split Tin, a French Stick, a Farmhouse, Cottage or Sandwich loaf. Most of our loaves are white or brown but we can buy ones made from rye or wholemeal flour. Do you know of any other loaves?

Bread is made of dough and baked in an oven. There is yeast in the dough to make it grow bigger. Long ago most people made their own bread and some mothers do so today. They mix the dough, put it somewhere warm so that the yeast will begin to work, then put it in the oven in tins or on flat shelves. Long ago, before people had ovens, they baked their bread on fires out of doors. A big, flat stone was put over the fire and the bread was baked on this stone.

We eat our bread with lots of nice things. What do you like best on your bread? Bread is a very important food and helps us grow strong. It has always been an important food. We can read, in history books and in the Bible, how people ate their bread, the main food for them each day.

Perhaps we have learned the special prayer which Jesus taught his friends. Part of it says, 'Give us this day our daily bread'. It may not have meant bread as we know it now, but it helps us to understand how important bread is to us all.


## 2   THE FARMER

Long before we eat our slices of bread and butter, someone has been planning and working so that our bread will be there for us. It all begins with the farmer who grows wheat in his fields.

Firstly, he prepares the ground, ploughing, to turn the soil and help it get fresh air. Then seed is put into the ground. The small seeds go down, down into the earth where they settle, warm and cosy. The rain falls and sinks into the earth to give a drink to the seeds. This helps them to grow and swell. Sometimes the snow makes a blanket over the earth to keep it warm. Then the sun shines, and its warmth reaches down to the little seeds. It makes them want to grow and stretch up to feel the sun.

After a while a little shoot comes bursting out of each seed, and reaches up through the soil until it breaks out of the ground into the daylight. Day by day the shoots grow. Each one grows very tall and at the top of the stem the 'ear' begins to form. This is the part of the wheat which is used to make the flour we need for making our bread.

The wheat turns from green to a golden colour until, at the end of the summer, we can see fields of golden corn, waiting to be harvested. Today the wheat is cut by a machine. Children who live in the country will know all about the combine harvester. They will see it at work in the fields. They may even have been able to ride on the platform whilst the harvester is driven round and round the field. The combine harvester cuts the wheat and separates the grain.

All kinds of people are busy throughout the year, making sure that there will be wheat to be gathered at harvest time. People working on the land, the farmer and his helpers, have different kinds of work to do. Some plough and some reap. The man who ploughs the field has to make sure the lines or furrows are kept straight. Horses may be used to pull the plough, but nowadays ploughing is usually done with a tractor. The people who look after the horses or use the tractor have to know all about them and how to make them work well. At harvest time the people on the farms are very busy and there is a lot of work to be done in a short time, so they work for long hours to make sure all the corn is gathered in and stored. In this way they see that there is enough to feed us in the winter.

The farmer, his family and his helpers, in doing their daily work, are helping God in seeing that we shall be fed. God sends the sun and the rain to help the grain grow, and man helps God, so that his people may be fed.

### 3   WINDMILLS

Have you ever seen a windmill? We can find pictures of them and, in some places in England, we can see the main part of a windmill standing. The sails may still be in place, but usually they are broken, as windmills are no longer used as they were long ago. If we had lived a long time ago, we would have seen many more windmills dotted about the countryside. These were the mills which ground the grain into flour to make bread.

The farmer would take his load of grain in a cart pulled by a horse and deliver it to a mill. The wind used to turn the huge sails or blades outside, while, inside the mill, the miller poured the grain between huge flat stones. The sails moving round and round worked the machinery which turned one stone to crush the grain into tiny particles of flour.

Long before windmills were built, or before anyone thought about making one, people ground their flour by crushing it between two big flat stones. It was very hard work and took a long time. Man has become very clever at making machinery, so making his work much easier when he wants to do things like milling. God has shown people all through the ages how to use their good ideas to build different kinds of machine and always people are trying to find ways of doing things more quickly. Windmills are no longer used to grind the grain into flour! Bigger machines are used instead.

Most of the grain used in Britain comes from a long way away—from large countries such as Canada, where very large open spaces are used to grow wheat, which is sent to feed us. The grain is brought here in large ships and instead of being packed into sacks as the farmer here packs it, it is kept inside the ship and taken to a mill which is close beside the river. The grain is then sucked into the mill through big pipes straight from the ship.

People working in the mills are often covered with the white dust of the flour—because the dust is so fine and it blows everywhere. They are almost like living snowmen! Just think how many people are working in the mills, in the ships and in so many other ways, so that the grain is made into flour and brought to the baker in sacks or packed into bags for our mothers to buy when they want to make the things we eat and enjoy so much.

## 4 THE BAKER

If you have watched mother making bread you will know that she gets her hands and arms white with the flour. This happens to the baker too. You may have seen him come into the shop with a tray of loaves. He wears a white overall and hat so that he can keep very clean.

The baker mixes the flour into dough and puts in some yeast to make the dough grow bigger or rise. When it is ready for baking, he cuts it into different shapes and sizes. He is very clever at making many kinds of loaf—large ones and small ones, square ones and round ones, plaited loaves, cottage loaves, bread rolls and lots of others.

The pieces of dough are put on flat trays or into tins and then put in the oven to bake. Do you like the smell of bread being baked? The delicious hot, fresh, crusty loaves are pulled out of the hot oven with a special kind of shovel that has a long handle.

Nowadays much of our bread comes from a large bakery, which is a kind of factory for making bread. A machine mixes the dough, cuts it up and puts it into tins. The loaves are baked in large ovens, then taken out of the tins, perhaps sliced by a machine, and wrapped in special paper to keep them fresh.

Bread from the bakery is delivered by lorries to your supermarket or grocery shop. Lots of people prefer fresh-baked bread made by the baker. But we can please ourselves and buy the kind we like best. Lots of people help to provide us with daily bread.

5 NO BREAD

Have you ever felt hungry? Really hungry so that you can think of nothing else? Oh, we sometimes wish that dinner or tea time would come soon, as we feel ready for some food. Most of us, though, are never in need of food for very long. We live in a land where we are sure of having sufficient food for our needs. Some of us have extra things to eat between meals—'snacks' we call them—to help us survive to the next meal!

All around us, on street posters, in books and magazines or on television, we see mouth-watering pictures of all kinds of food. Sometimes we are invited to collect wrappers, labels from food packages, to win a prize. This is to make us want to try that kind of food.

Think about the food you eat each day. First there is breakfast, eaten before going to school. We have a mid-day meal at school or at home, and another meal in the evening. We expect to have our food regularly and we take it all for granted, even grumbling at times because it may be something we do not like, or not what we wanted.

How would you feel if every day you were given just a small piece of bread, no butter or jam or anything else on it, or a tiny amount of rice, and were told that this was all the food you would have that day? Would you like that? Would you be very happy about it? But for many children in the world that is all there is to eat, day after day. They know there will be nothing else and so they are very glad to receive it.

For many reasons the food in the world is not spread out so that everyone can have a fair share. It may be that the country in which they live is not able to produce enough food for all the people that need to be fed. All this is very difficult for us to understand, but it is a sad fact that many, many children are hungry and cannot grow properly or be strong enough to fight off disease and illness, because they are not able to have enough of the right kind of food.

When you feel like grumbling or refusing to eat something prepared for you, try to remember the hungry children in the world—children who would be glad to eat the crusts you leave on your plate or the food you refuse. As you grow up, you may be able to help to see that there is sufficient food for everyone in the world to have a fair share. God has provided the means for us to be fed and He needs the help of many people in the world to see that nobody is hungry.

6   CAKES AND BISCUITS

Is there a special place in your home where mother keeps the tasty things you like to eat? Some families have a 'Cookie Jar', or perhaps a 'Biscuit Tin' or 'Cake Tin'—a special container. What do you find in yours? Biscuits and cakes made at home? Or ones from the bakery? There are so many different kinds of cakes and biscuits. We all have our favourites and look for these before trying others.

When you go with mother to the shops you will find so many to choose from. Have you ever counted the different kinds of packets of biscuits stacked on the shelves of the supermarket or on the shelves of the grocer's shop? There are biscuits of many shapes and sizes. Do you know their names?

Many years ago, before biscuits and cakes were sold in packets, the grocer kept his biscuits in special tins with transparent tops so that you could look into the tin and see the kind of biscuit it contained. Then, when mothers bought biscuits they were taken out of the large tin and weighed on the scales and put into bags to be taken home. Children then had some specially good times if they were allowed to help choose the biscuits, for they were able to have just a few of each kind to make a very tasty bag full of biscuits. Sometimes the grocer sold 'broken biscuits' cheaply.

Then, think about the cakes we are able to enjoy. There are those that are made at home and those displayed on the shelves in the baker's shop. Such delicious cakes, with jam and cream and sugar and icing! What are your favourites? Do you like to help mother make cakes?

So that we may enjoy such foods, a lot of work has to be done. Sugar has to be produced and flour and butter. Fruit is grown on trees and bushes in this country and other countries, then prepared for jam making, or dried to make currants, sultanas or raisins. All these are grown especially to help make the cakes and biscuits we enjoy. People try new ways of cooking—new recipes to make food attractive for us. These kinds of food are not really necessary for us to eat, but we do enjoy them. We must try to understand that we have so many extra and nice things in our lives that we should never be discontented or selfish.

God has given us so much in life that is good. Some of our food is very important yet perhaps rather ordinary. We know that some of these other enjoyable foods are extra and must remember that we are so well provided for.

### 7 MAKING CAKES

In a baker's shop I saw some birthday cakes waiting to be collected for some fortunate children's birthday parties. One cake was made to represent a football pitch, with goal posts and tiny figures arranged on the pitch as though they were playing football. On the cake was written 'Happy Birthday John'. Another cake was obviously made for a girl; it had ballerinas, tiny dancers on a stage, and again 'Happy Birthday' wishes, with a girl's name.

Sometimes we see cakes made to look like a basket with lovely flowers peeping out from the lid, or cakes made in the shape of a figure which tells us which birthday is being celebrated. They are decorated with candles, flowers, and good wishes. There are cakes made for Christenings, perhaps in the shape of a cradle with a little doll tucked in, looking like a baby in his crib. It seems such a pity to have to cut into these cakes—but they do taste good!

Christmas cakes with decorations remind us of the special time of Christmas with Santa Claus, holly or robins, and icing made to look like snow. Have you seen Wedding Cakes? Often these are made with more than one cake standing one above the other.

People who make such special cakes have to be very clever. The cake has first to be planned and thought about. The shape, the size and the decoration must be just right! Then the cake is made, sometimes with lots of rich fruit and all sorts of goodies. Or it may be a light and soft sponge cake specially made for children. After baking, the cake is decorated, and this must be done *very* carefully. Just one little mistake and the whole cake could be spoilt. Most of the decoration is made with icing. The icing sugar is mixed carefully and the cake covered with a layer of this before the special decorations are worked and put in place.

Cakes are made for many special occasions when people celebrate and each have a piece of the cake. As we enjoy these happy occasions with our friends and families, sharing our food with them, we thank God for food and fun and friends and families. They mean such a lot to us.

## 8   BREAD IN THE BIBLE

Moses was called by God to lead his people on a long, long journey to a new land. The journey took them many miles away from the land where they had been unhappy, to a new land which God was to show them. On the way the people began to grumble because they were hungry and had no food to eat. God spoke to Moses and promised that the people would soon find food to eat, and sure enough, one morning when they awoke, they saw on the ground something which looked like dew. But as the dew melted away they saw it was a special kind of bread. They called it 'manna', and they found it there each day that they needed it.

Many, many years later, Jesus was living on the earth and he was talking to people, making sick people well again, and making sad people happy. He was telling them wonderful stories, too. So many people had followed him one day and stayed with him until evening. By then they were all very hungry and there was no place nearby where they could get food.

One of the friends of Jesus told Him of a boy in the crowd who had brought some food with him. He had five small loaves and two fish. Jesus called the boy to him and asked him to share his food. Gladly the boy gave it to Jesus. After asking God to bless the food, Jesus began to break the loaves and fish into pieces which he gave to his friends to share out among the people. Five thousand people had enough food to eat that day, and the crumbs that were left over filled twelve baskets.

God provides food for us all and bread is the most important kind of food for everyone. These stories from the Bible, one from the Old Testament and one from the New Testament, show us how, on just these two occasions, people were fed in very special ways. God wants all his people to be fed and cared-for and he has provided food for us since the beginning of the world.

RELATED THEMES

1. As we fill ourselves with good food today, dear Lord, help us to remember that many people will have none. Bless those who try to help the hungry and make us thankful for all that we enjoy. *Amen*

2. Dear God, give us each day our daily bread; and teach us to be thankful for all the good things you give. *Amen*

3. Dear God, when we eat our bread we do not think very often of the people who work to make it for us. We thank you for their work: for those who get up very early so that we can have nice fresh bread each day; for the people who serve us in the shops and stores; and for all who labour so that we may eat, we say thank you, God. *Amen*

4. Dear God, when we pass the bakery and smell the lovely scent of newly baked bread, we remember that the baker has been very busy since early morning to prepare it and bake it. Thank you for bakers and the bread they bake. *Amen*

5. Father God, we love making things ourselves.
   We like to make cakes and biscuits
   And put them in the oven to bake.
   We like the lovely smell as they cook
   And we enjoy eating them afterwards.
   Thank you for providing us with food;
   Thank you for helping us to learn how to cook it;
   Thank you that we can enjoy it;
   And teach us to share it with others. *Amen*

6. For daily bread to feed our bodies,
   And lovely thoughts to feed our minds,
   We give you thanks, O Lord our God. *Amen*

7. Hear our prayers, O God, for those who give
   us our bread:
   For farmers who sow and reap the wheat,
   *Hear our prayers, O God;*
   For sailors who bring the grain from other lands,
   *Hear our prayers, O God;*
   For millers who grind the grain into flour,
   *Hear our prayers, O God;*
   For drivers who take the flour to the bakery,
   *Hear our prayers, O God;*
   For bakers who are skilled at making loaves,
   *Hear our prayers, O God;*
   For people who sell the bread in the shops,
   *Hear our prayers, O God;*
   For all of these we give you thanks. *Amen*

8. O Lord Jesus Christ, you said that you were the Bread of Life.
   Help us to remember that we need you just as much as we need
   our daily bread. *Amen*

9. Thank you, dear God,
   For all the fields of growing grain;
   For sun and rain which makes it grow;
   For the golden harvest gathered in;
   For those who grind it into flour,
   And those who make our daily bread. *Amen*

10. Thank you, God, for all bread we can enjoy; wrapped bread cut
    in slices, newly-baked crusty loaves and rolls, seedy loaves and
    French sticks, white bread and brown, all sorts of bread for all
    sorts of people. Keep up thankful for all we have to eat. *Amen*

11. Thank you, God our Father, for our daily bread. Help us to
    understand the importance of good food for our bodies and not
    waste the good things we receive from you. *Amen*

12. We say thank you, God, for the lovely fresh bread we can enjoy
    and for all those things we can spread on it to make it so tasty.
    *Amen*

HYMNS SUGGESTED

Father, bless our bread and meat
Hands of Jesus take the bread
Here in the country's heart
See the farmer sow the seed
Thank you for the world so sweet
The farmer comes to scatter the seed
When the corn is planted

BREAD IN THE BIBLE

| | |
|---|---|
| Famine in Egypt | Genesis 41; 28–57 |
| Bread in the desert | Exodus 16; 1–16 |
| Make me a cake! | 1 Kings 17; 8–16 |
| Feeding the 5,000 | Matthew 14; 13–21 |
| Breaking the bread | Luke 24; 28–30 |
| Jesus—the Bread of Life | John 6; 35 |

INTEREST WORK AND ACTIVITIES

*Books*

Here are some books on this subject which could be made available
in class for the children to look at and read.

BREAD *(Starters)*, Macdonald
BREAD *(Leaders)*, Ladybird
BAKERS AND BREAD *(Blackwell's Learning Library)*,
  Blackwell
THANK YOU FOR A LOAF OF BREAD *(Thank you books)*,
  Lion
CAKES AND BISCUITS *(Starters Activities)*, Macdonald
FARMING IN THE BIBLE *(Blackwell's Learning Library)*,
  Blackwell

*Helping others*

This theme might be taken in association with one of the special appeals for helping the hungry, e.g. Christian Aid Week, and the children encouraged to help hungry people to have their daily bread.

*Visits*

Visit a baker's shop so that the children can see for themselves the many different kinds of bread and cake that are on sale. If there is a bakery there too, it may be possible for small groups of children to see the baker at work or to have the baking process explained. The local bakery may also be willing to provide the school with any flour unfit for baking yet useful for the 'play dough' that can be made in school.

*Make a shop*

A baker's shop in the classroom can be used for many purposes. Bread, cakes and biscuits can be made with flour, salt and water (see recipe below). This will bake hard and can be painted or varnished. Shapes can be copied from those seen in the baker's shop.

Packets of biscuits, if emptied carefully, can be repacked using cardboard or any other 'filler' and the open end resealed for the shop. Encourage children to bring in any biscuit packets that they can obtain.

Prices can be put on the goods. Price tickets can be made and shopping lists prepared.

*Make a windmill*

A paper windmill (similar to those bought at fairgrounds or the seaside) can be made from squares of stiff coloured paper. Cut from each corner towards the centre. Fold the 'sails' over and pin through the centre to a stick. A bead between the paper and the stick will allow the 'sails' to move freely when caught by the wind.

A model of a windmill can be made quite simply from a cylinder of card, topped with a cap and suitably painted. The sails can be two strips of card glued in the shape of a cross. Lines drawn on these will represent the framework of the sails. These can be pinned to the tower, using a bead as above.

### Different kinds of bread

In a multi-cultural class children could be encouraged to bring in bread or similar products which are commonly eaten in their homes. Cypriot children might bring in their seed loaves, Jewish children their matzoth, Indians a chapatti, to name but a few.

### Make bread or cakes in school

It is quite common for small groups of children to make their own simple bread or cakes in school. Welfare assistants and parents may be able to help with this. There are lots of simple recipes for biscuits and cakes.

To make bread rolls:
    Mix 2 cups flour
            4 teaspoons baking powder
            1 tablespoon lard
    Add 1 egg
            ½ cup milk
Mix well to make dough. Make into rolls. Bake in a hot oven for 15 minutes.

To make play dough:
    You will need:
            Mixing bowl
            Water
            1 teacup flour
            1 dessertspoon of salt
            Food colouring (or powder paint)
    Put the flour in the bowl with the salt. Add the colouring to the water and then add water a little at a time, mixing it all the time.
    The dough will keep for approx. one week if kept in a plastic bag.

To make a chapatti:

Mix wheatflour with a little water and roll into small balls. Place on a flat surface and roll until flat. Cook on a metal plate over a gas ring or hotplate. Bake carefully, turning as necessary.

Cover one side with ghee or dripping. (Ghee is made by simmering butter in a saucepan for 1½–2 hours and then straining through muslin.)

There are other ways of making chapattis. Some, such as *puria* are deep fried. *Tandori Riote* is made from brown flour, is partly fried and then baked. *Prawnta* is a chapatti with a filling. Perhaps an Indian parent could come into school to demonstrate.

# 9   Water

*Of all the things around us, water is the most important. Without it life would cease. Yet it is one of the things that is most taken for granted and it is only in times of shortage that people begin to recognize its true value.*

*For most children it is a necessary evil. They have to put up with it when the time comes to wash themselves but perhaps it does not seem so bad when they can bath in it and play with their toys at the same time. And somehow getting wet in puddles or in the sea never seems as bad as having to wet oneself for washing purposes.*

*Here, then, are some thoughts about water as a necessary part of life, water to be enjoyed and water that can be a danger. It is a theme which can be developed in many ways, not least of which are a sense of thankfulness for a steady supply of pure, clean water and an awareness of the dangers of ponds, rivers and the sea.*

1   WATER FOR DAILY NEEDS

Before you came to school this morning, you probably turned on the tap to get some water to wash yourself. Perhaps you used the tap in the kitchen to fill the kettle or to get yourself some water to drink. No doubt you went to the toilet and pressed the handle or pulled a chain to flush it. Then you remembered to turn the tap once more so that you could wash your hands after using the toilet. How easy it all was! Just a small movement with your hand and there was all the water you needed—almost like magic.

But it wasn't magic. The water was there because a lot of people had worked hard to make sure that you, and millions of other people too, could have the water they needed without a lot of trouble in getting it.

Perhaps you have had a holiday in a tent or a caravan or on a boat. If so, you will remember that someone had to carry all the water that was needed from a tap that was a little way from where you were staying. No doubt you were very careful not to waste water. Perhaps you enjoyed not having much water for washing yourself. Maybe it was fun for a short while to have to fetch and carry all your water. But when you returned from holiday no doubt you were pleased to be able to use your tap again.

Not so very long ago in Britain there were no taps in many of the houses. People had to get buckets of water from a tap which they shared with people from other houses. Some of them had to get water from a pump, or even lower a bucket down a well. In many parts of the world people still have to do that today or even get water from lakes or rivers.

Just think of all the things for which you use water each day and think how often you would need to fill a bucket. Remember to say thank you for all the people who have made it so easy for us to get our water.

### 2 PURE WATER

Last time you wanted a drink of water, you probably turned on a tap, filled a glass or a cup and drank the water. Did you wonder whether it was poisoned? Or did you think it might be full of germs that would make you very ill? Probably not. We are so used to getting pure, clean water from our taps that we never think to ask ourselves whether it is fit to drink.

In some countries people get their water from rivers. So do their animals. People wash their clothes in the rivers too! Imagine drinking water that animals have been in or in which people have been washing themselves or their clothes. And these are only two things that may have happened to that water. It is not surprising that many people in those countries become ill and die.

Your local river will be very dirty, too. Lots of things will have gone into it as it flows towards the sea and these could make you very ill. *Never* drink river water or water that has been standing in ponds or lakes.

Yet the water that comes out of your tap is the same water. It is taken from a river or a large lake or reservoir but, before it reaches your home, several things are done to it. Firstly it is allowed to stand so that bits and pieces in the water can sink to the bottom. Then it passes through a sand-bed which takes out most of the germs. Very small amounts of a chemical called chlorine kill any germs that are left.

The pure water is then pumped into a large tank or water tower, from which it flows through pipes into your house. So today we can enjoy the pure, clean water which refreshes us and will not make us ill.

### 3  NO WATER!

Have you ever felt *really* thirsty? Perhaps you have been playing or have gone for a long walk on a hot day without being able to get a drink. Your mouth and your throat feel very, very dry. You go to the tap, fill a cup or glass with water and take a long drink. You soon feel very much better because you have done so.

People need water. If we do not drink water we shall die because we have to replace all the water that is used up by our bodies. Our bodies use a lot of water every day.

In Britain we are never likely to run out of water because we normally have plenty of rain to fill the rivers and lakes from which our water comes. When was the last time it rained? It is not often that we go more than a few days without rain. Just think what it would be like if it had not rained for months or even for years. There would not be much water anywhere. Lakes and ponds would dry up and so would many of the rivers. There are countries in some parts of the world where it has not rained for so long that everywhere has dried up. The ground has cracked, plants have withered and many people and animals have died.

The people who live in lands like this have to dig deep into the earth to find water that has settled a long way down. When they have dug a well, they have to bring up water from the well by using a bucket or large jar on the end of a long rope. It might just be enough water to keep them alive but it will not be enough to make their food grow. And, because their food does not grow, these people become very, very hungry. Lots of children in these lands die before they are as old as you are.

Today we have to be thankful that we have the water we need and we ought also to remember those people in many parts of the world who are not as fortunate as we are.

### 4  RAIN, RAIN, GO AWAY!

Sometimes when we set out for school it is pouring with rain and we have to wear special clothes to keep us dry. On go the macs which keep the rain off our clothes and the Wellies to keep our feet dry. We may wear some kind of hood or carry an umbrella or perhaps

Mummy comes with us with her big umbrella so that we are still dry when we get to school.

Sometimes it is fun to be out in the rain and to splash in the puddles but it is very silly to play in the rain without a coat or to splash in puddles in ordinary shoes or slippers if we cannot change into dry clothing afterwards.

No doubt there have been lots of times when you have looked out of the window and been very disappointed to see that it was raining. Perhaps you wanted to play with your friends or your parents were going to take you out for the day. You may have said, 'I wish it would stop!' Or you may have told the rain to go away:

> *Rain, rain, go away!*
> *Come again another day!*

But it didn't make much difference. The rain carried on as long as it wanted to and possibly spoiled your plans. Maybe at times we do not like the rain but we need it. Farmers need it to make their crops grow. And we all need it for lots and lots of reasons, for it is the rain that soaks into the ground and then fills the rivers and lakes that provide the water in our homes.

We do use lots and lots of water. Think how much you use yourself. Think how many people use water in your house, in your street, in your town or city. Where does it all come from? From the rain.

So, next time it rains, don't be too upset, even if it does spoil your plans. We can't do without it. Just thank God for the rain.

## 5 MAKING WATER WORK

Have you ever stood by a river and watched the water flowing past you? You may have thrown a stick into the river and watched it float away. The river is always moving. Nothing can stop it. Anything that is in its way can be pushed aside. People in boats on rivers know how strong the river can be.

Swift-flowing rivers can be very dangerous, too. Anyone who falls in can be swept away by the river and perhaps drowned. It is always sensible to keep well away from a river bank in case you slip in. Some of the most dangerous parts are those where the river has to squeeze between some rocks and the stream of water becomes very powerful as it is forced through the narrow space.

Long ago, people learned that rivers could be made to work for them. Perhaps you have seen a building beside a river with a large wheel on the side. Boards or paddles fixed to this wheel are pushed by the water so that the wheel is turned. As the wheel turns it works machinery inside the building.

People in many countries have used water wheels for lots of different purposes. People have also discovered that water forced through a narrow space can drive machinery to make electricity.

But there are lots of other ways in which water is used to do special work for people. A motor car needs water to cool the engine. Firemen need water to put out fires. Dairymen need water to clean the milk bottles. Farmers and gardeners need water to make their plants grow. Cooks need water to prepare our meals. Can you think of other ways in which water is used?

Water is one of the most valuable things we have. Do we remember this? And do we remember to thank God that we have enough water?

6  WATER IS FUN

We are not very old before we discover that water can be fun. There are so many things that we can do with it or in it. If you have a little baby brother or sister, see what happens next time baby is put into the bath. Arms and legs splash away in the water; mother gets soaked; and when bath-time is ended there is probably nearly as much water on the table or floor as there is remaining in the bath. It's such fun! And baby probably does not know what he is doing.

No doubt you, too, have fun in the bath. Perhaps you have learned not to splash and to keep the water *inside* the bath; but have you your special toys to play with in the bath? A rubber duck, some plastic boats, or other toys? It is much more fun than having to wash yourself! As people get older, some still have fun with model yachts or motor-boats that can be sailed on the pond.

Perhaps you enjoy boats that are big enough for you to get inside. Many children like to have a boat on the boating lake at the seaside, or perhaps to ride in a canoe or a rowing boat with older brothers and sisters or with Mum or Dad. Grown-up people sometimes like to take boating holidays or spend weekends on boats that are big enough to live on. Boats can be fun.

Of course, people who like to play by ponds or enjoy themselves in boats have to be very careful and very sensible to do everything they can to keep safe. One very important thing is to learn how to swim. Can you swim? If you can, you will soon know how much fun you can have doing that too—swimming, racing, diving and really enjoying the water. And the sooner you learn to swim, the better.

Perhaps you enjoy looking in water to see what interesting creatures live in it; or maybe you enjoy it in other ways. Thank God for water and for all the fun we can have with it.

### 7 AT THE SEASIDE

There are lots of interesting things to do when we go on holiday to the seaside. Usually we cannot wait to go down to the beach with our buckets, spades and all our other bits and pieces so that we can start digging in the sand and making sandcastles.

Sometimes we are disappointed. When we get to the beach we find that the tide is in and there is very little beach for digging. In any case the dry sand is not as good as the wet sand for making castles.

When we have built our castles, we like to dig a moat round them which we can fill with water to protect our castle from any 'enemies'. Sometimes we carry the water in buckets, but it soon soaks away. Sometimes we dig a channel to the edge of the sea, but we know that it will not then be long before our castle will be washed away as the sea comes in. We may try to stop the sea but we know that we cannot. Nothing will stop the sea.

A long time ago there was a great king named Canute. His followers told him that he was so great that even the waves would stop if he told them to. So one day his throne was taken down to the beach as the tide was coming in and he sat on it close to the water's edge. Then, in a loud voice, he spoke to the sea: 'I command you to come no further!'

But, of course, the sea took no notice. Canute got his feet wet and he proved to the people around him that no one, not even a mighty king, can tell the sea what to do. Twice a day the tide comes in and goes out so regularly that we can work out just when high tide and low tide will be.

What we cannot be sure of is how safe the sea will be. Sometimes we can play in it quite safely but at other times the waves can be so big and strong that it is too dangerous for us to go near.

As we stand on the shore the sea stretches out as far as we can see and we know that there is a lot more beyond the horizon. The mighty seas and oceans form a very large part of this wonderful world which God has given us.

## 8  LIFEBOAT

The seas that we can enjoy in summer can sometimes be very dangerous for those who have to sail on them to catch our fish or bring our food.

Imagine a cold winter's night when the wind is blowing hard and the waves are very big. A ship is battling through the waves when one very large wave goes right over the ship. It breaks open the hatch where the cargo is stored and begins to fill the ship with water. The captain knows that his ship will sink and so he sends up a rocket which will tell people he is in trouble. He sends a message by radio too.

On shore a coastguard receives the signal and decides that the lifeboat should put to sea as soon as possible. A loud noise is made which calls the lifeboat crew and they all rush for the lifeboat. Apart from the engineer they are not full-time lifeboatmen. Three are fishermen, one works in a garage, one in an office and one in a shop. Soon they are all on the lifeboat.

Without wasting any time, the lifeboat is launched and heads out to sea. It will be a dangerous night's work. They will probably be soaked through by the icy seas and will feel very cold. They may even have to be tied to the lifeboat so that they are not swept into the sea and drowned. But there are men on the ship who may die if they do not go to help.

In the darkness the lifeboat comes alongside the ship and the men get some ropes aboard. One by one the crew climb down to the lifeboat as their ship sinks lower and lower into the water. A few hours later they are all safely in harbour, thanks to the lifeboatmen who have willingly given their service quite freely to save life.

The Lifeboat service is not run or paid for by the Government. It finds all the money it needs by asking people for help. We can all help by giving a little money that will save the lives of sailors.

*The Royal National Lifeboat Institution*

The R.N.L.I. had its origins in 1824. Since then, lifeboats have been instrumental in saving thousands of lives around our coasts.

The work is maintained entirely by voluntary contributions. The boats are donated: the crews, other than the engineman, are volunteers. Many schools are pleased to support the R.N.L.I. during Lifeboat Week as one of their special appeals.

RELATED THEMES

---

PRAYERS

1. Dear God, we enjoy playing with water.
   There are so many things we can do with it.
   It is so useful too.
   Yet people in many lands do not have enough.
   We say thank you that we have so much
   And we feel sorry for those who do not. *Amen*

2. Dear God, we think about the rain which freshens the earth,
   fills the rivers and lakes, and gives us all the water we need: and
   we say, 'Thank you for the rain.' *Amen*

3. O God,
   Our land has water all around it:
   Sailors must sail it to bring us our food;
   Fishermen must sail it to get us our fish.
   But sometimes there are storms;
   Sometimes there are big waves and strong winds;
   Sometimes the sailors and fishermen are in danger.
   Bless them and keep them safe, we pray. *Amen*

4. O Lord Jesus Christ, who protected your friends in that storm
   on the Sea of Galilee, watch over all who sail the seas today and
   bring them safely into port. *Amen*

5. Thank you, Father God, for the rain which falls:
   For the sweet smell when it has fallen on dry ground,
   For the new life that it gives to growing plants,
   For the water it provides for our daily needs.
   Thank you for the rain. *Amen*

6. Thank you, God, for the lifeboatmen. Please keep them safe
   and bless all those people who help them. *Amen*

7. Thank you, O God, for the pure fresh water we have to drink
   and for all those people who have learned how to make it safe to
   drink. *Amen*

8. Today, O God, we think about people who are hungry and thirsty in many parts of the world because they do not have enough water. Bless all the people who help them to find water in their dry lands. *Amen*

9. Today, O God, we think of all that water is used for. We know how important it is for us to have it and so we say, thank you for the water . . . and for giving us plenty of it. *Amen*

10. We thank you, God, that there is always plenty of pure, clean water for us to use and that, when we want it, all we have to do is to turn on our taps. Thank you for all the people who made it fit for us to drink and for all those who help to bring it to us in our homes. Give us grateful hearts. *Amen*

11. We thank you, God our Father, for water,
    For cool, refreshing water to drink,
    > *We thank you, God our Father;*
    For clean water for washing and bathing,
    > *We thank you, God our Father;*
    For lots of water for cooking and cleaning,
    > *We thank you, God our Father;*
    For water we use for swimming or playing,
    > *We thank you, God our Father;*
    For seas and rivers, ponds and lakes,
    > *We thank you, God our Father;*
    For rain and dew to refresh the ground,
    > *We thank you, God our Father;*
    For all our water we say thank you. *Amen*

12. We thank you, O God, for all the fun we can have in the water when we are on holiday or outings. Help us to take care so that we do not get into danger in the water or cause worry to those who look after us. *Amen*

# 9 WATER

Down came the raindrops
Down the air, everywhere
God made the shore
I love the sun
I saw raindrops
Little drops of water
Water in the snow
We praise thee for the sun
When lamps are lighted

## WATER IN THE BIBLE

| | |
|---|---|
| Noah and the flood | Genesis 7; 1–5 and 11–24 |
| Digging wells | Genesis 26; 16–25 |
| Bitter water | Exodus 15; 22–25 |
| Elijah and the drought | 1 Kings 17; 1–7 |
| Dangers at sea | Psalm 107; 23–32 |
| Jesus and the fishermen | Luke 5; 1–11 |
| Paul shipwrecked | Acts 27 |

## INTEREST WORK AND ACTIVITIES

*Books for the book corner*

I AM A DROP OF WATER *(Who am I?)*, Blackwell
RAIN/THE SEA *(Starters)*, Macdonald
WATER/MAN ON THE SEA *(Leaders)*, Ladybird
WATER/LAKES AND DAMS *(First Library)*, Macdonald
WATER *(Waste not, want not)*, Burke
LET'S FIND OUT ABOUT WATER *(Let's find out)*, Watts
WATER AND THE WATER WORKS/LIFEBOATS AND
LIFEBOATMEN *(Blackwell's Learning Library)*, Blackwell
THANK YOU FOR A DRINK OF WATER *(Thank you books)*, Lion
RAIN *(Head-Start)*, Burke
THE RAIN *(Young Nature)*, Angus and Robertson
THE LIFEBOATMEN *(Easy Reading)*, Ladybird

*Sea (or water) project*

This is a subject which can lend itself to a school project if so desired. Each class or group take one aspect to be developed over some time and displayed for all classes (and visitors) to see.

A sea project could include: Sea and shore; ports and harbours; ships; animals that live in the sea; sea birds; fish; fishing; safety at sea; sailors.

*Class pictures or friezes*

Make a colourful frieze or large picture using cut-out umbrellas and Wellington boots. The umbrellas can be of many colours with black boots as contrast.

*Painting and drawing*

Paint or draw pictures on various aspects of the theme, e.g.
Ourselves at the seaside,
A storm—or a rainy day,
A lifeboat,
Fishing (Deep sea fishing or angling).

*Making models*

A ship on the sea. An oblong piece of card (A4 size or similar). Fold across the card from one end in zig-zag fashion (as when making a fan). Leave the last three or four inches unfolded. This will stand up at the back behind the 'waves' to provide a background. On this paint sun and sky. The 'waves' can be painted blue and white.

On a smaller piece of card draw and paint a ship or boat. Cut out. A strip of card pasted or glued to the back of the cut-out and extending beyond the stern can be used to manipulate the ship so that it slides along the folds between the waves.

Make a model lake using a mirror. Reeds and plants can be made from junk materials. An old loofah or foam sponge could usefully be included in the junk material box.

*At the seaside*

Make a 'Seaside Book'. Include as many aspects of the seaside as possible. Encourage the children to bring holiday postcards. Tell about their own holidays by the sea.

*Making music*

Use water for making music. Collect a number of jars that are the same size. Partially fill with water to varying levels. Tap the rims of the jars with a pencil. See if a simple tune can be played.

*Water activities*

What do children discover from playing with water? Give opportunity for children to try things out with water and talk about what they do.

*Visits*

Visit any nearby water—pond, lake, reservoir, river, canal, sea. Make sure there is adequate supervision. This may provide opportunity to reinforce any instruction that has been given in safety precautions.

*Water creatures*

We need water, but so do many creatures and not just for drinking. Frogs and toads, for example, must have regular access to water.
Water is 'home', not only for fish but for many small creatures. Find out about the wild life that uses any local water (pond, river, or sea).
Start (or observe) a school aquarium with a few fish and perhaps other creatures. Let children enjoy looking at the aquarium but stress the need to find out beforehand how to look after anything kept in home or school and the importance of taking good care of anything that thereby becomes dependent upon us.

## 9 WATER

---

### Swimming

This is naturally associated with the theme. Schools with a learner pool will have an advantage but those without might take the opportunity to discuss who is learning to swim elsewhere. Where? And with whom? Stress water safety.

### Sailors

Collect pictures and stories of seamen, fishermen and any others who work on the water. Talk about their work. We often ask God's protection for them. Many of them have a strong belief in God, e.g. Psalm 107; 23–32 and the Breton fisherman's prayer:

*Dear God, be good to me. The sea is so wide*
*and my boat is so small.*

Perhaps a sailor could visit to talk to the children.

### Lifeboats

Find out more about Lifeboats and Lifeboatmen. The R.N.L.I. will willingly supply posters and have films available for free loan. During Lifeboat Week the children could be involved in fund-raising.

# 10    Letters and news

*The telling and hearing of news is so much a part of everyday life it is taken for granted. Every day the postman delivers letters: every day the newspapers are produced. On those occasions when for some reason the newspapers, letters and other forms of communication are denied us, we begin to appreciate just how much we depend on others.*

*Young children are usually very ready to impart news. Their own particular item of news is **the** most important to them, and they enjoy the telling of it. This section deals with the subject——letters, newspapers, and the people concerned with them. These people play an important part in our everyday life and we attempt to help the children to be aware of the services rendered.*


1   THROUGH THE LETTER BOX

RAT-A-TAT-TAT ... the special kind of knocking on the front door told everyone in the house that the postman was here and had delivered some mail. The children, Peter and Julie, raced to the door, each wanting to be the first and to pick up the assortment of letters lying below the letter box.

There were several letters addressed to Father, one for Mother and there, with their names and address written in large letters, was one addressed to Peter and Julie. Although Peter was the eldest he very kindly allowed Julie the privilege of opening *their* letter. Inside was a gaily decorated notelet. 'Please come to my party' it began. They carefully read the rest of the invitation. One of their friends was to have a birthday party and had invited them both to join in the fun. It was very exciting to get a letter specially addressed to them and even more exciting to find that it contained an invitation.

'When you receive an invitation such as this you must write a reply and accept the invitation,' Mother told them. So that evening, after tea, Mother helped them with their reply. They got out some paper, an envelope and some pens. They thanked their friend for the invitation and said how pleased they would be to attend the party.

Do you like to receive letters? Just think of all the kinds of letters that are delivered every day. Envelopes are of different shapes and colours—brown, white and some brightly coloured. Those are usually the 'happy' letters which bring invitations or birthday cards. Sometimes when fathers and mothers open brown envelopes they make a face: then we know they have probably received a bill to be paid!

There are all kinds of letters. Friends and family who live a long way from us write to give us all their news, happy or sometimes sad, perhaps news of a new baby or of someone not very well. There are birthday cards, Christmas cards and picture post cards from friends who are away on holiday.

When we write letters we have to address an envelope very clearly so that the postman can read the address and deliver the letter to the right person. We must know how to spell all the names correctly.

The sending and receiving of letters and cards is an important part of our lives, and the postman, and many other people, help us to send or to receive these.

2 THE POSTMAN

Peter was talking to his father and telling him about his friends and their families. 'You know John, in my class. He says his father is a postman,' said Peter. 'That's a nice easy job, putting letters through the letter boxes on people's doors.'

Father chuckled . . . 'I don't think John's father would agree with you,' he said.

There is a lot more to the work of a postman than just delivering the letters. He has to get up very early in the morning and go to work at the large post office where all the postmen start their day. It is often very dark when he leaves home. When he arrives at the post office he finds lots of letters to be sorted. Other postmen have opened the mail bags and sorted the letters into areas for delivery. This kind of sorting is called 'setting in'.

Our postman has to sort his letters into the order in which he will deliver them. He ties the letters into bundles and puts these into his post bag. He fastens the bag so that it is comfortable for him to carry and off he goes. Sometimes the bag will be very heavy when he begins his round of delivery.

Whatever the weather the postman carries on with his daily task. It may be a lovely bright, sunny day: it may be cold and wet with the rain trickling down his neck, and his shoes getting very wet, so that he is glad to get home and change into dry clothing. He may have to make his way through snow, mist and fog.

We expect the postman to be on duty and we know that he usually is. It is a very important job he is doing and we rely on him to do his work well so that we may receive our mail. Remember to say thank you to the postman sometimes, when you see him at work.

### 3   POST OFFICE

Peter was still very interested in the subject of letters and postmen and he asked his father many questions. 'Were there postmen when you were a little boy? When Grandad was little, too? And great-great-grandad?'

'We have had postmen for many years,' said his father, 'but they have not always been the kind of postmen we have today.' He told Peter and Julie about the early days of postmen.

Long, long ago there were no postmen to carry letters. King Henry the First was one of the first kings of England who liked to write letters himself, and when he wrote his letters he had special messengers to take them.

He was careful in choosing the right sort of people to carry his letters. They had to be brave, honest and able to ride fast on their horses. They only carried the King's letters. Then, messengers began to carry letters for other people as well as the King. They wore a special uniform and were called 'postboys'. They rode their horses very fast along bad roads and the horses became very tired. Fresh horses were kept at inns along the road and the postboys were able to change horses at these inns. They were allowed to ride over fields but the farmers were not very pleased about this and attacked them. Postboys were also attacked by highwaymen, who stole the letters in the hope that money would be inside them. So it was rather dangerous work, being a postboy.

As more and more people learned to read and write, more letters were written and more messengers were needed. Letters were put in mail bags and delivered to the post inns by mail coach. A man at the back blew a horn so that people knew the mail was coming. People had to pay for their letters when they collected them. If they had no money, they could not have their letters.

Then someone invented stamps. Letters could be paid for before they were delivered. The first stamp issued was the 'Penny Black'. It cost one penny and showed Queen Victoria's head on the stamp. Great Britain was the first country to issue stamps. At first they were cut out by hand: now stamps are printed in sheets with rows of tiny holes so that one stamp can easily be torn from a sheet. Now we can send letters all over the world. The letters are carried by ship, aeroplane, van and train, and many people are busy so that we may receive our mail.

### 4   SORTING THE LETTERS

Peter noticed that Father and Mother had been very busy writing letters. 'There must be thousands and thousands of letters sent every day. How do they sort them all out?' he asked. So Father continued his account of the Post Office and its work today.

When our letters have been written, we post them in a pillar box. The very first pillar box was set up when Queen Victoria was on the throne of Great Britain. Before that, postmen, who were called letter carriers, walked through the streets ringing a bell. When people heard the bell they went out to give him their letters. Today we can post letters in the post office or in pillar boxes standing in streets or post boxes set in walls.

A postman collects the letters from the pillar box and puts them into a bag which is taken to the sorting office. At the sorting office some wonderful machinery deals with the letters. Firstly the letters are carried along a moving belt and sorted into different shapes and sizes. One machine puts all the envelopes the right way up and another stamps a postmark on each stamp. The postmark shows the date and place where the letter was posted. Then the letters are sorted into different boxes, called 'pigeon holes' in a frame on a wall. This is done by postmen sitting in front of the frame.

Not all letters are sorted by hand. There are machines that sort letters and are worked by a man who sits at a kind of typewriter. After sorting, the letters are ready to go on their journey. All letters for the same town are tied into bundles, put into mail bags and loaded into vans. These vans carry the letters to railway stations, where they are put on to trains. Ordinary trains carry some mail, but there are also special mail trains which are like travelling post offices with sorting offices inside. Mail trains can also pick up bags of mail without stopping. As the train rushes through the countryside, postmen are busy sorting letters into their pigeon holes so that people may have their letters next morning. No time is wasted; they work all through the night. Letters and parcels to and from other countries are carried in ships or on 'planes.

So our letters, and millions of others, are safely delivered each day.


5  KEEPING IN TOUCH

Peter and Julie began to understand how important it is to keep in touch with people through letter writing, and they began to write letters themselves, usually short notes to put in the letters being sent by their mother and father. They understood how much it meant for people to hear their news, because they liked to receive letters too.

It is very important too that we should write 'Thank you' letters after Christmas and birthdays when we have received presents and cards from people. Because people have made us happy, we must show them that we appreciate their kindness and their thoughts.

Some people are very lonely, especially older people who live alone and it is such a pleasure for them to get letters so that they know they are not forgotten. People in hospital are glad to receive 'Get well' cards and letters from friends who are thinking about them and hoping they will soon be well.

Some of the nicest and happiest letters and cards sent to people in hospital are those we have made ourselves, with pictures drawn and messages written especially for the person we are sending them to. Many people, children and grown-ups, too, have been made happy by receiving letters and cards like these.

When people have to move away to a new place, it is good to receive letters from their old friends and neighbours, from their classmates and friends. Of course, they will soon make new friends and settle down in their new home and school, but they will like to hear from time to time, all the news of their friends left behind. And the friends left behind will no doubt like to hear news of them too.

All over the country and all over the world people are keeping 'in touch'—families and friends want to feel they are still close to each other. We have learned to read and write so that we may enjoy so many things in life. Sending and receiving letters are ways in which we can enjoy these skills.

Has anyone received letters recently from families living overseas? Has anyone received letters from friends or relatives living in another part of England? Or Scotland? Wales or Ireland? We can give pleasure, as well as receive happiness, by making sure we 'keep in touch' with people.


## 6   NEWSPAPERS

Much earlier in the day than the postman called there was a different kind of 'thump' on the floor. Something much larger than a letter was pushed through the letter box. Julie and Peter knew what this would be—the daily paper, brought by the boy who did the paper round. He delivered papers for Mr. Knight, the Newsagent whose shop was in the High Street.

If you look on one of the newsagent's counters you will see lots of different newspapers. There are special newspapers for business men, for teachers, and other people. In another part there are rows of magazines which tell people about things they especially enjoy—their interests and hobbies. Some people collect their papers from the shop, but many others, like Peter and Julie's parents, have them delivered. Boys and girls get up very early to do a paper round. They help the newsagent as they earn some pocket money for themselves.

The newsagent has to be up very early. The papers are delivered to his shop. Then he has to sort them out and find out which papers have to be delivered to which houses. He writes the numbers of the houses and street names on the papers, then helps the newspaper boys and girls to load their bags. It is very important that the papers are clearly marked and none left out, as people are waiting to read their newspapers, perhaps before they go to work or as they travel to work.

The newsagent knows that some papers will be read by lots of people: others are read by only a small number. But all newspapers are important to the people who read them, because they bring news of what is happening in lots of places. Local papers bring news of places and people near home: national daily papers bring news of people and places farther away. There are items of news to interest everyone—stories of people, animals, happy news, sad news—all keeping us in touch with the world outside our home.

'I think I would like to do a newspaper round when I am older,' said Peter.

'Plenty of time to think about that,' said Father, 'We will wait and see if you still want to do it when you are more grown up. Remember you have to get up very early, even if you would rather stay in bed, and go out to deliver the papers on cold and rainy days as well as the sunny, warm days.'

'Meanwhile,' called mother from the kitchen, 'just remember the boys and girls, the newsagent and his helpers who *do* start work very early so that we may have our newspapers brought to us each day.'


7   NEWSMEN

'Where do newspapers and magazines come from?' Peter asked his father. 'I know they are delivered to the shop and then sold to people, but where are they made, and who makes them?'

'A lot of people make the newspaper,' Father told him. 'Let me show you.'

Father brought his newspaper for Julie and Peter to see. He showed them how to look for the names of people who had provided the news and stories for the paper. There were names of reporters who went out to find the news that would make a good story. Then there are sports writers who give all the news of games and teams. There are pages especially for women about clothes and fashions, cooking and make-up. A doctor may write an article to help people or a vet about care of pets. Many people read the papers and they have many interests, which must all be remembered when the paper is made.

These people who write for newspapers are called journalists. They have to be able to write in a way people will find interesting, to spell correctly and be careful to report things truthfully. Many people help to make a newspaper. After the reporters and writers have prepared their work it is seen by important people in the newspaper office. Most important of these is the Editor, who decides what will go into the paper and how it will be set out. When all is ready, the paper 'goes into print' as newspaper people say.

Local papers give news of people living nearby and are printed in the same area. The big daily and Sunday papers are printed in large cities such as London, Manchester and Glasgow. Newspaper buildings are very big. They hold large machines on which the papers are printed. Huge rolls of newsprint—the special kind of paper used for newspapers—pass over the rollers which print the words and pictures. The machine cuts and folds the finished paper ready for sale.

After printing, cutting and folding, the papers are tied in bundles and sent out. As they are printed during the night when we are safe and warm in bed, it is still very early and dark when the papers are loaded on to vans and trains to be sent to towns and villages all over the country. When we read the papers at breakfast time, we do not always remember how many people have worked during the day and night so that we can read the news early each day. So many people, working for us!

## 8 GOOD NEWS

The best kind of news—the kind everyone likes to hear—is the good news. It makes people happy. Peter had heard his father say, 'That's good news,' and knew his parents were happy about something.

Sometimes a man selling papers will call out in a loud voice—something like 'Read all about it', and people hurrying along the street will wonder what it is they should read about.

People who have good news usually want others to share it. It is so important to them that they are sure it will be important to others, too. If something very special happens in your family, how you long to see your friends and tell them about it.

Many years ago, Jesus came to live among ordinary people on this earth. He was very special, sent by God to tell people all about God. He made some close friends who went with him, listened to him and helped him in his work. Jesus was able to teach and heal people who were sick or comfort those who were sad. He helped and taught many people, but they did not understand all he tried to tell them.

The day came when Jesus had to go away—away from all his friends who loved him and had worked with him. His friends were very sad for a while. Then something happened: something so wonderful that at first they could not believe it, but they began to understand that Jesus had not really left them. In a very special way he could still be with them, although they could not see him.

This was wonderful news—really good news—and the friends of Jesus wanted to tell everyone their news. Not everyone would believe them, but they still wanted people to know. So some of Jesus's friends thought they should write all about the work Jesus did, and how he helped people. They tried to remember all the wonderful things that had happened, and the things Jesus taught them and told them. Those friends who could write well, decided to write it all down, something like a big, special newspaper for people to read for themselves or to others. We call this the 'Gospel', which means 'Good News'.

We can read this today in the part of the Bible called the New Testament. This is a very special good news, which is still news for people after many hundreds of years. We can read it for ourselves and learn of the good news that Jesus came to tell us: God is always with us, and around us and interested in us, every one.

RELATED THEMES

*Family far away*                                                page 22

THE 'GOOD NEWS'
*from The Good News Bible*

'I am here with good news for you, which will bring great joy to all the people. This very day in David's town your Saviour was born—Christ the Lord!'                    *(Luke 2; 10–11)*

'The Good News was promised long ago by God through his prophets, as written in the Holy Scriptures. It is about his Son, our Lord Jesus Christ . . .'                    *(Romans 1; 2–3)*

'Jesus went to Galilee and preached the Good News from God. "The right time has come," he said, "and the Kingdom of God is near! Turn away from your sins and believe the Good News!"'
                                                            *(Mark 1; 14–5)*

'. . . this Good News about the Kingdom will be preached through all the world . . .                    *(Matthew 24; 14)*

1. At the beginning of the day, O God, we think of the news that we have had this morning about . . . We ask that you will bless all who need our prayers today [*especially* . . . ] *Amen*

2. Dear Father God,
   Every day our parents enjoy reading the newspaper
   And sometimes find things especially for us.
   Thank you for all who make the newspapers
   So that we can enjoy them. *Amen*

3. Dear Father, we are thankful for the greatest news of all, the Good News told by Jesus that you are our Father and you love us. Help us to be the very best we can for you. *Amen*

4. Dear God, I enjoy it when the postman calls and brings a letter that is just for me. Help me to think how much pleasure I may give to other people when I write to them. And help me to do something about it. *Amen*

5. Dear God,
   My newsagent's shop is a very interesting place.
   There are so many newspapers and magazines
   That people enjoy reading;
   There are lots of other things to see too,
   Like toys and books, felt-tip pens and pencils;
   There are lots of pretty greeting cards
   For birthdays, Christmas and other occasions;
   And there are all those jars of sweets
   And bars of chocolate that make my mouth water.
   Thank you, God, for shops like these
   And for the busy shopkeepers who are so helpful. *Amen*

6. How nice it is, dear God, to be able to keep in touch with our friends and relations in other parts of the world! Thank you for all the people in many countries who make it possible for us to do so. *Amen*

7. Thank you, dear God, for all the people who prepare the newspapers, magazines and comics that we enjoy. They are people we do not know but they do give us a lot of pleasure. *Amen*

8. Thank you, dear God, for the Good News about Jesus Christ and how he came to help us to know you better. Help us to learn from him and so do your will. *Amen*

9. Thank you, God, for postage stamps. There are so many different ones and some of them are very pretty. Some of us like collecting them to see how many different ones we can save. Thank you for all the things which give us pleasure. *Amen*

10. Thank you, O Lord, that there are so many interesting and happy ways to send our good wishes to our friends:
We like to send happy greetings at times like
    New Year, Christmas, and other special occasions;
We remember people on birthdays, anniversaries,
    Mothers' Day or Fathers' Day;
We send postcards to our friends at home when
    we are enjoying a holiday;
We can send telegrams for very special days
    such as weddings or anniversaries;
We sometimes send 'Get Well' cards when our
    friends are ill or in hospital;
And we can always send letters to tell our
    friends about ourselves.
Thank you, O Lord, for all these things. *Amen*

11. Today, O God, I am thinking about *my* postman.
I know he has a busy job to do:
He has to be out early and in all weathers,
But that does not seem to trouble him
And he seems to enjoy bringing our letters:
So thank you, God, for my special postman. *Amen*

12. We say thank you, dear Father God, for all the people who mean a lot to us and for all the ways in which we can keep in touch with them. *Amen*

HYMNS SUGGESTED

For all the things which we enjoy
Glad that I live am I
God make my life a little light
Hands to work and feet to run
Morning has broken
Thank you
When Jesus lived in Galilee


NEWS AND GREETINGS IN THE BIBLE

| | |
|---|---|
| A news report from long ago | 1 Samuel 4; 10–17 |
| Solomon and Hiram exchange messages | 1 Kings 5; 1–9 |
| The Good News of Jesus Christ | Mark 1; 1–6 |
| | John 3; 16–17 |
| Paul's greetings to Corinth | 2 Corinthians 13; 11–13 |
| Paul's greetings to Colossae | Colossians 4; 7–18 |
| Paul's letter to Philemon | Philemon |


INTEREST WORK AND ACTIVITIES

*Books*

Have available a number of books which can be read and handled
by the children. A few simple ones are:

POST *(Starters)*, Macdonald
THE POSTMAN *(Early Reading)*, Ladybird
LET'S GO TO THE POST OFFICE *(Let's go)*, Watts
POSTMEN AND THE POST OFFICE *(Blackwell's Learning
    Library)*, Blackwell
THE TELEPHONE OPERATOR; THE REPORTER *(What
    do they do?)*, Macmillan
NEWSPAPERS *(Blackwell's Learning Library)*, Blackwell

Large-print copies of the gospel in the *GOOD NEWS FOR
MODERN MAN* series might also be available or some simple
books of Bible stories about Jesus.

*Collections*

A small collection of postage stamps could be encouraged and also stamped envelopes received from overseas so that children can see how the envelopes are addressed, stamped and post-marked.

Collect newspapers, magazines and comics. If enough are brought in they could be used as a class 'shop'.

*Letters*

Practise writing letters to each other, to friends and families. Construct a pillar box for use in the school. This may be made from a large cardboard container with a slit cut in the front. Paint red with a white panel on the front giving times of collection. An alternative is to construct a round pillar box from corrugated cardboard, with base and top. Decorate in the same way. An opening has to be made in the back of the box to remove the letters.

Arrange for a postman or postmen to be appointed to 'clear the box'. All ages can take part in this. Sorters from the older classes will be needed to sort the letters into groups or classes for delivery at certain times of the day.

Equipment may be made—i.e. a peaked cap or caps for the postmen and suitable bags for collection and delivery.

*Newspapers*

Find from local papers items of news of special interest to the school. (Parents will be needed to help here.) These may be mounted and displayed, or copied in large print suitable to be read by the children.

Children can make their own newspaper—in classes or groups—by contributing items of news about themselves and their families, the school, and other local interests. Children's 'news', written carefully, can be illustrated and displayed on sheets or in large news books. Snapshots may be used to illustrate news but great care must be taken that they are returned in good condition.

*Visitors*

Invite a local postman to visit the school to show the children his uniform and his bag and to talk about his work—getting up early, going out on cold mornings.

A newsagent may be invited—to tell about his work. Any adult known to the children who works in printing of newspapers, may be able to visit. All these people work the kind of hours that may make it possible for them to come in school time.

Any visitor from overseas may be able to talk about the delivery of letters or newspapers in his own country. In New Zealand, for example, people living in remote areas have their letters left by the roadside on frames, specially constructed to take a bag. The full bag is collected by a bus driver. The same bus driver will deliver a newspaper in a remote area by throwing the rolled up paper out of the bus window over the roof of the bus, to land in a field. This is later collected by the recipient.

*Visits*

Nearby sorting offices may be visited by older children. It would not be practical for small children to join in such visits.

# 11   Light and darkness

*Lights of various kinds are so much a part of our daily lives that we tend to take them for granted and we are seldom really aware of their importance to us. It is only when we are plunged into darkness, or when lights cease to work, that we are brought face to face with the chaos and confusion that ensues.*

*Without doubt most people prefer the light to the darkness and are thankful for the longer days of the summer months. It is small wonder that people of long ago had their light festivals to mark the turning point in midwinter and to celebrate midsummer. The association of evil with darkness and of good with the light are to be found expressed in various religions.*

*Lights have a fascination for children, whether they be candles, fairy lights, lanterns and illuminations, or the great lights of the Universe. So in this theme we focus attention on many kinds of light; we evoke a sense of thankfulness or appreciation; and we teach a few simple parables.*

## 1  DAY AND NIGHT

Keep very, very still . . . Can you feel the world moving? No? Because you can feel nothing, it may *seem* as though the world is standing still. But it isn't. At this very moment you are travelling very fast through space on a long journey round the sun, which is going to take one year to complete before it starts again. At the same time, our world is spinning round and round . . . and we can't feel that either.

Because the world is turning round and round, there are some times when our side of the world faces the sun and there are other times when we face away from the sun. When we are facing the sun we enjoy the daylight; then, as we spin round, it becomes dark.

People used to think that the sun travelled round the world. They could not feel the world moving so they believed it stood still. In the morning they saw the sun rise; during the day it travelled across the sky; and at night the sun set. Now we know that the sun keeps still and it is the world that moves.

The sun is like a great ball of fire, very hot and very bright. We can feel how hot the sun is, especially in summer . . . and that heat has travelled 93 million miles through space! We know too that the sun is very bright because we cannot look at it. If we try to do so without using a special darkened glass we can damage our eyes.

At night we cannot see the sun but we have other lights in the sky. The largest of these is the moon. Unlike the sun, the moon *does* travel round the world. It takes about a month for it to make one journey round the world. At night the moon gives us light but it is not its own light: it is light reflected from the sun. So the moon gives light without being hot.

Also at night we see lots of stars. They are all balls of fire like our sun but some of them much stronger. They seem so small because they are millions and millions of miles away in space. Like the sun, they are very hot but we do not feel any warmth from them because they are so very, very far away.

Also at night we may see planets, some of them brighter than the stars. They are other worlds which travel round the sun like our planet, Earth.

We call all these things—sun, moon, stars and planets—the Universe. It is so wonderfully made that we know for sure that our seasons will come each year; and we know for certain that night will follow day and day will follow night.

What a wonderful universe our God created!

## 2   LIGHTENING THE DARKNESS

Do you like it best when it is light or when it is dark? Most people prefer the light because they can see things much more easily. Sometimes when there is no moon the streets and the countryside can seem very, very dark. But it is never completely dark out of doors. Once our eyes become used to the darkness we can usually see the shapes of objects even though we may not see what they are really like.

There are not many places where it is ever completely dark, where no light is ever seen. There are some deep caves where you can never see anything if the electric lights are switched off. Imagine not even being able to see your hand if you hold it right in front of your face! Most people like it when the lights are switched on again.

If we are going anywhere where we know it will be dark we usually make sure that we have some means of seeing our way.

---

Often we take a torch, which is easy to carry and can be switched on when we find ourselves in the darkness.

Motorists often need to be able to see their way along dark country roads and so all cars are fitted with powerful headlights which can show where there are bends in the road long before the motorist reaches them. They show any people, animals or dangers that might otherwise not be seen by the driver.

Sometimes we use very powerful lights which make the night-time almost as bright as the day. No doubt you have watched football matches, which are played in the evening under lots and lots of floodlights. Floodlights are also used to light up important buildings so that they can be seen easily in the darkness. Floodlit buildings look very nice when all around them is dark.

So we have lots of ways of lightening the darkness but none of them is quite the same as the daylight. We can switch on lights in our homes but they are never as bright as the sunshine which streams in through the windows when we pull back the curtains. Nowadays most people like to have large windows in their homes or their offices to let in as much light as possible.

Often we welcome the daylight at the end of a night that may have seemed particularly long. It is also very nice to see the daylight at the end of a long tunnel that we may have been travelling through.

Sometimes you will hear people talking about their bad times as times of darkness. How nice it is in such times to have special things to brighten the darkness—a comforting word, the smile of a friend, or the feeling that God is near.

3  STRIKE A LIGHT

If it is dark and you need a light, what do you do?
[*Children's answers.*]

The easiest way to get a light is to press the switch on the wall so that the light comes on. Just like magic isn't it? It may *seem* like magic but it isn't really. The light comes on because there is electricity there and because many years ago a man discovered how to make electricity light up in a bulb.

Suppose you wanted a light somewhere and there was no electricity. You might use a torch with batteries in it. That is one way in which you can take some electricity with you. Or you might use a lamp. How would you light the lamp? No doubt you would take a box of matches and strike one by rubbing the head of the match against the side of the box. There is something in the head of the match which catches fire easily and give you the burning light you need.

A long, long time ago people had no electricity or torches and they had no matches because people had not discovered how to make them. All they had was fire. But how could they light a fire without any matches?

Rub your hands together hard and see what happens. Notice how warm they get. If you rub things together for a long time they get hotter and hotter. Long ago people discovered that, if two pieces of wood were rubbed together for long enough they would become so hot that one would begin to burn. They also discovered that some stones, called flints, would make sparks if they were hit. The sparks could set fire to very dry materials which we call tinder.

What a lot of trouble just to get a light? Aren't you thankful for electric lights, battery torches and boxes of matches?

Once those people of long ago had lit their fires they could take sticks from the fire to light their way. Perhaps you have seen pictures of people carrying blazing torches like this.

Long ago people invented another kind of light too. It was a lamp. It was like a bowl and was filled with oil. In the oil was something like rag or string which we call a wick. The end of the wick was lit and it kept burning as long as there was oil in the lamp. This was much better than a burning piece of wood for giving light in a house.

Today we have many different kinds of light or lamp and simple ways of lighting them. We are much more fortunate than people of the past and than people living in some other parts of the world today.

## 4 HELPFUL LIGHTS

How often have you been especially pleased to see a light? Perhaps it has been a light that has been particularly helpful when you have wanted to see your way. Travellers in the country have often been pleased to see a light in a window which tells them they are getting near a house.

Sailors have often been pleased to see the helpful light of a lighthouse, which has guided them past dangerous rocks. They have also looked for much smaller helpful lights at the entrance to the harbour, which show them where to go.

How many helpful lights can you think of in town? [*Shop lights, car lights, traffic lights, warning lights, street lights . . .* ] Some of the most helpful are the street lights because they help us to see so many things when it is dark. Have you noticed how different it is if any of the street lights are not alight? And how dark the country roads seem when you leave the town lights behind.

Motorists on country roads are helped by another kind of light. Most roads now have a line of 'cats' eyes'. They are small pieces of glass, set in rubber. They do not have any light inside them but reflect the lights that shine from the car. Cats' eyes are very small but very helpful.

Lights do not have to be large to be helpful. In fact the smallest lights can brighten a dark place. There are some people who do not like sleeping in a dark room and so they have a small light which burns all night. It is called a night light and it is like a short, fat candle.

How many other kinds of candle do you know? There are the plain white candles which we sometimes use at home; there are pretty coloured candles in fancy shapes which we use for decoration; and there are special candles sometimes seen in churches or other places of worship. There are fat ones, thin ones, pretty ones and plain ones. Some stand in plain candlesticks and some in very pretty or ornamental ones—but they all give the same kind of light once they have been lit.

Jesus once told his disciples that they should let their light shine—helpful lights that would show people something of God.

So we should let our lights shine in the world today. And it does not matter whether we are big or small, fat or thin, plain or pretty, white or coloured. Nor does it matter whether we are in a simple or a fancy home. We all have the same kind of light and we can all let it shine.


5   WARNING LIGHTS

'I'd better put the lights on,' Dad muttered half aloud. The family had just been to visit Grandma and were on their way home in their car.

'Why do you want your lights on?' George asked. 'I can see where we are going.'

'So can I,' Dad replied, 'but the lights on a car are not only to help you see your way. They are also to help other people to see you so that there is no accident. The only lights on a car that help the driver to see where he is going are the headlights and they also help other drivers to see us in fog or heavy rain as well as when it is dark. The other little lights in the front of the car, the ones we call side lights are only there to make sure we are seen. What other lights are there on our car?'

George and Sandra started answering together. They thought of the red lights at the back of the car and the bright red light that goes on when the driver puts his foot on the brakes to warn others that he has done so. There are the flashing lights which warn that the car is going to turn right or left; there are white lights which come on when the car is being driven backwards; and there are special fog lights on some cars.

Dad explained that ships have lights too. They are called navigation lights and they give information to the captains of other ships. Ships that are in trouble, or ones doing special jobs so that they cannot move out of the way of others, carry other lights too as warnings. He also told them about lots of other warning lights that help sailors such as the buoys which mark sandbanks or wrecks, the lighthouses which warn of rocks and different kinds of harbour light.

'Next time you hear an aeroplane at night, see if you can spot it by its lights,' Dad went on. 'You will notice that the lights flash on and off. Why do you think they do that?'

Dad always liked the children to have something to do on a car journey: it helped to keep them quiet. He told them to think of all the other warning lights they could.

'Red lights on masts and chimneys,' said George.

'Lights round a hole in the road,' added Sandra.

'The lamps Mr. Wilson hung on his rubbish skip.'

'Traffic lights.'

'Orange beacon lights at zebra crossings.'

'Reflectors on the back of bicycles and cars,' said Sandra.

'And the ones which show where the road bends,' George added.

So we have lots of lights which warn us of danger and help us to keep safe on journeyings. Jesus once said that he was the Light of the World. He came to help us to have a safe journey through life, avoiding dangers which would spoil our lives or keep us from really knowing God.

## 6   HAPPY LIGHTS

Steve was enjoying himself. It was his birthday and he had some of his friends at home for his birthday party. Mum had said that they could come to tea and then stay to play games with him until it was time for them to go home. As they arrived they brought him presents and there was great excitement when he unwrapped them to see what he had been given.

Then came the birthday tea. There were all sorts of thing that the children would enjoy including jelly, trifle and lots of pretty, cream and iced cakes. And there in the middle was the birthday cake. Mum had made it and decorated it with icing. It had the words on it, 'Happy Birthday, Steve', and one candle for each year of his age.

When they had eaten most of the other food, Mum lit the candles and told the children that they should sing 'Happy Birthday' to Steve. They all did. Then it was Steve's turn to do something. 'You must blow out all the candles with one breath,' he was told. He took a deep breath, blew until he thought he would burst, but managed to blow them all out. It was one of the highlights of his party, a very happy occasion.

Have you ever thought of some lights as happy lights. Those lights on the birthday cake certainly were—even though they were only alight for a short time. There are other times, too, when we have happy lights which help us to enjoy something special.

Most people enjoy having fairy lights at Christmas time. We put strings of fairy lights on our Christmas trees or elsewhere in the room. Sometimes they flash on and off. We get a lot of pleasure from these and other coloured lights. No doubt you have enjoyed the ones you have seen at the seaside, on fairgrounds or in parks.

Other happy lights are fireworks with their pretty colours. People watch rockets soar into the sky and then burst into colour. You will hear a loud 'Aah . . .' from the crowd, which tells that they are enjoying the display. People in many countries enjoy their fireworks and other pretty lights too, sometimes in coloured lanterns, on special occasions when they want people to know how happy they are.

Perhaps another kind of light is a happy face because a happy face can always bring a lot of brightness to people who may be feeling sad and in need of cheering up. It is one way in which we can *all* help to make the world a brighter place.

Is yours a happy face?

## 7   FESTIVAL LIGHTS

Most of our happy lights are ones which we think of at special times of the year when we have something to be especially glad about. Birthdays are a special time for us because a birthday is our own special day. There are some days when lots and lots of people are happy at the same time. We call these days festivals.

One of the happiest of these festivals is Christmas, when people all over the world remember how Jesus Christ came into the world. Our candles and coloured lights are just one way of showing our happiness at Christmas.

There is one special day when many people let off fireworks. That is Guy Fawkes Night, 5th November. It is not a religious festival but a time when people long ago were happy because the king and the Houses of Parliament had not been blown up.

People in many parts of the world have their happy days. In India there is a very special festival called Divali. It is a time when people light all sorts of candles, lamps and lanterns. In the big towns and cities there are lots of coloured lights and people enjoy their fireworks too.

Divali is the time when people remember a story of how, thousands of years ago, there lived a good king named Rama. His wife Sita was a very lovely person. One day, while Rama was away from home, the demon-king of Sri Lanka, whose name was Ravana, came to the house, captured Sita and took her to his home.

After many adventures and battles, Rama defeated Ravana and rescued his queen. They returned to their own kingdom, where the people shouted with joy. From that day to this the people have enjoyed Divali—the Hindu festival of light. In many parts of the world, wherever Indian people live, there is happiness at Divali when the people remember how the good king overcame the bad king. They have new clothes, enjoy special foods and give presents, much as Christian people do at Christmas.

There are lots of times during the dark months of the year when people have festivals of lights. In China and Japan the lights are put in colourful lanterns. In other places candles are lit.

One of these places is Sweden. On St. Lucia's Day, 13th December, girls dress as St. Lucia and wear crowns of lighted candles. Then they go from house to house with trays of cakes and coffee.

So people in many parts of the world keep their special days and light their different lights which bring a lot of brightness and happiness to others as well as to themselves.

## 8  LIGHTS THAT REMIND

Do you remember why the Indian people have their special lights at Divali? It was because the good king Rama had won his battle against the bad king Ravana.

Often we hear people talk about the light when they mean good things and darkness when they mean bad things. Lights can always brighten the darkness, so it is not surprising that people put on lights when they want to remember how good overcomes evil.

Jewish people keep a very special festival towards the end of the year, when they remember how bad things were destroyed long ago. The festival is called Chanukkah. They remember how a little group of Jews, over two thousand years ago, won a battle against a powerful ruler.

Those Jews had been told that they must not worship God. Their scriptures had been destroyed and the temple where they worshipped had been used for evil things. Their leader, Judah, attacked his enemies for three years until he drove them out of the holy city. He cleared out the temple and went to light the light that always burned there. There was only enough pure oil for one night but by a miracle it lasted for eight days.

So Chanukkah is a festival which lasts for eight days. During the festival, a special candlestick is used, which has holders for eight candles. On the first evening one candle is lit; on the second, two; and so on until the eighth evening when there are eight.

The lights of Chanukkah are a reminder of how a small group of people, with God's help, overcame great evil. Light had overcome darkness.

About the same time, some Christian people are lighting Advent candles. Advent is the time just before Christmas when Christian people remember how God had said he would send Jesus to help people. On each Sunday of Advent an extra candle is lit in some churches until there are four on the Sunday before Christmas. Then, at Christmas there are lots of lights which can be enjoyed, making it a very bright and happy time.

A few weeks later, on 2nd February, comes the festival called Candlemas. This is a reminder of the time when Jesus was taken to the temple by his mother to be presented to God. An old man took the baby Jesus in his arms and said Jesus was the one who had come to be a light to show people in a dark world how to find God.

So the lights of Advent, Christmas and Candlemas are a reminder of the very special person who said that he was the Light of the World.

RELATED THEMES

1.  Accept our thanks, O Lord God, for every blessing we have received from you, and for your light which has guided our way. Teach us to walk in your light so that we may live good and useful lives. *Amen*

2.  Dear Father God, we need never be in darkness because there are so many ways of making light. Thank you for all those people who discovered how to do so and people who have made it so easy for us to have light wherever we need it. *Amen*

3.  O God our Father, when we think of the sun, moon and stars, we remember how great you are. Thank you for looking after us, who are so small. *Amen*

4.  O Lord Jesus Christ, who said that you were the Light of the World, let your light shine into our hearts so that we may try to be like you in all we do. *Amen*

5.  Teach us, O God, to look for the right way to live, so that our lives may be pleasing to you and we may bring a little brightness and happiness to others. *Amen*

6.  Thank you, dear God, for all those lights which bring happiness into our lives. Help us to remember that happiness is one of your great gifts to us. *Amen*

7.  Thank you, dear God, for the comfort and help that even the smallest light can give. Help me to let my little light shine so that it brings comfort and help to others. *Amen*

8.  Thank you, God our Father,
    For all the lights which help us to see,
    And those that guide our way:
    Thank you for Jesus, the Light of the World
    Who showed us how to find you.
    May we follow the path he has shown us. *Amen*

9. Today, dear Father God, we think of all the brightness that has come into our lives because of the love of others and the good things they have given us. Teach us always to be thankful and to show our thanks by being bright and cheerful ourselves. *Amen*

10. We remember, God our Father, how often, in the past, dark and evil things have been overcome by good things and how you have helped good people in their fight against evil. Help us to follow their example. *Amen*

11. When the world seems dark and dreary, O God, help us to remember the brightness that comes from your love, and your light which helps us to see our way to enjoy life. *Amen*

12. When we remember all your gifts to us, O God, we are very happy to know that you care. Show us the right things to do so that we may always try our best to please you, for this is the best way we know to say Thank you. *Amen*

HYMNS SUGGESTED

A little child may know
Can you count the stars?
Click goes the switch
God make my life a little light
God who put the stars in space
I have seen the golden sunshine
I love the sun
I love to think that Jesus saw
Jesus bids us shine
The great round sun we love to see
Twinkle, twinkle, little star
We praise thee for the sun

# 11 LIGHT AND DARKNESS

*Books for the book corner*

WE DISCOVER SUN MOON AND STARS *(We discover)*,
  Arnold
SUN *(Starters)*, Macdonald
MOON/STARS *(Starters Facts)*, Macdonald
LET'S FIND OUT ABOUT THE SUN/MOON *(Let's find out)*,
  Watts
WE DISCOVER LIGHT, LENSES AND COLOUR *(We
  discover)*, Arnold
WINDOWS *(Do you know about?)*, Burke
LIGHT AND COLOUR *(First Library)*, Macdonald
LAMPS AND LIGHTING *(Blackwell's Learning Library)*,
  Blackwell

*Night and Day*

Demonstrate night and day on a globe, using a torch for the sun.
This is best done in the dark if the room can be blacked out.
  Paint pictures on themes of night and day—darkness and light.

*Lamps*

Make a collection of different lights and lamps and discuss when
each is used. Allow children to handle and examine where possible.
Include various kinds of electric lighting and torches, fairy lights,
hurricane and other lamps, flashlights for photography, spotlights
and candles of various sorts. If possible include some of the industrial types of lamp, e.g. miner's safety lamp and those used to mark
roadworks.
  Add interest by including pictures of any kind of light which
cannot be brought into school, e.g. a lighthouse, floodlighting, a
searchlight.
  Think about special uses for lamps and candles other than for
giving light, e.g. candle clocks.

Make a note of all those lights which help or warn, e.g. policeman's blue lamp, traffic lights, rockets. Find pictures of these and make into a 'Helpful lights' book.

*Effects of light or darkness*

Do a few experiments or talk about the different effects of light and darkness.

Note the effect upon eyes and how they change in appearance when the light is switched on after a period of darkness.

Experiment with seedlings. Place identical seedlings in different surroundings—one in a bright place and one in a dark place. Compare regularly and note differences in rate of growth, colour and strength.

Demonstrate the differences when a room is blacked out or the lighting is poor. Note the effect on sight. Which is best for health?

It may be appropriate to consider briefly the rainbow and other matters of light and colour.

# 12 Signs and symbols

*We are surrounded by signs and symbols of many kinds, some more obvious than others. We are very familiar with traffic and warning signs but there are those many other signs which we can 'read'— such things as weather lore and health symptoms.*

*On the whole, signs are messages without words, though many do bear words, particularly the warning signs. Many early signs originated because people were unable to read. They were the visual aids of their day. Some of our characteristics and expressions of feeling are also wordless signs, sometimes indicating feelings in such a way that words would be superfluous.*

*Through this section there will be some very important lessons to be taught in helping children to recognize the danger signs and certain basic facts that will be useful to them. Perhaps, without expecting too much of them at this stage, one might initiate a spark of pride in belonging.*

*Whilst not referred to directly in the 'stories' which follow it will be obvious that a few signs to show the children during assembly will be very useful visual aids and will bring home the messages more clearly.*

## 1 SIGNS ALL AROUND US

How many of you, on your way to school today, noticed any special signs which were set up to tell people something they ought to know? Did you come across a zebra crossing? What do the black and white stripes tell motorists? What do they tell people who want to cross the road?

Was there a school crossing patrol—a lollipop man or woman? What did he/she have in his/her hand? What does this tell people? Would a policeman need to carry a special sign? His uniform is a sign of a different kind. We recognize him by his uniform. It is a sign that he belongs to the police and people can recognize him a long way off.

Perhaps you noticed some signs on posts by the side of the road. There are lots of signs that have been put up so that motorists and others can be helped to keep safe on the roads. Most schools have a sign nearby to warn motorists that there are children about. It may not have the words 'Children' or 'School' on it. Does anyone know what it looks like? Can you think of any other road signs that look something like this? What do they tell motorists?

These signs tell in a kind of picture language what the motorists need to know. Then it does not matter if they cannot read the words. Some motorists come from another country where they speak a different language. They may not know English but they would recognize the sign because they probably have one in their own country that looks similar and has the same meaning.

The most important signs for any of us are those which warn of danger. They may have the word DANGER written in large letters ... but there may be people who cannot read. So we have one special colour which stands for danger. Do you know what it is . . .? Think of the traffic lights. Which colour means STOP? It would be very dangerous to drive past this red light. When might you see a red flag flying on the beach? Always be careful if you see a red flag, a red notice or a red light. It may be a warning of some kind.

Perhaps you can think of other signs that have been put up for people to see. There are lots and lots of them. See how many you can spot on your way home.

## 2   WARNING SIGNS

Do you remember which colour is used as a sign of danger? It is put near the danger spot for people to see. Sometimes it is necessary to use another kind of sign for people to see *and* read.

If anyone were to put a red board by the gate of a field you might ask, 'What is dangerous there?' But if there was a notice which said BEWARE OF THE BULL you would know that you should keep out of the field because some bulls can be dangerous. Perhaps you have seen a notice on somebody's gate which says BEWARE OF THE DOG.

Sometimes the notices or signs say simply NO ENTRY, or KEEP OUT. They do not say why but we should do what they say because it may be for our safety. There are other signs, which we might see, which are not signs of danger but are put there for a very good reason. KEEP OFF THE GRASS is a warning of a different kind. It would be harmful to the grass, not for people who walk on it, because too many people would damage it. PRIVATE is also a warning we should heed too. It means that the owners do not want on their property people who have no right to be there.

So whatever notices you see, remember to do as they say for your safety and for the sake of other people.

The signs we have thought about so far have been ones you see. But there are other warnings too. Some very important signs are ones that you hear. What happens in school if there is a fire? No doubt you remember the last time you had a fire drill so that you would know what to do in case of fire. What was the warning like?

And if a fire engine did have to come to put out a fire, how would it warn traffic to keep out of the way so that it could reach the fire quickly. Every car carries a warning sign too. Have you ever been hooted at by a driver to warn you to keep out of the way?

Some of the simplest warning signs are given with the voice. Someone may shout STOP, or RUN, or FIRE, or GO AWAY and wave his arms at the same time to make sure you see him. Animals give danger signs too. Have you ever put out your hand to stroke a dog, when he has started growling and bared his teeth. That is a good warning sign for you to keep away.

And, of course, there are people like that too. Do you know anyone who loses his temper and hits out or kicks people? Usually he goes very red in the face first—a good warning sign to keep out of his way as it may be dangerous to get too close.

Always take notice of warning signs of any kind.

3  SIGNS THAT POINT THE WAY

Some signs are used to tell people of something they will find helpful or to show how to find something.

Without using any words, can you tell me where the piano is? . . . And where is the door? . . . And the ceiling? You could show exactly where they were just by pointing your finger in the direction of the object you were thinking about. Pointing is another sign that we often use.

Sometimes we point with our fingers but sometimes we need to have a sign which always points the way for anyone to see at any time. It may be in the shape of a hand with a finger pointing or it may be an arrow. Have you any in school? Is there a sign pointing towards the Head Teacher's room? Or the school office? Or one which says WAY OUT. This is a pointing sign that we see in lots of different places and we are often pleased to see it.

People are often looking for other signs which point to places they want to find—toilets, a car park, the seafront or a special show that is being held

No doubt the commonest pointing signs are the signposts that we see at road junctions or crossroads so that travellers know which road to take when they want to go to a particular place. There are lots of people who have been pleased to see a signpost when they have lost their way or have not been sure which way to go. Nowadays on busy roads, such as motorways, there is a different kind of sign a long way before the place to turn off, because cars on motorways travel very fast.

There are signposts that point the way for sailors, too. They are not signposts like the ones by the roadside. Can you think what they are? There are lots of them round the coast. They are usually painted white, red and white or black and white so that they can easily be seen by day. By night they have a bright light. They are lighthouses. And when it is foggy so that they cannot be seen, they make loud noises that sailors can hear. Lighthouses point the way to a safe course into harbour or past dangerous rocks.

In the Bible we are told that God's word is like a lamp to show up the path. So our holy books can be signposts too, to help us live good lives and to find our way to knowing God.

## 4  SIGNS WE RECOGNIZE EASILY

If you were to see a red cross on a white background, what would you expect to find there? It might be a hospital. It might be a first-aid tent on the beach. It might be painted on an ambulance or on a hospital ship. It is probably the best-known sign in the world and one which is recognized by people all over the world.

It is a very special sign because it means that there are people there who are looking after others who are very ill or who have been hurt very badly. Even in war time, when people are fighting and killing each other, they usually try to do nothing to harm those people who are helping others under the sign of the red cross. A similar sign is a red crescent, in the shape of a new moon, used in countries where the people are Muslims.

There are other signs which help us to find people who are ready to help others. You will often find a blue lamp outside a police station. In many places, too, you find a yellow sign with black letters AA—the sign or symbol of an organization to help motorists. Can you think of any other signs that people would find especially helpful at times?

All the signs we have thought of so far have been ones that people have put there. There are other signs that have been given to us by God.

Have you ever heard Mum and Dad say, when you have been on holiday, 'Red sunset! That's good. It should be a nice day tomorrow.'? Or perhaps one morning the curtains have been opened and Dad has said, 'Red sky! Don't like the look of that.' There is an old saying:

> *Red sky at night, shepherds' delight.*
> *Red sky in the morning, shepherds' warning.*

The sky can often tell us what kind of weather we can expect. There are lots of signs like this.

There are also signs that tell us to expect other things, too, which may not be very pleasant. What would it be a sign of if your nose started running or if you started sneezing? It is a warning that you will not feel too well for a few days. Our bodies are wonderfully made and give us lots of warnings that things may not be quite right with us. If we are wise we see our doctor and follow his advice by taking some medicine or going to bed.

We remember that God has given us wonderful bodies and a lovely world. And God expects us to take notice of the signs he gives us.

## 5   SIGNS WE ALL USE

Tommy wasn't feeling very well. He had come home from school feeling all hot and bothered. He didn't want to go out to play, as he often did, and he did not feel much like eating his food. Mum looked at him.

'Is something wrong?' she asked, although she could tell that he just wasn't his usual cheerful self.

'I don't feel very well,' Tommy replied.

Mum put her hand on his forehead. It felt very hot. 'I think we'd better take your temperature,' she said. So she took out the thermometer and put it under his tongue. After a minute or so she took it out, looked at it and knew she had been right. Tommy had a temperature that was higher than it should have been.

Soon Tommy was on his way to bed. Mum tucked him in so that he was comfortable, kissed him on his forehead and left him to sleep.

Mother had read the sign that all was not well. A high temperature is always a sign that something is wrong with the body. And Mum had given Tommy a sign too. That kiss on his forehead was a sign that she loved and cared for him. We often kiss people as a sign of affection or love. It is a way of showing our deep feelings so that other people know how we feel.

There are lots of other things that we do which show how we feel about something.

When was the last time you had a good cry? Perhaps you had fallen and hurt yourself. Maybe someone had said something unkind. Or perhaps you had lost something you treasured. The tears just came into your eyes and there was nothing you could do to stop them. It was a sign to everyone that you were hurt or unhappy.

There are some times when tears do not mean that. Have you ever seen someone laugh so much that tears have come as well. Laughter is another sign—a sign that we are very happy about something. A smiling face is another sign. How nice it is to know people who usually have a happy face'.

Some people always seem to look miserable. They scowl at almost anything. It is a sign that they are certainly not very happy people.

What kind of person are you? What signs do you give other people to see? Do they see you as someone who is always selfish, miserable, or bad-tempered? Or do they see you as someone who is always cheerful, happy, kind and loving?

I think we all know which it is best to be.

## 6 CLUES

There is a very well-known story about a man named Robinson Crusoe, who was wrecked on a desert island. He thought there was no one else on the island until one day he saw some footprints in the sand on the beach. They were not his, so he knew that there was somebody else on the island. The footprints were a sign that told him so.

Sometimes we call signs like these clues. They are the kind of signs that are very useful when we want to find out something. When a policeman goes to a house where things have been stolen, he looks for signs or clues that will help him to find the person who broke into the house.

Is there any sign that a door or window has been forced open? If a window is open, are there any footprints in the earth underneath the window? Are they large or small? That will tell whether it was a man or a boy. Were they made by boots or slippers? Are there any special marks, such as patterned heel marks which they would recognize again?

Inside the house they will look for fingerprints on anything that has been picked up or moved. Take a look at your fingertips. Can you see all those little lines on them? Did you know that the patterns on everyone's fingers are different? Your fingerprints can be taken by putting them in special ink or paint and then pressing them on to a piece of paper. Sometimes the police find that the fingerprints in a house that has been burgled match up with the fingerprints of someone who has been in trouble before. Fingerprints are a very good clue or sign.

Some people like to look for clues out of doors which tell them about animals or birds. Often, in the country, you can see the footmarks that animals have left in muddy places. What kind of animal was it? The footprints may tell. Perhaps you have found some birds' feathers. What were they like? They may be a clue which will tell what kind of bird had been there.

People who look for clues are often called detectives. You will find as you get older that you can have lots of fun being detectives and seeing what you can discover yourself from any clues there may be.

Remember, too, that we give other people lots of clues which tell them things about ourselves. Whether we like it or not we give all sort of clues that they can use. Sulking, laughing, offering to help, snatching things from others, comforting someone who is sad, spiteful behaviour, working hard, playing fairly—these are all clues which tell people what we are really like. What kind of clues do you give?

7 SIGNS OF BELONGING

It was a bright afternoon, sunny but a little on the chilly side. Robert was walking with his dad towards the local football ground. He was feeling rather proud because he was dressed rather like his father. Round their necks were nice warm scarves in the colours of their local team. They both wore woolly bobble hats, also in their team colours, and had large rosettes on their coats. There was no doubt whom they supported.

There are lots of times when we wear a sign of belonging, perhaps clothing or a badge. You have probably seen children wearing a school uniform. Anyone seeing them can tell from the colour of the blazer which school they attend. There are lots of grown-up people, too, who wear a uniform. Men and women in the army, for example, wear a uniform and that uniform also shows which part of the army they serve in. Sailors, policemen, firemen and air stewardesses all wear uniforms. So do boys and girls in The Boys' Brigade, Brownies, Guides and other organizations. How many others can you think of?

Many of these also wear badges. A badge is a special sign of belonging which can be worn by people if they are not in uniform. How many of you have badges to show that you belong to a special group of people? What do the badges mean?

The idea of wearing badges is not a new one. Long ago, when knights rode into battle, they carried shields which had markings on them by which they could be recognized. One of these was a white shield with a specially shaped black cross on it. They were Knights of the Order of St. John of Jerusalem. You will still see that badge today—worn by members of the St. John Ambulance Brigade.

A cross is found on lots of badges because it is the special sign of those people who call themselves Christian. They are people who follow the ways of Jesus Christ who was put to death on a cross. So the cross is a special sign for Christians—just as the Star of David is a special sign for Jews. There are signs for people of other religions, too.

Crosses are also found on lots of flags. The flag of England is a red St. George's Cross on a white flag. Scotland has a white St. Andrew's Cross on a blue flag. Ireland has a red St. Patrick's Cross on a white flag. Long ago they were all put together to form the flag we now call the Union Flag or Union Jack. Lots of people are proud to wave their Union Jacks to show that they are British. It is another sign of belonging—in this case to a particular country.

It is nice to belong to something that we believe is good and to be proud to let everyone know that we belong.


## 8  TRADEMARKS

Karen had gone shopping with Mum. They had gone to the supermarket, each with a shopping bag because Karen liked to carry some of the shopping home as well. It made her feel as though she was grown up if she could do the sort of things that Mum did.

They looked around the shelves and began taking the goods they needed. 'We need a tin of baked beans,' Mum said. So Karen walked over to the shelf and was just about to pick one up. 'No! Not that one!' her mother said. 'Get one of those over there.' So Karen did as mother had said. She couldn't understand why. They were both baked beans; they were both the same size; and they were the same price. So mother explained. She had tried all sorts of baked beans and she liked some better than others. 'I always buy those,' she said, 'because I know they are good. Do you see that name? And that special badge or mark? We call those the registered name and the trademark. You can always rely on goods that have those on them. They are always good.'

So Karen began looking at other goods too. She found lots of them that had special names or trademarks and she pointed them out to Mum. Her mother told her, 'It is always a good idea to buy things with a special name or trademark because the people who make it want you to be satisfied. If you like it you will buy the same thing again next time—and that is good for business. So they try to make sure that anything in a tin or packet that has their special sign or badge is the best they can possibly make it.'

On the way home, Karen was thinking about what Mum had said. Anything in the tin or packet that had a special name or badge had to be the best that could be put into it. She had a school blazer and a badge that had the name of her school Was she the best kind of person who could be put into it?

She went to Sunday School. Her church had a sign—a cross, and a special name—Christian. Was she the best she could be there, too?

Whatever it is that we belong to, whether it is a school, a church, an organization or even a whole country, we should aim always to be the best we can, so that other people who see us will feel that we belong to something worth belonging to. It is all too easy to do wrong things which let the side down. If we are proud to belong to something we should always try to be the best we possibly can.

RELATED THEMES

SYMBOLS OF THE PRINCIPAL RELIGIONS

(a)  JUDAISM: The Star (Shield) of David
(b)  CHRISTIANITY: The Cross (Many shape variations)
(c)  BUDDHISM: The Eight-spoked wheel (Eightfold path)
(d)  SIKHISM: The Khanda
(e)  HINDUISM: The OM or AUM—part of all Hindu prayers
     ISLAM: None. The star and crescent moon appearing on many emblems is not a religious symbol.

1. All around me, O God, I see signs:
   Signs that warn me of some danger;
   Signs that help me to know what to do;
   Signs that show me where to go;
   And signs that tell me useful things.
   Help me to know what they mean
   And to heed what they tell me
   For my own good
   And for the sake of others. *Amen*

2. Dear Father, help us to recognize those signs which mean danger; and make us wise always to take notice of them. *Amen*

3. Help me to remember, O God, that my face tells people what kind of person I am. Help me to grow up to be a cheerful person with a happy face that spreads sunshine wherever I go. *Amen*

4. My Father God, I know that roads can be dangerous places and I must be very careful. Help me to learn how and where to cross the road in safety. *Amen*

5. My Father, God, when I wear a badge which shows that I belong to something, help me to be proud to belong and to do nothing that would give it a bad name. *Amen*

6. O God, help me to remember that people who use a trademark try to make sure that all goods having that sign are always the best they can be: and help me to remember that, if I am a member of any group that has a special badge or sign, I should be the best kind of member that I can be. *Amen*

7. O God my Father, if sometimes I do not know why a sign or notice has been put up, help me to realize that there must be some reason and to take notice of what it tells me. *Amen*

8. O Lord, in all our work and all our play, show us how to do and be the best we can. *Amen*

9. Sometimes, O God, we are not sure which way to go.
   Thank you for signposts which show us the way;
   Thank you for people who are ready to help us;
   Thank you for any who guide us
   And show us how to live good lives
   As true children of our heavenly Father. *Amen*

10. Teach me to use my eyes, O Lord,
    To be aware of things that others may not see,
    And to learn from all these things
    So that I may enjoy your world. *Amen*

11. Thank you, O God, for all that helps us to know you:
    For the Bible and all holy books;
    For Jesus who came to teach us;
    And for holy people who have helped us.
    Like signposts they have pointed the way
    And we say thank you. *Amen*

12. Today, O God, we think of all the things to
    which we belong:
    There are our homes and our families;
    There is this school and our own special class;
    There are organizations, where we enjoy being with others;
    There are Sunday Schools and churches or other
    places of worship;
    There is the country in which we live.
    Make us *good* members of them all. *Amen*

HYMNS SUGGESTED

Daisies are our silver
Give to us eyes
God, whose name is love
Hands to work and feet to run
Look for signs that summer's done
Lord, I love to stamp and shout

INTEREST WORK AND ACTIVITIES

*Books*

It may be possible to include a few books in the classroom that deal with particular aspects of signs and symbols.

> SYMBOLS AND SIGNS/MAPS AND SYMBOLS/TRACK-
> ING ANIMALS *(Blackwell's Learning Library)*, Blackwell.
> FLAGS/HERALDRY/SAFETY/SIGNALS/SIGNS  *(First look)*, Watts
> ROAD SENSE, Ladybird
> CHILDREN AND TRAFFIC, Books 1 and 2, Macmillan.

*Danger and warning signs*

Make a list and draw pictures of warning signs. Note any that are in the school environment.

Look for any that are of particular relevance to the children, e.g. 'Children crossing', 'Bus stop'. Put up copies in school so that children, including non-readers, can familiarize themselves with these signs.

*Road signs*

A project on road signs would not be amiss, with special emphasis on road safety. Make copies of the most important signs and such things as traffic lights. Have a model road in the playground or school grounds and use it for play so that children become accustomed to the signs.

*School badge*

If there is a school badge, explain to the children what is the meaning of any symbolism or heraldry thereon. If there is none, maybe they could try to design one.

Extend this to a consideration of town, county or national badges or emblems.

---

*Uniformed organizations*

If any children are members they could talk about the badges of their organizations. Members could wear uniforms to school to display their badges. Distinguish between badges of membership and badges that are earned.

*I-Spy*

Encourage children to look for badges and make notes about any they may spy. Some, such as the AA and RAC will be familiar.

It may be possible to have a collection of badges for display but especial care will need to be taken of any that are to be returned afterwards.

# 13    People who help

*Those people, who are a part of our everyday life, depended upon to help us when they are needed—Policemen, Firemen, Dustmen, Shopkeepers—are accepted by the children as part of the society in which they live.*

*We take a look at the work of these people in this section, giving some details of their work and service. In bringing these to the attention of the children it is hoped that they may appreciate more the part such people play in their lives and realize how different life would be if these services were not available.*

1  OUR FRIEND, THE POLICEMAN

Police Constable Burrows was a welcome visitor to the school. The children knew him and liked to talk to him. He frequently called in to see them, to meet any new children and ensure all was well.

It was because the children had so many questions to ask P.C. Burrows that he was invited to the school specially to tell the children about his work as a policeman and about the police force. This was a city school and P.C. Burrows explained to the children that the work of a policeman varied in lots of ways according to where he worked or lived, but everywhere there was some central place where police could be contacted. In towns and cities there were police stations, whilst in a country area the policeman's house also served as the police station.

He told the children about the beginning of the police force. Before then there were watchmen who kept a watch for people doing wrong, but this did not work very well. Then, in London, Sir Robert Peel started a police force. The policemen were then called 'Bobbies' or 'Peelers'. 'I wonder if you can think why?' asked P.C. Burrows.

Today there are policemen in every city, town, and country area. They have to be prepared to work at all times of the day and night. Very early in the morning, very late at night and all through the night, policemen are on duty, protecting, watching and helping. There are many different kinds of duties performed by the police. They try to catch people who break the law—thieves and all sorts of people who hurt others or cause damage.

When crowds of people get together, perhaps to watch a football match or to march in the streets about something, police have to be on hand, ready to make sure that the crowd is kept in order and people are not hurt. A policeman has to be strong; he must be patient; and he has to obey any orders given by his officers.

When a policeman reports for duty at a police station, he is inspected by an Inspector, and has to have all his equipment with him and in good order. A note book, a whistle and a truncheon are important when he is on duty. The policeman is told his duties but he has to be ready to do all sorts of things. He has to direct traffic when traffic lights break down or if traffic is heavy. He has to see people safely across the road, or deal with an accident on the road, or check on a break-in at a shop or house. He has to keep his eyes and ears open for any sign of trouble or anything that is unusual.

He is able to keep in touch with other police at the station and in cars by means of a radio which he carries with him. This 'walkie-talkie', as it is called, can be switched so that he can talk to other police and also receive messages from them. So, very quickly, he can be called to help another policeman, or he can himself call for help if he needs it.

There are so many different kinds of duties a policeman can do, that P.C. Burrows thought it would not be possible to tell the children in one visit. So he arranged to come another day and tell them more.

Meanwhile he wanted the children to remember, always, that the policeman is a friend—someone who is at hand to help in time of trouble. 'If ever you need us, if you are lost, or in trouble of any kind, please find a policeman or a policewoman and say that you need help,' he said.

The children felt they really had some good friends in the police force—men and women who were kind and helpful.


2  POLICEMEN AND POLICEWOMEN

On his next visit P.C. Burrows told the children more about the police. He introduced P.C.W. Green, who was a policewoman, and he explained that there were some kinds of work that police-women did, especially with children and ladies. The policewoman is always at hand with policemen and faces the same dangers every day.

He went on to tell of many different kinds of police work. Lost children are often cared for by policewomen, or even by the wife of the policeman until they can be taken home by their parents.

There are lots of special kinds of work that are done by policemen. Some policemen work with horses and dogs. Some patrol in cars, on motor cycles or on rivers in powerful boats.

The police dogs are usually Alsatians, which are specially trained to help catch robbers or other law-breakers. They each have one policeman who looks after just that one dog. He is called a dog-handler and the dog is always with him, usually living at his home.

The Mounted Police are very splendid. Their horses are well groomed and cared for and they are especially trained for the work they do. They help to keep back crowds on special occasions and at times of disturbance. They lead parades and look very proud animals. The horses have to be trained so that they are not frightened by loud noises or by things being waved in their faces. The policemen or policewomen who ride them are specially trained in their work, too.

In country areas the policeman has other duties to do. He has to see the farmers and make sure, when there is infection or disease among animals, that the animals are treated and 'dipped', and supervised by a vet. He may not be involved in large gatherings of people or big football matches but he has many special jobs to do. He has to know a lot about the area and about all the rules and laws which affect the lives of people living there.

There are police motor launches which patrol large rivers. On the Thames there is a 'floating' Police Station near the heart of the city and from this station the river police are controlled, keeping a watch on shipping on the river.

Some policemen do not wear a uniform but work in ordinary clothes. They may be detectives. They have to know how to look for clues, perhaps fingerprints, or footmarks, even bits of thread or . . . 'What else, do you think?' asked P.C. Burrows. All kinds of things which may seem unimportant, help a detective to find criminals.

Today police have to find people who do many kinds of wrong and some are specially trained for this kind of work. There is a special drug squad, for example, and a 'flying squad' which gets to the scene of a crime in double quick time.

All day and all night, while we go about our ordinary life, waking or sleeping, our police are there on duty. We owe a great deal to them for the ways in which they help us.

And always remember—they are our friends.

### 3  LOLLIPOP PEOPLE

Lollipops! What do you think of when you hear this word? A sweet lollipop on a stick? A boiled sweet? Or perhaps cool ice lollies, so refreshing on a hot day?

Just now we are thinking of a different kind of lollipop. It is the big 'lollipop' carried by the lady or gentleman who helps us to cross the road safely. Their proper title is 'School Crossing Patrol', but, because the sign they carry is shaped like a huge lollipop, they have come to be called 'Lollipop man' or 'Lollipop lady'. Their 'lollipop' sign has the words 'Children Crossing', which means that cars and other vehicles have to take notice of them. When the sign is shown to them, they must stop their vehicles to allow the children to cross the road safely.

These people are employed by the police to help them in their duties. This means that a policeman is able to be busy with other duties while 'Lollipop' people see that children cross the road. Some of them are older folk who have retired from their daily work and want to work for a short time during the day doing a job that is helpful. Some are mothers who feel this is a job they would like to do.

They have to be there in their place whatever the weather. Be it cold, snowing, foggy or wet, they still have to go out, collect their 'lollipop' and take it to the place where they control the crossing. They have to understand a little about the traffic and know when is the best time to stop it to take the children across. If they stopped the cars and lorries every minute or so, there would be a long line of traffic waiting, so they have to judge when is the right time and sometimes wait until there are several children waiting to cross.

Children get to know them and become good friends with the 'Lollipop' people. The 'Lollipop' people also get to know the children. They hear all about the school and special things that are being planned. They know if children are unhappy or anxious and often have a cheering word for them. Parents are pleased to know, when their children go to school that there is someone who will escort them safely across a busy road.

This is a very important work these people are doing in looking after children. Don't forget to say thank you to your 'Lollipop lady or gentleman'. Say how thankful you are for being looked after so well.

### 4  THE FIREMAN

When we hear a loud siren wailing above all other sounds, we all look to see what may be making the noise. It could be a police car, an ambulance, or a fire engine. When the siren raises its voice, cars, cycles, lorries and buses, all make an effort to pull over to the side of the road to leave a space so that the emergency vehicle may get quickly through the traffic and to the place where it is needed. It is so important that it gets there as quickly as possible.

With its siren sounding and its shiny red paint showing up on even the dullest day, the fire engine goes racing along the road to where it is needed. Paul's father is a fireman and, after P.C. Burrows had told the children so much about the work of the police, he was invited to tell them about the work of a fireman. He was glad to come along to the school and talk to the children. He told them that the fireman has to be ready to go to a fire at any time of the day or night when he is on duty.

A telephone call to the fire station, usually through the emergency service, when we dial 999 or call the telephone operator, tells the officer on duty where the fire is and the alarm is sounded. Immediately the firemen jump into action. Each man knows exactly what to do and which position is his on the fire engine. If they are in a fire station which has part of its building upstairs, the firemen may slide down a pole to get down really quickly to where the fire engine is kept. This is much quicker than running downstairs. Sometimes Paul's father may be the driver. At other times he will have a different place on the fire engine.

At the sound of the alarm, some firemen run to open the doors of the fire station, others to their places on the engine. They have to wear special clothing, helmets to protect their heads, waterproof clothing to keep them dry and big boots, like your 'wellies' but much bigger and stronger. When they get back from a fire, they have to prepare their clothing ready for the next time. The boots and trousers are put in the right position so that the firemen can step into them quickly without wasting a moment of time.

In between fires, the firemen have to work on their engine, keep it in good running condition, clean their equipment, and do all kinds of things to make sure everything works well. It is important that they keep very fit, too. They need to be strong and brave to face fire dangers. How glad we are that people like Paul's father want to be firemen and work in this way to help us.

### 5   MORE ABOUT THE FIREMAN

On his next visit to school, Paul's father told the children about the special equipment a fireman has to use. He carries a small axe in a kind of holster on his belt. This may be needed if he has to break down doors or windows.

We have all seen the long hoses which the fire engine carries. The hose is wound in a special way so that it is easily unwound at the scene of the fire. The water is turned on and the hose is pointed towards the place where it can best be used. We call this 'training' the hose. It is quite difficult to 'train' a hose as it is heavy and needs more than one fireman to hold it when the strong jet of water is coming through it. The fireman has to know just where the water should go. He learns all about fires and decides which is the best spot to aim for.

The water may be directed from the ground or it may be directed by a fireman who has climbed up a big ladder on a fire engine to get nearer the fire. This ladder can be moved around on a turn-table so that the fireman is in the best position to use the hose. This ladder is also used to rescue people who are trapped in a burning building. Firemen have to learn how to help people trapped in this way. Sometimes they carry the person they are rescuing down the ladder to safety and there is a special way of carrying such people. Sometimes they lower the people to safety instead.

Firemen are called out to help on other occasions than fires. They are sometimes asked to help rescue people who are trapped somewhere out of reach, perhaps on a tall building or on a ledge on the outside of a building. They have been known to rescue cats which are trapped in the boughs of tall trees or to help people, children and grown-ups, who have managed to get themselves trapped in some way, such as putting their heads through railings and not being able to get them back again. This is not very sensible and it gives the firemen work to do which could prevent them from being able to fight a fire somewhere else.

The children at the school were very fortunate. Paul's father was allowed to bring his fire engine to the school for the children to see. They sat in the driver's seat, sounded the siren, helped use the hose and tried on some of the helmets. It was a very interesting and enjoyable visit and the children did like talking to the firemen and asking questions.

All the children were glad that we have people like these brave firemen to look after us. And some of the boys were quite sure they knew what they would like to do when they grew up—to be firemen!

Our firemen are brave and we are greateful to them for all they do for us.

## 6  THE AMBULANCEMAN

Like the fireman and policeman, the ambulance man must be ready to go wherever he is needed at any time of night or day while he is on duty. As the siren wails its warning, traffic on the road makes way for the ambulance to go through. The ambulance men are racing to an emergency, which may mean saving the life of someone.

They may be going to a road accident or to a house where someone is very ill and has to be taken to hospital quickly. There are usually two people with each ambulance. One is a driver and the other looks after the person who is sick. They work together to take good care of the patient. After an accident they have to decide how the person is injured so that they do not move him in the wrong way. They may have to give first aid treatment to make the patient comfortable until reaching hospital. They take the sick or injured person on a stretcher and carefully place the stretcher inside the ambulance before hurrying as fast as possible to hospital.

While the driver is intent on the road and driving quickly yet carefully, his partner is taking care of the patient, talking to him, comforting him and looking after him if he is in pain.

Ambulance men, too, have lots of different kinds of work. Apart from emergencies, they may have to meet trains, or ships or 'planes at airports, to take people to hospital. They may sometimes drive the kind of ambulance that is like a minibus, collecting people from their homes to take them to hospital for treatment. Usually these are old people who cannot easily get to hospital by themselves. When they have all seen the doctor or had their treatment, the people are helped into the ambulance again to be taken back home. This is a great help to them. Some people who are handicapped and unable to move about by themselves are taken by the ambulance to centres where they can be with other people for a time to talk with them or make things and enjoy each other's company.

Ambulance men are usually very cheerful, kindly and caring people. They make jokes to cheer people up. They see so many people who are sick or hurt and it must sometimes be hard for them to be so cheerful and comforting to people. Yet they are and we should be glad there are people like this who work for us all.


## 7   DUSTMEN AND ROADSWEEPERS

Of all the people who come to our homes and give us service perhaps the dustman is the one who has the least pleasant job to do. We often hear people grumbling when the dustman is not very careful and spills rubbish on the path or on the pavement, but when we think about the amount of rubbish the dustman has to move every week, we know that there is not much he leaves behind.

Usually a dustman is part of a gang. Three, four or even more men work with the dust-cart and they have several ways in which they organize their work, carrying the bins out to the dustcart, emptying the bins and taking back the empty bins to the house. Sometimes the rubbish is in plastic sacks. In schools and some other places the rubbish may be put into a large bin on wheels, which is wheeled out, fastened to a 'lift' and tipped into the lorry.

Whichever way the bins are emptied, there must be times when the rubbish spills out on to the dustman and he gets very dirty whilst tipping other people's rubbish to empty their bins. It is not the kind of work everyone would like to do.

The name of 'dustman' came from the sweepings on the floor and coal dust, and we still call the men dustmen, but their proper title and one which sounds nicer is 'refuse collector'. That after all is just what they do—collect the refuse, or rubbish, for us. It is taken to a tip, or some other place, where it is disposed of by being burned or buried.

Another person who does similar work to the dustmen is the 'Road Orderly', or roadsweeper as we know him. His job is to sweep the gutters and the pavements of the streets. This is sometimes difficult to do, as there are vehicles parked along the road, but when the gutter is clear the sweeper can take his big strong broom and sweep up the rubbish. He will sweep until he has a pile of rubbish and then, if he has a little hand-cart with him and is working alone, he will pick up the pile of dust and dirt with the shovel and put it into his cart. If he is working with a gang he will be part of a team which sweeps and leaves the piles for another member of the gang to pick up and put into a lorry.

Both the dustman and the roadsweeper have dirty and unpleasant work to do. They need to change their clothes and wash as soon as possible after finishing their work. Sometimes, especially in winter when the mornings and evenings are dark, they need to wear special bands on their jackets so that they can be seen in the dark. These are bands of the kind some children wear for safety, that reflect in the light and show motorists they are there. Traffic is just one of the dangers for such workers; they may be worried by dogs or slip on wet roads.

Without people like these we would soon have our rubbish piling up, causing disease and infection. Where rubbish is not cleared, it rots and attracts rats or other kinds of unpleasant visitor. So we are glad that there are people who are prepared to do this work so that we may live more comfortably. It would be nice for us to say thank you to our dustmen and road sweepers next time we see them.


8  SHOPKEEPERS

Nowadays much of our shopping is done in supermarkets, or perhaps hypermarkets—enormous places where it is possible to buy just about everything we need. There are, however, many people who still like to use the small shops which we see along our High Street, or in the centre of the village, or in some street near to where we live. Sometimes these shops are called 'corner shops' and they are very useful to people living away from the shopping centre or perhaps not very close to bus stops so that they would find it difficult to travel into town.

Some of these small shops stock almost anything that may be needed. Others sell one kind of thing. The shopkeeper may be a grocer, greengrocer, chemist, butcher, baker or newsagent. It may be a shop selling knitting wool and needlework goods, toys, tools or electrical goods. There seems to be a shop for almost everything we need. When we look up at the shopfront, over the window, we can usually see the name of the shopkeeper. 'A. Brown and Son, Butcher', 'D. Enever, Baker', 'R. Patel, Newsagent, Tobacconist'. These really mean something to us, as they are the names of the actual people who may be found serving in the shop.

Shopkeepers who have these kind of shops learn to know which goods are most likely to sell in that area—the kinds of thing the people like best. They also get to know families, so that if you are shopping for Mum and are not quite sure of the kind or brand of goods she would like, the shopkeeper is quite likely to know just what she usually gets from him. There is a homely, cosy family feeling about these shops which we find very helpful if we are not quite sure about things.

Some of the small shops help in another way. They have, at one end of the shop, a 'sub-Post Office', which means that they can sell stamps, postal orders, and many of the things we find in the big post offices. They are particlarly helpful to elderly people who are able to go there to get their pensions. The shopkeeper gets to know them and can be very helpful in so many ways, such as telling people how to fill in forms or write addresses. These shopkeepers have to learn about Post Office regulations beside being knowledgeable about the other goods they sell.

Being a shopkeeper is a busy life and sometimes a little worrying, but shopkeepers are often people who help us in all sorts of ways while doing their daily work. Perhaps you can think of some who have been especially helpful to you.

RELATED THEMES

---

PRAYERS

1. Dear Father God, some people are very untidy and leave a lot of rubbish lying around. Thank you for all those people who help to keep the streets and the countryside clean and tidy. *Amen*

2. Dear Father God,
   We like to go shopping to buy all sorts of things.
   Thank you for all the shops
   And for the shopkeepers who are so helpful. *Amen*

3. Dear God, it is so nice to have so many people who help us. Thank you for them all. *Amen*

4. For all those people who help me day by day, help me to be thankful, dear God. *Amen*

5. O God, bless all the brave firemen who risk their lives when there is a fire. Keep them safe from harm and danger. *Amen*

6. O God, our Father, it is not very nice to have to empty dirty, smelly dustbins but somebody has to do it and so we say thank you for all who help get rid of our rubbish. *Amen*

7. Thank you, dear God, for the lollipop man/lady who sees us safely across the road when we come to school, whatever the weather may be like. Thank you for people like him/her who like to help children like us. *Amen*

8. Thank you, Father God:
   For all those people who help us day by day,
   > *Thank you, Father God;*
   For people who keep us from harm and danger,
   > *Thank you, Father God;*
   For people who help us to have the things we need,
   > *Thank you, Father God;*
   For those who teach us how to do things,
   > *Thank you, Father God;*
   And for all who love and care for us,
   > *Thank you, Father God. Amen.*

9. Thank you, O God, for our village [*local*] policeman, who is always there to look after us and help us, and for all policemen and policewomen. *Amen*

10. Thank you, O Lord, for firemen and fire
    brigades:
    For bright red fire engines, always ready for use;
    For all the gear used for putting out fires;
    .For ways of saving people trapped by fire;
    And for all the brave firemen who use these things;
        Thank you, dear God. *Amen*

11. Today, O God, we think of lots of policemen:
    The men and women who walk the streets on their beat;
    Those who patrol in cars or on motor cycles;
    Mounted policemen on their fine horses;
    Policemen in motor boats on the rivers;
    Plain-clothes policemen and those with police dogs;
    And lots of others. Thank you for them all. *Amen*

12. We think of lots of people, O God, who help us in so many ways. Help us to help them by not doing anything that would give them extra work or cause them trouble. *Amen*

HYMNS SUGGESTED

Click goes the switch
For all the things which we enjoy
Here we stand on the pavement
I'd like to be a milkman
Somebody's coming down our street
What do we see when we go to the town.

INTEREST WORK AND ACTIVITIES

*Books*

A selection of books available for the children to look at and read could include some of the following:

POLICEMEN AND THE POLICE FORCE/FIRES AND FIREMEN *(Blackwell's Learning Library)*, Blackwell
THE POLICEMAN/THE FIREMAN *(Easy Reading)*, Ladybird
THE SHOPKEEPER/THE FIREMAN/THE DUSTMAN/THE POLICEMAN/THE AMBULANCE MAN *(What do they do?)*, Macmillan
FIGHTING FIRES, Dinosaur
SHOPS *(Starters)*, Macdonald
LET'S GO TO THE SHOPS *(Let's go)*, Watts
AT THE SHOPS *(Head-start)*, Burke

*Picture and news books*

Books could be made in respect of each of the services referred to in this section, e.g. collect pictures of policemen in any of the branches of the force. Find newspaper cuttings and news items. Make into a book or wall frieze. Similar for the others.

*Art and craft*

Paint pictures of policemen/firemen in action. Make junk models of fire engine, police car, ambulance, dust cart.

*Visits and visitors*

Visits to fire station, police station, ambulance station, including any part of special interest, e.g. police stables.
 It is usually not difficult to have a policeman, fireman or ambulance man to come to school to talk about his work. It is sometimes

possible to arrange a special interest visit, e.g. a fire engine or a mounted policeman with his horse.

The local newsagent or other shopkeeper might also be pleased to come in to talk to the children about his work, involving a lot more than merely standing behind the counter.

### Shopping

The classroom shop will be a useful interest in connection with this theme. Remind the 'shopkeeper' to be courteous and helpful. This might follow usefully a shopkeeper's visit as referred to above.

### Safety

An ideal opportunity to introduce safety training—road crossing and safety drill, fire drill.

Learn how to raise alarm for fires by telephone or other means. Point out dangers of giving false alarms.

# 14  People who care

*The people we think about in this section are some of those whose work involves service to others in a special way. The work of doctors, nurses and priests frequently extends well beyond the bounds of duty. Society accepts that such people will always be there, and we can go to them for help and relief.*

*Also included are those who care for the old and the young.*

*It is as well for the children to know that such caring has often come through insight, knowledge and a basic caring for people. They need to understand, too, that knowledge has to be sought and acquired, and that effort has to be made to reach a standard necessary to be of real service to others.*


1  DOCTOR

Stephen felt very funny. His head hurt; his throat hurt; and when he coughed, as he was doing quite a lot, it all hurt even more. He was glad Mum said he must stay at home: he really felt he did not want to be in school with his friends.

Next day he was still not very well and Mum said he must see the doctor. 'Open your mouth—wide,' said Dr. Lawson. 'Say Aah . . .' 'Hmm!' said the doctor. Then he picked up his stethoscope, put the two ear pieces into his ears and carefully placed the other end firstly on Stephen's chest and then on his back. 'Deep breath . . . and again,' said the doctor as he moved the stethoscope from place to place.

When the doctor had finished, Stephen had a question to ask. 'What does that do?' he asked—meaning the stethoscope. 'Why do you put it in your ears?'

'It's something like a telephone,' said the doctor. 'Through it I can hear all kinds of sounds which help me to decide what is making you feel unwell.'

Then Stephen couldn't ask any more questions for a while as the doctor had taken out a thermometer, shaken it and put it into Stephen's mouth. After the doctor had gone Stephen had more questions to ask his mother. 'Does the doctor do that to everyone he sees?' he asked.

Mum told him a little about the doctor's work, how he tries to find out what makes people sick and then decide how he would make them well again. 'Doctors have to work hard and learn such a lot before they can be doctors and help people,' she said. 'Some of them call at people's houses and see people in their surgeries but there are also doctors in hospitals and clinics, on ships and at airports. Some doctors learn more and more about special things and are called "specialists". The special doctor for children is called a Paediatrician.'

'That's a long word,' said Stephen.

He stayed in bed for a day or two. With the care of his mother, and the medicine prescribed by the doctor, he was soon well and looking forward to seeing his friends again.

'I'm glad we have doctors to make us well when we are ill,' said Stephen. His mother agreed. She was glad, too, that he was once again his noisy, busy self.


## 2 NURSE

Sandra went to hospital and had to stay there for a few days. She hated it when her mother went home and left her there, but Mum promised she would be back again to see her once she had seen that Dad and the others were all right.

It all seemed very strange to Sandra. There were lots of other children, some of them in bed and others out of bed, looking at television, reading or playing with toys. The nurses were very kind and made up a little for Mum not being there. Sandra especially liked one they called Nurse Jones. She was the one with laughing, twinkling eyes looking at you out of a smiling face. She was a great favourite with the children. Everything she did was kind and gentle yet firm, which made them feel safe.

After a day or two, Sandra felt quite settled and had made new friends. She felt she had a special friend in Nurse Jones. In fact she thought she might be sorry to say good-bye to them all when she went home at the weekend.

Nurse Jones was leaving the ward then, and going to look after grown-ups in another part of the hospital. The children learned from her and the other nurses of the work they did—making people comfortable, washing them, treating sore wounds and bandaging, taking temperatures, feeling a pulse, giving people their pills and medicines, giving injections and encouraging people to eat or drink. All day they were very busy, some of them nursing children, some nursing grown-ups, very old or very sick people. Sandra thought the nurses looked very smart in their uniforms.

'I'm going to be a nurse when I'm grown up,' she told her mother on the way home from hospital.

'That would be fine,' said her mother, 'but you will have to learn a lot, and study and work very hard.'

Sandra said a special 'Thank you' prayer that night in her own bed at home. 'Thank you, God, for nurses.'

## 3   HEALTH VISITOR AND DISTRICT NURSE

Shirin went with her mother to take her baby brother Jamal to the baby clinic. Shirin's mother did not know very much of the English language. She had lived in Bangladesh and so spoke her own language, but Shirin had been in school in England for a time and was now speaking and understanding some of the language. So Shirin went with her mother to help her understand.

At the clinic there were other mothers with their babies. Among them she saw a face she knew—it was Donna's mother. Shirin and Donna were friends. They each had a baby brother and talked together a lot about them.

Donna's mother smiled and said, 'Hello.' Then she helped Shirin and her mother to understand what they had to do.

A nurse came along and spoke to the mothers about the care of their babies and answered their questions. The babies were weighed, played with and examined by the nurses, who seemed to know such a lot about babies and children. Shirin recognized the nurse who spoke to them. It was the same lady who visited them at home and talked to her mother about the baby and her other little brother who was almost old enough to start school. She was really just like a friend and they were all getting to know her quite well.

One day in school, Donna and Shirin saw their nurse from the clinic. Their teacher said she was a Health Visitor. At first their nurse had looked after people in hospital and now she had special work to do with mothers and babies at home and at the clinic, in schools and in the area where they lived. Shirin and Donna were glad they knew their special 'Health Visitor'.

\* \* \*

Another kind of visitor came to a neighbour's house. Andrew and Jane were busy with their garden patch in the front garden when they saw her arrive in her little car. Old Mrs. Green lived next door. She was not able to go out, and could move around very little. Their mother did Mrs. Green's shopping and went in to see her quite often. Andrew and Jane sometimes said 'Hello' to Mrs. Green and waved to her, but didn't stay in the house for long as they felt they had to be very still and very quiet. But they knew Mrs. Green liked to see them and talk to them sometimes.

Mother saw the visitor arrive. 'Good morning, Nurse,' she called.

'Why is a nurse coming to Mrs Green's house?' the children wanted to know. Mother told them all about the visitor, who was a District Nurse. These are nurses, Mother told them, who care for people in their own homes. Elderly people who are sick or unable to walk or move very much, mothers with young babies, anyone of any age, who needs nursing or being cared for without being in hospital, can all be helped by the District Nurse.

Doctors call to see the people sometimes, but the nurse goes regularly to take care of them, to change dressings and bandage sore places, to wash people, give injections or medicines and make them nice and comfy.

The District Nurse may have a car or may go on her bicycle to help people. She may look after people in country places, in cottages or in a town or city. The District Nurse takes her bag and tends the people. Usually working alone, she does a special kind of work which is so important to the people she cares for.

## 4 DENTIST

Jamie and Susan went to see the dentist. They waited in a room, where there were books and comics for them to read. Then the nurse came to take them to the dental surgery. They went together, with Mother.

The first thing they noticed was the big, big chair. 'Now!' said the dentist, 'Who is going to have the first ride?' The children both went forward but Jamie managed to climb into the chair first. The children always had this competition when they visited the dentist.

Jamie sat in the chair and he looked quite small in such a big one. The dentist operated the chair so that it went up and down, up and down. He tipped the chair back so that Jamie leaned back, and then sat him upright again.

The dentist put a kind of bib round Jamie's neck, let back the chair so that he could see into Jamie's mouth and began his examination. Susan watched until it was her turn, and then it was Jamie's turn to watch while the dentist examined Susan's teeth.

When they first went to see him the dentist had let them look at his instruments, carefully arranged for him to use. Among them were tiny probes, some rather sharp, and a little mirror which helped him look at the back of their teeth.

Jamie needed a little treatment. Susan didn't need anything done this time. The dentist talked to them about caring for their teeth, remembering to clean them regularly and properly so as to reach into all the corners, to brush them up and down as well as from side to side.

As they cleaned their teeth before going to bed that night, Jamie had some questions to ask. 'How does a dentist know about teeth? How does he know what to look for and how to fill and scale them? How did he know how to make the chair go up and down?'

Father explained that the dentist learns all these and lots of other things about people's teeth by studying very hard and learning in hospital. Like a doctor and a nurse he has to study to learn all about his work as a dentist.

## 5   RELIGIOUS LEADERS

Teresa came into school one day with some great news. She had made her first Communion at Church on Sunday, and this was a very special day for her. 'What does she mean?' one of the children asked their teacher. They sat down with their teacher who talked about these special days. Teresa had been to a Christian church. The man who had given the Communion and was the leader of that church was a priest.

The children talked about the places they went to and how they worshipped God. Some of the children attended a church where their leader was called a Rector, or Vicar or Minister. Some of them went to a Mosque where an Imam led the worship: they were Muslims. Some, who belonged to Jewish families, went to the synagogue, where they had a Rabbi or Minister.

Their teacher explained that in all places of worship there was someone who led them. More than that, the Priest, or Rabbi, or Minister, or Imam was important to the family in many ways. When babies were christened or taken for a blessing to the place of worship, when people were married, when people in a family were unhappy because someone had died, or when they were in some trouble, this special friend was there to help. He also teaches people to understand the Holy books.

The Vicar, or Priest, the Minister, Rabbi or Imam, would know the family and try always to be at hand to help them learn more of their faith. He would also help them through the happy, gay or sad times in life.

### 6   CARE FOR THE OLD

On the way home from school the children watched as a minibus drew up and stopped outside a house. An elderly lady was helped down from the bus and up to her front door. The lady knew some of the children and smiled at them after waving to her companions still in the bus. She had been to her club, where she went on some afternoons to meet other people, to make things, chat and drink tea.

Mary and Peter knew a little about the club because their mother helped elderly people. She drove a van, which took dinners to old people living alone, who were no longer able to shop and cook meals for themselves. Mum had told the children, how, while they were having their lunch in school, the 'Meals on Wheels' helpers took the lunches round as quickly as possible so that older people could have their meals at the right time. They would take the dishes to the houses and, if the old people could not come to the door, the helpers would go in and see that they were given the food. Then they collected the dishes from the dinner of the day before.

One day, Peter and Mary knew that their mother had gone along to help an old gentleman who had been alone for a long time and now found it difficult to cope with being in his house alone. He needed help each day and so a place had been found for him in a special house where he would be able to live with someone to look after him. Mum had gone with him after helping him decide what he would like to take with him from his own home. She had helped him to settle in.

'I'm sure he will be happy there,' said Mum. 'He will have other ladies and gentlemen to talk to or to play cards and dominoes with. He will be able to sit in the garden and perhaps help a little, with the gardening.'

Mum sometimes went along to see how he was settling down in his new home and she took the children to see him and the other people living there. They enjoyed these visits and the older people enjoyed seeing children, talking to them and hearing their news.

'It's just like having lots and lots of Grans and Grandads,' said Peter and Mary.

7   CARE FOR CHILDREN

Many years ago some people thought a lot about children who had no homes, whom nobody wanted or cared for. One gentleman was Dr. Barnardo. A friend took him to the places where he knew these children slept at night. The children they found were huddled in corners, in dustbins, on roofs or hidden away with no covering and no food. They could only eat food they could find or steal. They had no homes or families who cared.

Dr. Barnardo decided he must do something to help and so he made a home for a few boys at first. Then, in the years that followed, he worked to provide homes for thousands of children. Another gentleman who cared was Lord Shaftesbury. He also made homes for children to live in. Today there are places provided so that no child need be left homeless. There are people who care.

Some other children have to go away from home for a while if there is no one to look after them at home. They are cared for until they are able to return home to their families. Other people make sure that children are not ill treated. Yet others help parents who are in need of help so that their children do not suffer. There are all kinds of organizations who will help a child in need.

Well-known children's homes, such as Dr. Barnardo's and the National Children's Home, which was started by Dr. Stephenson, have existed for many years and have cared for many children. Apart from these large homes there are many smaller houses, caring for a few children who need that help. There are also foster parents who look after children, perhaps with their own families, so that children in need of care are made to feel safe, happy and cared for.

What a wonderful work people like these have been doing. The kind doctors and Lord Shaftesbury long ago, and the people who look after children today have all had the same kind thought—to care for children.

## 8 FATHER BORELLI

One day in 1950, a Roman Catholic priest named Father Borelli went to see his Archbishop to ask if he could do something that many people would think strange. In the city of Naples, in Italy, where he lived, there were lots of children who roamed the streets because they had no home. Father Borelli wanted to go to live among them so that he could help them.

The Archbishop was not sure that this was a very good idea. There were lots of things Father Borelli could do as a priest—looking after a church or a school or perhaps doing some other work. Father Borelli was troubled. He had set his heart on helping these children. He was sure it was what God wanted him to do. But there was still hope. The Archbishop had not said 'No'. He would think it over and give Father Borelli his answer ten days later.

Father Borelli went away and prayed to God to show him what he should do. Suddenly an idea came into his mind. He telephoned a friend, who was a photographer, and together they went out into the city to take photographs of children begging, cooking and sleeping in the streets.

When next he went to see the Archbishop, Father Borelli had with him a collection of these photographs. But it was not really necessary. God had given wisdom to the Archbishop to see that he should allow Father Borelli to go ahead with this work.

So he went into the streets and made friends with the homeless children. There was a lot of hard work to be done but before long he had a home in which some of them could live. A few of the unwanted children had found that they *were* wanted because God had shown one of his people that this was what he should do.

RELATED THEMES

CARING AGENCIES

This theme can be developed further by reference to the various organizations which care for their fellows in various ways. Many of these have information which they will readily supply on request. These are but a few, their activities not necessarily limited to the headings under which they are listed.

CHILDREN: Dr. Barnardo's; National Children's Home; Shaftesbury Society; N.S.P.C.C., Save the Children Fund; Spastics Society; Bible Lands Society.

OLD AND NEEDY: British Red Cross; Cheshire Homes; Church Army; Help the Aged; Royal British Legion; St. Dunstan's; Salvation Army; Samaritans; Women's Royal Voluntary Service.

SEAMEN: British Sailors' Society; Missions to Seamen; Mission to Deep Sea Fishermen; Royal National Lifeboat Institution.

OVERSEAS AID: Christian Aid; Oxfam; The overseas (missionary) departments of Christian churches.

ANIMAL WELFARE: People's Dispensary for Sick Animals; Royal Society for the Prevention of Cruelty to Animals.

---

1. Dear Father God, be with all who are ill or lonely or sad; and help them to feel that you are close by to help them. *Amen*

2. Dear Father God, give us happy faces and loving hearts. When we look around us we see so many people who are sad, lonely or in need of help. Show us how we can be cheerful and kind, being good friends to all we meet today, and bringing a little brightness into our world. *Amen*

3. Dear Father God, teach me how to look after myself so that I keep fit and well; and make me thankful for so many people who care for me and help me keep well. *Amen*

4. Help us, dear God, to look after our teeth so that they do not go bad or ache; but if they do, make us thankful for dentists who can do something to help us. *Amen*

5. O God, many of the things which we enjoy we have because of great men and women of the past who cared. Thank you for these people and for all the people today who care for others. *Amen*

6. O God our Father, you have loved us and we want to love you. Help us to show our love by being helpful and kind to others. *Amen*

7. Thank you, dear Father, for our homes and families. Today we think of children with no families or homes like ours. We ask that you will bless them and those who care for them. *Amen*

8. Thank you, dear God, for all the people who help us when we are not well; for all doctors, nurses and people who work in clinics or hospitals. We are thankful that there are so many who care. *Amen*

9. Today, O Lord, we are thinking about nurses.
Lots of them work in hospitals
Caring for people who are ill or hurt:
Others work for doctors or dentists
In surgeries or clinics:
Some visit our homes or our schools
To help us keep healthy:
Thank you for them all. *Amen*

10. We know lots of old people, O God
Some of them need a lot of help
Because they cannot do things for themselves;
Some of them are weak or ill
And have to stay in bed or in a chair;
Some live on their own
And they often feel very lonely.
Show us how we can help them. *Amen*

11. We praise and thank you, O God, for all those people who help
us to learn of you and who help us when we are in need. We
remember all priests, ministers, rabbis and others who care for
us in the places where we worship you. Thank you for all the
help they give us. *Amen*

12. We remember those children who have no homes or families
and ask that you will hear our prayers, O God.
For all homeless children, everywhere,
*Hear our prayers, O God;*
For children's homes where they can live,
*Hear our prayers, O God;*
For the men and women who run the homes,
*Hear our prayers, O God;*
For those who care in many lands
*Hear our prayers, O God.*
Help us, O God to look for ways in which we can help those
who are less fortunate than we are. *Amen*

For all the strength we have
God who made the earth
He's got the whole world in his hands
I love God's tiny creatures
Kum-ba-yah
Look out for loneliness
Thank you
When I needed a neighbour

SOME BIBLE STORIES

| | |
|---|---|
| David cares for Mephibosheth | 2 Samuel 9; 1–3, 6–7, 13 |
| Jesus shows compassion | Matthew 9; 27–36 |
| Jesus and the ten lepers | Luke 17; 11–19 |

INTEREST WORK AND ACTIVITIES

*Books*

Have books available including simple ones which introduce those
not-so-pleasant or perhaps feared experiences. A few that would be
useful are:

HOSPITALS *(Blackwell's Learning Library)*, Blackwell
AT A HOSPITAL/AT THE DOCTOR/AT THE DENTIST
   *(First Time Books)*, Macdonald
LET'S TO TO THE HOSPITAL/DOCTOR/DENTIST *(Let's
   go)*, Watts
GOING TO THE DOCTOR/GOING INTO HOSPITAL/
   VISITING THE DENTIST, Dinosaur
GOING TO THE HOSPITAL *(Starter Facts)*, Macdonald
THE NURSE *(Easy Reading)*, Ladybird
THE DISTRICT NURSE/THE VET/THE NUN *(What do they
   do?)*, Macmillan
THE CLINIC *(Terraced House Books)*, Methuen
TOM VISITS THE DENTIST/JOHNNY GETS SOME
   GLASSES/LUCY LOSES HER TONSILS/PETER
   GETS A HEARING AID, Nigel Snell, Hamilton

---

*Play activities*

Have a 'Hospital Corner' for play. Make available nurses' aprons and caps. Doctors' white coats can be made easily from old white shirts.

*Visits to school*

The school doctor, school nurse or health visitor could be invited to the assembly. It could provide an opportunity for the children to say a word of thanks to them.

Invite the local clergy and spiritual leaders of any Christian churches and other faiths in the neighbourhood of the school. Perhaps they could speak to the children particularly on the subject of caring as it pertains to their work.

*Get well*

If any children are ill or in hospital, write notes, draw pictures or make Get Well cards to send to them.

*Caring news*

Collect news items, cuttings and pictures of people who care. These need not be the 'professionals' but stories of ordinary people who have seen a neighbour in need and have cared enough to do something practical about it.

The stories have not included caring for animals but this is an obvious extension of the theme to include veterinary surgeons and animal welfare organizations.

Make the cuttings into a scrap book about 'People Who Care'.

*A 'Helping' project*

Involve children in some kind of project to help people in the vicinity of the school.

Make contact with any nearby homes for elderly people. Groups of children could visit on special occasions, e.g. at Christmas, to sing to them. Produce from the school harvest festival could be taken there. If any have few or no relatives it might be possible to work out an 'Adopt a Gran or Grandad' scheme. Visit regularly; find out birth dates; take small presents and send cards.

Support any efforts that are being made to raise funds for organizations responsible for the care and welfare of young or old.

# 15 Animals

For most children animals hold a fascination, especially those that are furry and cuddly. Most of them have pets of one kind or another in their homes. Many of them are aware of wild animals in the wider world around them and, of course, big wild animals feature largely in their story and picture books.

Here we endeavour to bring home to them the need to care for all animal life and especially any that have been committed to their care, whether at home or in school.

No doubt there will be animals in school: rabbits, guinea pigs, hamsters, gerbils or others will give practical experience in caring. Even fish in the aquarium will give some insight into this.

In the wider sense the children will realize that many animals are more than just wild creatures or pets. Some people are very dependent upon their animals.

Indeed, in this great world of ours the dependence of one part of nature upon the other is one of the wonders of creation.

## 1 PETS AT HOME

There was a knock at the door. Christopher went to answer it. Very soon he was back again looking very excited.

'It's Mr. Robertson from along the road. He said he wondered whether we would like a kitten because he's got two that he doesn't want. It's a little black one and . . . can we have it, Mum?'

Mum looked at Dad and Dad looked at Mum. Then they both looked at Haggis, who was snoozing on the mat. Haggis was a Scottish terrier and he didn't like cats. In fact, if a cat dared to come into their garden he was out there like a flash, barking furiously.

'Haggis would never allow a cat in the house,' Dad said.

'But this isn't a cat,' Christopher replied. 'It's only a kitten. Perhaps it would be all right.'

Christopher's sister Miriam had been listening. 'Can we see what happens?' she asked.

'All right,' Dad answered. 'But we shall have to see that the kitten doesn't get hurt.'

Soon afterwards Miriam came back from Mr. Robertson's house

with a little bundle of black fur in her arms. 'Isn't she lovely,' she said, 'so nice and soft and cuddly.'

Very gently she put the kitten on the carpet. Haggis had already sensed that something was going on. What was this? A kitten? In *his* house? He got to his feet, slowly moved forward and went to sniff at the kitten. He soon had the surprise of his life ... and so did everyone else. The kitten sprang to life, arched her back, gave a loud Pfssst and hit out with her tiny paw. Haggis jumped back, took another look at the kitten and disappeared under the table, where he decided to stay.

'It looks as though she has come to stay,' said Mum. 'We shall have to find a name for her.'

'Blackie' ... 'Kitty' ... 'Cuddles' ... The children had lots of suggestions. Then Miriam said, 'Black cats are said to be lucky. Let's call her "Lucky".' So it was agreed.

'I hope she is lucky,' Dad said. 'She has found a home but I hope she will have been lucky enough to find two children who will look after her properly. If you want a pet you must always care for it. It is not something to make a fuss of now and then get tired of.'

That is something we must always remember if we have pets. They rely upon us for so many things and we must not let them down.


2  MAN'S BEST FRIEND

One day the piano tuner called at the school to make sure that their piano in the hall played all the right notes. When the children went into the hall he was still there. Sitting beside the piano was his dog, waiting patiently until he had finished. Susie was a very special friend and helper to the piano tuner. He was blind and Susie was his Guide Dog.

The children watched as he stood up and took hold of the special harness that Susie wore. Everywhere he went she guided him, making sure that he did not bump into anything that was in his way and, when in the street, stopping at the kerb until it was safe to cross the road.

Their Headmistress explained to the children that it cost a lot of money to train a Guide Dog but, once the dog had been trained, it would be like eyes to the blind man. Lots of blind people have been thankful for their Guide Dogs, who have become real friends to them; and they have also been thankful to the people who have collected the money that is needed to pay for the training of the dog.

How many of you have dogs at home? What kind of dog? Some people like to keep large dogs such as Alsatians or Labradors; others prefer smaller ones such as Terriers, Spaniels or Corgis. Many of them are just kept as pets because people enjoy having them in the house, taking them for walks and caring for them. Lots of people think of a dog as a faithful friend. There is an old saying that 'a man's best friend is his dog'.

But there are lots of dogs too that are not just pets. They work for their owners. The Guide Dogs are like that. How many others do you know? Perhaps you have seen a shepherd at work with his sheepdogs. Each whistle or call is a signal to the dog to move in a certain direction or take some action which will drive the sheep where he wants them to go. A good sheepdog is a very clever animal.

No doubt you can think of other dogs that work, dogs that race, dogs that help policemen and dogs that people keep for all sorts of other reasons.

Sometimes we hear of people who do not look after their dogs properly, but it is good to know that most people who keep dogs enjoy their friendship and try to care for them as well as they can.

3  HORSES AND PONIES

Miriam and Christopher had gone for a walk together along a lane near their home. They often came this way, and for a very special reason. There was a field in which there were several horses and they liked to go to see them.

One was their particular favourite. He was a very friendly animal with a lovely chestnut-coloured coat. Often he was standing by the gate but, if not, he would come ambling over when he saw the children, no doubt hoping that they would have something tasty for him to eat, as they usually did. They loved to stroke his nose as he reached over the gate: it was so soft and he seemed to like them doing it. They didn't know his name but they called him Ernie because Chris had once said that the horse reminded him of one of the boys in his class.

Sometimes the children had watched others riding their own horses and ponies. They always looked very smart in their riding outfits and seemed to enjoy their riding. Miriam thought it would be nice to have a pony of her own and once asked her father if she could have one.

'I am afraid you can't,' Dad replied. 'They cost a lot of money and then you have to buy their food. You will have to content yourself with your dog and kitten.'

So, if they couldn't have a horse of their own, Ernie was the next best thing. At least they could pretend he was theirs and they could help look after him.

Dad told them that the place where the horses could be seen in the field was one that cared for horses that had spent their lives working by pulling carts. Now they had retired from work and could enjoy the field, the grass, the sunshine and the care of the people who looked after them. There are lots of places like this where old horses and donkeys are cared for.

'It is very nice,' Dad said, 'to think that horses that have worked for so many years can find people who want them and care for them when they are getting too old for work.'

## 4 ANIMALS ON THE FARM

'Come on, Daisy,' said Farmer John, 'it's your turn to be milked.'

One of the black and white cows in the farmyard looked up and gently pushed her way between the others, making her way to the milking parlour where the milk was to be taken from her to be sent to the dairy.

Christopher and Miriam were watching. Dad had known the farmer for a long time and he had taken the children when he went to visit his friend.

'How does she know her name is Daisy?' Christopher asked.

'I can't tell you how she knows,' Farmer John replied, 'but she certainly does know, and she always comes when I call her. So do all the others when I call their names.'

'How do you know which is which?' Miriam asked. 'They all look the same to me.'

'Then take another look,' the farmer told her. 'Look closely and you will see that they are all different.'

She soon saw how right he was. They were all black and white but the patterns of the colours were different. Some cows were a little larger than others and their faces were not quite the same, just as people's faces are different. Miriam still thought the farmer was clever to know them all. Then she remembered a story she had heard from the Bible about the Good Shepherd knowing all his own sheep by name and the sheep recognizing his voice. Fancy knowing the names of so many animals!

People who work on farms know how important it is to get to know their animals and the sort of things they may do. The better they know the animals the better they can care for them. The animals come to know the farmer, too, as the person who looks after them and they are not afraid of him as they are of strangers who they do not know.

Miriam was very quiet in the car on the way home. She was still thinking how wonderful it was that the farmer knew all his animals so well. She thought again about that story from the Bible. Jesus had said he was the Good Shepherd. How lovely it was to think that Jesus or God could know everyone by name and care for each one. Many people have found it a great comfort to know that.

## 5  ST. JEROME AND THE LION

We hear of lots of people who keep dogs or cats, cows or sheep, but sometimes we hear of people who look after other sorts of animal. There is an old story which tells of a very good man named St. Jerome, who made an unusual friendship.

One day St. Jerome was sitting outside the monastery where he lived, with some friends. Suddenly a big lion came towards them. People were very frightened. They were sure the lion would kill them, but Jerome waited to see what the lion would do. It came close to Jerome and lifted up its paw. Jerome saw that it was swollen and painful, with a thorn in the pad. He gently pulled out the thorn, bathed the sore paw and made the lion comfortable.

The lion wanted to stay with Jerome. In the morning, when Jerome awoke, the lion was still there. However much he tried to send it away, the lion would not go. 'Well,' said Jerome, 'everyone who lives in this house has to work, and you must work, too. You will go with the woodcutter and the donkey to the forest every day and guard them.' So every day the lion did so.

One warm day, the lion fell asleep. When he awoke there was no donkey and no woodcutter. The lion lifted his head and sniffed. He could smell men. Robbers had taken the donkey. He went slowly back to the monastery, looking so ashamed that Jerome knew what had happened. 'You must take the donkey's place,' he said.

So every day the proud lion did the work of the donkey. One day there came by a company of people with a long line of camels and horses, all carrying fine things: in front was a donkey! With a great roar the lion sprang towards them. He recognized the stolen donkey. The merchants were terrified and ran. The lion chased them all the way to the door of the monastery.

The merchants asked Jerome to forgive them for stealing his donkey and he did. So, once again, Jerome's donkey carried the firewood and the lion faithfully served St. Jerome.


6 AT THE ZOO

There was great excitement as Christopher went to school one morning. It was the day of a school visit that the children had been eagerly awaiting. There, outside the school gates, was the coach that would take them to spend a day at the zoo.

Christopher had heard quite a lot of stories about animals and he had seen lots of pictures but this would be the first time he had been able to see some of the animals. He could hardly wait to get to the zoo.

The first animals he saw were some deer in a paddock. They were lovely animals, so gentle-looking, but Christopher wanted to see the really big animals like elephants and giraffes. There was also the baby bear that had been born in the zoo recently and had been in the news, with photographs in the papers.

But perhaps the most exciting would be the big cats, the lions and tigers. They would probably be very fierce and roar or snarl as soon as the children came near. He was rather disappointed when they came to the enclosures where these animals were kept. They didn't look at all fierce and they didn't make any noise at all. In fact they looked very sleepy. One lion opened an eye, took one look at the children, then closed it again.

'I am sure he would let me stroke him,' he said.

'I don't think so,' his teacher told him. 'Lions may look harmless but I wouldn't chance going near one. It is always best to keep at a safe distance from wild animals.'

Christopher enjoyed the elephants. Their trunks were held out for any food that people would offer them. He took out a piece of bun which he had taken for his lunch. It was funny to see the elephant take it in her trunk and put it in her mouth. He liked hearing the sealions bark and watching them dive into the water.

After lunch teacher looked at her watch, then took the children back to the lions. They were prowling around and growling. It was time for them to be fed. They looked much fiercer as the large pieces of meat were tossed to them.

Then it was time to go home. It had been a lovely day. Christopher was pleased that people had found so many animals for him to see.

'I think I'd like to be a zoo keeper when I grow up,' he thought to himself. 'I'd like to look after animals.'

7  ANIMALS IN SCHOOL

'Who would like to be a zoo keeper?' teacher asked on the day after the children had been to the zoo.

Christopher's hand shot up. So did the hands of lots of other children too. Most of them had enjoyed seeing the animals and thought it would be nice to look after them.

'Well now,' teacher said, 'you can't all do it at once. Christopher and Tariq can be first and then the others can have their turn.'

The two boys looked puzzled. What did she mean about their being zoo keepers? They had no lions or elephants. How could they be zoo keepers?

Mrs. Macdonald smiled and walked over to the stock cupboard in the corner. When she came back she had a cage in her hands. The children eagerly looked to see what was in the cage but they couldn't see anything at all. Then Mrs. Macdonald opened the wire top, put her hand into the bed space in the corner and brought out a hamster. 'There you are,' she said. 'Isn't it lovely.'

Teacher put the hamster on a table for the children to see. It moved around slowly with its nose twitching all the time. Perhaps

---

the hamster was feeling strange with all these children. Some of them wanted to hold it in their hands and they were allowed to do so before Mrs. Macdonald decided that the hamster had been handled enough and put it back in the cage.

She explained to Christopher and Tariq that they would have to keep the cage clean or it would smell. They would also have to see that the hamster was given food and clean water. One of them would have to take it home at weekends so that it was not left for too long.

That afternoon it was a very excited Christopher who ran home from school.

'Mum! I've got to look after our class hamster. Can I bring it home on Friday?'

'Of course you can,' Mum replied. 'I had better come to meet you and carry the cage in case you drop it. We have to take care of it, you know.'

Christopher learned a lot in the next week or two. If you have the job of looking after animals, you must always do it properly, even when there are other things you would like to do. Being an animal keeper is a very responsible job.

## 8 CARING FOR ANIMALS

One evening Miriam stepped into the garden and stepped back indoors quickly. 'There's something funny out there,' she said.

Dad went to the door and could hear a strange snorting sound. He smiled. 'It is only a hedgehog,' he said.

The whole family watched as the prickly hedgehog made its way across the lawn and disappeared under the garden shed. 'I expect the rest of its family is under there too,' he said.

Soon the hedgehogs had been accepted as part of the family. At night the children put out food and drink, then watched out for the animals. It was nice to have wild animals as well as their pets.

One day Miriam noticed that one of the hedgehogs had been hurt. She told Dad, who put on his thick gardening gloves so that he would not get hurt on the spikes, then picked up the hedgehog and put it in a box.

'That needs to be seen to,' Dad said. 'We had better get it round to the P.D.S.A. straight away.'

'What is the P.D.S.A.?' asked Christopher.

'The letters stand for People's Dispensary for Sick Animals,' Father replied. The man at the P.D.S.A. is an animal doctor or, to give him his proper name, a veterinary surgeon. We usually call him a vet. It is easier to say.'

'But doesn't he only look after pets?' Miriam asked.

'No,' her father replied. 'Vets treat any animals or birds—large animals such as horses or cows as well as small ones like mice. Of course most of the animals are cats and dogs because these are the ones most frequently kept as pets, but you will find that P.D.S.A. vets often have wild animals to treat, even snakes.

When they reached home again, with the hedgehog that had now had its leg treated, Dad explained that the P.D.S.A. never turned away any animal, even if the owner had no money. Lots of people give money so that the P.D.S.A. can do this.

'It is nice to think that so many people care,' Dad said. 'God has put lots of animals in the world for us to enjoy. It is up to all of us to do what we can to look after them.'

RELATED THEMES

1. Dear Father God, thank you for all who look
      after animals:
   For Vets who treat them when they are sick;
   For animal welfare organizations such as the P.D.S.A.;
   For kind people who care for animals that have
      been treated badly;
   For those who keep retired horses and donkeys;
   And for all who look after animals in zoos.
   Thank you, Father God, for all people like these. *Amen.*

2. Father in heaven, we thank you:
   For all the animals we can enjoy,
                 *Father in heaven, we thank you;*
   For animals that are very helpful to people,
                 *Father in heaven, we thank you;*
   For animals that give us companionship,
                 *Father in heaven, we thank you;*
   For animals which we look after,
                 *Father in heaven, we thank you;*
   Make us kind towards them all. *Amen*

3. I like animals, dear God.
   I like their soft furry bodies;
   I enjoy holding or cuddling them;
   I enjoy just watching them, too;
   I like animals, dear God.
   . . . I hope they like me! *Amen*

4. O God, you have put many different animals in our world.
   Some I like better than others. Help me to remember that you
   made them all and that I should care for them all. *Amen*

5. O Lord Jesus Christ, help us to know that you are the Good
   Shepherd who knows all about your flock, even those of us who
   are so small; and teach us to know that you care for us. *Amen*

6. O Lord, make me kind to all animals, wherever I may find them and especially help me to do all I can to look after those that have been put in my care. *Amen*

7. O Lord, may we be kind to all living creatures, especially our pets in school and at home. *Amen*

8. Thank you, dear Father God, for the Guide Dogs which help blind people. Thank you for those who train them and those who pay for them to be trained so that more blind people can be helped. *Amen*

9. Thank you, God my Father:
   For horses and ponies and donkey rides;
   For cows and sheep and pigs on the farm;
   For cats, dogs and other pets;
   For animals I can see in zoos:
   Thank you for so many different kinds. *Amen*

10. Thank you, God our Father, for the pets which share our homes; for dogs and cats, rabbits and guinea pigs, hamsters and gerbils, budgerigars and canaries, and for other animals and birds that we enjoy keeping. Help us to look after them well. *Amen*

11. Thank you, O God for horses:
    For big, strong horses that pull carts;
    For sleek, fast racehorses;
    For graceful horses used by policemen;
    For gentle horses that people ride on;
    And for ponies and donkeys too.
    Thank you for them all. *Amen*

12. Today, dear Father God, we think of lots of animals:
    Large wild animals that live in other countries;
    Wild animals that live in our own land;
    Animals that are looked after by farmers;
    And the pets we have in our homes.
    Help us to remember that you made them all
    And you expect us to care for them. *Amen*

All things bright and beautiful
All things which live below the sky
Stand up, clap hands
Think of a world
The duck goes 'quack'
The flowers that grow in the garden
The kitten's fur is warm


BIBLE STORIES ABOUT ANIMALS

Jesus rides on a donkey                          Matthew 21; 1–9
The Good Shepherd                                  John 10; 1–18


INTEREST WORK AND ACTIVITIES

*Books*

It will not be difficult to find a large number of books on animals.
Here are some.

DOGS/CATS/HORSES/VERY SMALL ANIMALS *(Starters)*,
    Macdonald
ANIMALS/KEEPING PETS/ZOOS *(Blackwell's Learning
    Library)*, Blackwell
BIG CATS AND LITTLE CATS/BIG DOGS AND LITTLE
    DOGS *(Magpies)*, Hulton
PUPPIES AND KITTENS *(Learning to Read)*, Ladybird
TAME ANIMALS *(Beginners' World)*, Macdonald
TAME ANIMALS *(Our World)*, Burke
WE DISCOVER PETS/WE DISCOVER ANIMALS ON THE
    FARM *(We discover)*, Arnold
CATS/HORSES AND PONIES *(First Library)*, Macdonald
BABY ANIMALS *(Leaders)*, Ladybird
LET'S GO TO THE VET/LET'S GO TO THE ZOO *(Let's go)*,
    Watts
WHO'S AT THE ZOO *(Head-Start)*, Burke

GOING TO THE ZOO *(Starters Facts)*,
ANIMALS *(Waste not, want not)*, Burke
SAVE THESE ANIMALS/ANIMALS KEEPING CLEAN/
  ANIMAL DEFENCES/FARM ANIMALS *(First Interest)*,
  Ginn

*General decor*

Have an animal theme for the school with pictures and art work of
all sorts. Small animal shapes can be cut out of card and suspended
as mobiles from wire coat hangers or canes on threads of various
lengths. Shapes of larger animals can be made to hang on to
projections, e.g. monkeys with arm extended and hand hooked;
others to hang by tail.

Encourage children to look for animal pictures, which can be
mounted or put in class books.

*Pets*

Children to talk about their own pets and how they look after them.
It may be possible to have some pets brought to school for a short
period. If there are school pets, and it is possible to do so, bring them
to a central point for all to see. Encourage visits between classes or
groups to see the different pets and talk about them.

*Visits to see animals*

A zoo outing is an obvious choice if there is a zoo within reasonable
distance. Talk about some of the animals that will be seen and what
the children should watch out for. If it is a large zoo, be selective.

A safari park or a park containing a herd of deer would also be
profitable for a visit.

If there is a farm nearby or a shelter for retired horses, see if a visit
can be arranged.

*Visitors*

Anyone who works with animals could be invited to talk to the children, e.g. a vet, a pet-shop owner, a livestock farmer, a breeder, a zoo keeper.

*Things to make*

Animal friezes. Cats of all shapes and sizes cut out and mounted. Similar friezes of dogs, rabbits or children's own pets.

Horses. Old socks stuffed with newspaper make good horses' heads. Fur fabric strips can be used to make manes. Arrange a display of the heads so that they are looking over a fence or hedge. Alternatively mount on old broom handles or other suitable poles to make hobby horses.

A model zoo or farm. A suitable base and background of cages or buildings can be made. Use small model animals already in school or those belonging to the children.

Models can be made from plasticine.

*Animal welfare organizations*

Find out about the work of the P.D.S.A., R.S.P.C.A. and bodies providing refuge, shelter or sanctuary for horses, donkeys and other animals.

It may be possible to support the work of any of these.

# 16 Birds

*Most children are interested in birds and like to care for them. They like to feed the ducks on the pond and the wild birds in the garden. They feel protective towards the young fledgling cowering by the wall or in the playground. They like to look after the birds in their homes, the chickens in the yard or the pigeons in the pigeon loft. No doubt many envy the bird's ability to fly and wish they could do likewise.*

*This general interest in birds is a useful starting point on which to build, for the lessons that can be learned from and about the birds are numerous. Moreover there are lots of possible activities associated with the subject, many being on the theme of caring for or protecting weaker creatures.*

## 1 HIGH IN THE SKY

A little sparrow sat on the branch of a tree and looked around him. Everything was quiet and there on the ground were some crumbs that he wanted to eat. So down he flew and soon he was joined by several others who had seen him eating and thought they would do so as well.

But the sparrows were not the only creatures looking for food. Slowly a cat crept along the flower bed. 'One of those sparrows would make a nice dinner,' it thought. But just then one sparrow saw the cat, chirped loudly and flew quickly with all the others to the safety of the branches above.

When all was safe, they came down to finish their meal but they were soon disturbed again when a man opened the door of the house and came out. Was he a friend or an enemy? They did not know. So once again they spread their wings and flew away to somewhere where they could feel safe.

What might the birds think of you? Are you a friend or an enemy? Are you always kind to birds? Or do you ever do anything that would harm them? I wonder what the birds think about people when they are flying high in the sky! Do they take any notice of all those people rushing about in the towns or working patiently in the fields? I know the seagulls take notice of the fishermen when they have scraps of fish to throw away and there are many birds which take notice of us when they need to be fed, especially in the winter

213

---

when there is not very much natural food to be found. Birds soon get to know where food is put out for them. And they soon get to know kind people who care for them. There are lots of wild birds that will take food from people's hands or even hop into their kitchens.

It must be nice for a bird to be able to fly away from danger but it must also be nice to know that there are kind, helpful people who will care for them. We cannot fly like the birds, nor can we run away from things we do not like but we do know that there are many people who really care for us, in our homes, in our school, in our church and in lots of other places too.

And the Bible tells us that God, who cares for the birds, also loves and looks after us, his children.

## 2  ST. FRANCIS AND THE BIRDS

St. Francis was a kind, gentle man, who lived several hundred years ago. He was the son of a wealthy merchant but he gave away all his riches then went around helping people, especially those who were ill or poor. They enjoyed listening to him too as he told them about God and his love.

But it was not only to people that St. Francis spoke. Often he stopped and spoke to the birds and the animals. He called them his little brothers and sisters. They could tell that he loved them and they allowed him to touch them without showing any fear. There are many lovely stories told about St. Francis and his little friends.

One day he was preaching to a lot of people but they could not hear him very well because some swallows were twittering loudly. St. Francis looked towards the birds and spoke to them very kindly. 'Little sisters. You have said what you wanted to. Now it is my turn. Listen to the word of God and be quiet until I have finished.'

The story says that the birds did as he asked them. Another tale is about a wolf which kept attacking people in a village. When St. Francis heard about it, he went to look for the wolf, not fearing that it would harm him. When he did find the fierce animal he made the sign of the cross, then told the wolf that all the people were God's children and should not be harmed. From that day the wolf became tame and did not harm anyone again.

Many other stories are told of St. Francis and animals, birds or flowers. Of all the saints he is remembered most as one who loved God and everything in God's world.

## 3  BABY DUCKS

I was sitting by a small pond one day and heard a 'quack-quacking' which told me a duck was nearby. Sure enough, there was a mother duck leading eight little fluffy yellow ducklings along the path on the other side of the pond. The path was rather high above the water of the pond.

They waddled along until they reached the place Mother Duck thought suitable. She said something to her babies, then opened her wings a little and with a gentle plop, she landed on the water, then turned to face them on the bank. Her baby ducklings stood in a row watching her and looking fearfully down—it would seem a long way for such small creatures.

Mother faced her young, talking to them all the time. 'Quack, quack, quack,' it sounded to me, but I think she was probably saying something like 'Come on, I am here. I will look after you and see that you come to no harm. You must learn to swim. You have walked with me for the first time, now you must swim in the water with me.' She went on talking to them, reassuring them and encouraging them to join her.

The ducklings looked at her; they went nearer to the edge. One or two looked as though they would jump. They opened their wings to balance and tipped forward a little. Then, one brave little duckling went right up to the edge of the bank, teetered, used his wings to keep his balance and then with a big jump—PLOP—he took the plunge and landed beside his mother.

After that, the others followed. One after another they went to the edge, put out their wings and plop, plop, plop, sometimes one, sometimes two little ducklings took the plunge and soon they were all safely in the water with their mother.

Mother Duck quacked happily and turned, calling to her babies to follow her. They paddled hard with their little webbed feet and so they formed a line behind her, swimming away to the far end of the pond.

They had learned a very important lesson in their lives. They had taken their first steps and their first swim in the water. They trusted their mother even though they were probably nervous, and then found that, once they had taken the step and made the big jump, it was much easier than they thought.

It was a very proud mother and proud and happy ducklings that swam across the pond that day.

## 4 BABY COOTS

In the springtime a pair of coots built a nest beneath the bushes beside a river. It was made mainly of sticks and it floated on top of the water. The mother coot laid her eggs in the nest and sat on them until, one day towards the end of May, they hatched out.

Soon there were four tiny little chicks, little black bundles with red heads, nothing like their parents' with their greyish-black feathers and white foreheads. Father spent the rest of that day swimming back and forth, finding food and taking it back to Mother, who, in turn, fed the children.

It was not long before the little chicks were moving around in the nest, climbing over the side and sitting by the water's edge. Now Mother and Father were both busy gathering food. They made sure their young ones were snug in the nest that night.

On the following day the young ones became braver. Suddenly two of them swam away from the nest and were soon being carried quickly away on the fast-moving water. It was a dangerous thing to do. They could have drifted right away or they could have been eaten by a large fish. Pike like small birds for dinner!

Father coot swam after them and managed to get them to the water's edge. Then mother followed and encouraged the little ones to swim behind her back to the nest. What did she say to them? We don't know—but the first thing she did was to see them lovingly to the nest and give them something to eat.

Jesus once told a story of a boy who left home, and did silly things but then went home, where his father made him welcome. He said that God is pleased when his children who have strayed come back to him again, because he loves them.

## 5 BIRD SONG

All birds have their own particular sound or song. Can you tell me the sound made by a duck ... or a cockerel ... an owl ... or a cuckoo? They are all well known and easy to recognize.

Some bird sounds are not very musical. Rooks flying round the trees make a harsh cawing noise. Seagulls have a mewing call. Many water fowl have only a single sharp cry. Swans make a little hissing sound.

Often the birds make noises to scare other birds, animals or humans away from their nests or their young ones. They are very protective and make loud squawking or chirping noises until the danger has passed. Sometimes the sounds they make are to attract other birds, especially during the mating season.

Some birds are known as song-birds because of the lovely sound they make. One of the most famous is the nightingale but you are probably more likely to hear the fine sounds of the blackbird or the song thrush both in the town and the country. There are lots of other small birds such as the warblers, which sing away for much of the day. In the country, one of the best known songs is that of the skylark which flies high into the air singing merrily the whole time.

Lots of people enjoy listening to the birds and trying to recognize which birds are singing.

Birds sing at different times for lots of reasons but there is one time when many of them join together. If you are awake very early, when the day is dawning, you will hear lots and lots of birds begin to sing. We call it the 'dawn chorus'. Why do they do it? Perhaps they are glad to welcome each new day.

What better way to start each day than with a cheerful song—a song of thanks to God our maker.

## 6 HOMING PIGEONS

One summer evening a man was standing near a brightly coloured shed in his garden. He was looking into the distance and became quite excited when a speck appeared in the sky heading towards him. It was one of his pigeons which had been on a long journey and was now coming home. Soon, that, and other pigeons, had fluttered safely down to rest and feed after their long flight.

Some time before, they had been put into baskets and taken a long way off with pigeons which belong to other people. Each had a ring on its leg with a number on it. They were homing pigeons and were taking part in a race to see which reached home in the fastest time.

When they had reached the place where the race would start, all the baskets had been opened. The pigeons flew into the air, circled a couple of times to get their bearings and then headed straight for home. How did they know which way to go? No one knows. There is something about homing pigeons which makes them do that. Homing pigeons have often been used to carry messages, sometimes by soldiers who have wanted to get information past an enemy.

A homing pigeon is trained to fly straight and quickly. It will be flying through an interesting world in which there are lots of other things to do. It could stop in a cornfield for food; or it could rest in a tree with other birds; but it has to head straight for home.

Life is something like that! We are starting on a journey which will last for many years. We know that God would have us lead a good, straight life until we reach the end. There will be many wrong things we can do but we must not allow ourselves to do anything that would keep us away from God.

## 7  MIGRATION

In springtime you may hear someone say, 'I've just heard the first cuckoo!' Its song, easily recognizable, 'cuckoo ... cuckoo ... cuckoo ...' is always a sign that spring has come, because the cuckoo is one of the birds that only spends the summer in Britain. By August all the cuckoos will have gone again—back to the warmer land from which they came.

About the same time lots of other birds arrive too. Swallows come from their winter homes in Africa and spend the summer raising their families. As summer comes to an end, the swallows gather in large numbers ready to fly away. You may sometimes see lots of them perched on telephone wires ready for their long journey—hundreds of miles over land and sea.

Why do they leave us? Well, if you have watched swallows during the summer, you will have seen them darting through the air or skimming the river to catch insects on which they feed. But by the autumn there are very few insects about. Many of them have died and others have hidden themselves away for the winter. So the swallows, and lots of other birds, too, which feed on insects, have to go to the warmer countries where there is still food to be found.

Every year there are millions of birds which fly from one part of the world to another in the spring and autumn. How do they know where to go? There are no signposts to show them the way.

It is an even greater puzzle to know how the young birds can know where to go. When the cuckoos fly away, they leave their young ones behind to find their own way. There is no one to tell them which way to fly nor when they should do so—but they do fly at the right time and to the right place.

How they do it we don't know but we live in a remarkable world and there are lots of things we do not understand.

## 8  GOD LOVES THE SPARROWS

Which birds do you like best? Or which do you think are the most interesting? There are lots and lots of different birds. Most of them can fly. Some, like eagles, have very powerful wings. Seagulls can spread their wings and glide through the air. Other birds cannot fly. Ostriches are very large birds which cannot fly—but they can run very fast. Penguins cannot fly, or run, but they are very good swimmers. Some people enjoy watching birds such as blue-tits which can be quite amusing as they twist and turn to get at nuts which are hung in the garden for them to eat.

Lots of people like to care for wild birds by putting out food for them. Others enjoy having birds in their homes—brightly coloured budgerigars which chatter away in their cages, yellow canaries or other song-birds. Some people keep parrots or mynahs, which can be taught to say words. People living on their own may like a bird for company.

Some of these birds have very beautiful feathers. Parrots and other birds which normally live in hot countries may have bright red, yellow, green and blue feathers. Perhaps you have seen a peacock with his beautiful tail spread out. Other birds are very plain. Rooks and crows may seem very dull with their black feathers.

There are some kinds of bird which are seldom seen and people get very excited when they see one of these rare birds. Other birds are very common. There are more blackbirds in Britain than there are any other kind of bird. There are lots and lots of sparrows too—so many that people take very little notice of them. But when Jesus wanted to talk about God, he chose ordinary sparrows for a lesson to help people understand how God cares.

He said that, although they could be bought very cheaply, they are important to God, who knows all about them and cares for them. He said that if even one sparrow was hurt or 'fell to the ground' God would know. Isn't it wonderful to think that God knows all about the smallest of his creatures and cares about every one? If God cares for little birds, of course he must know about us and care for us too.

I am sure God likes to think that we help him in his work by looking after the birds and his other creatures.

RELATED THEMES

GOD MADE THE BIRDS

God made the birds that fly high in the sky,
    That rise up on powerful wing:
God gave them voices to praise Him at dawn
    And taught them the songs that they sing.

God gave them feathers, some plain and some bright:
    He loves every one he has made:
Even the sparrow that falls to the ground
    God cares for—so Jesus once said.

Thank you, O God, that you care for the birds
    That fly in the heavens above;
But thank you much more for caring for us
    And keeping us all in your love.                        R.P.

---

PRAYERS

1. Accept our thanks, dear God,
   For all the birds which cheer our lives;
   For cheeky little sparrows in the garden;
   For song birds with their cheerful music;
   For the noisy seagulls round the harbour;
   For . . . [*add any that may be relevant*];
   Thank you for all of these. *Amen*

2. As the birds sing your praises at dawn, O God, may we, your
   children, be glad for all your great gifts and sing your praises
   day by day. *Amen*

3. Dear Father, we are pleased that you made birds;
   We like to see them flying high in the sky;
   We love to listen to their cheerful songs;
   We like to watch them as they eat their food;
   We enjoy looking at those which come into our garden,
   Especially those that are not too frightened by us.
   Help us to care for all the birds;
   To be kind to them;
   And to do what we can to help them. *Amen*

4. Dear God, we enjoy seeing baby birds but we know they need
   looking after. Help us to do nothing that would harm them in
   any way. We remember that you care for them and we ask that
   we may do so too. *Amen*

5. In these cold days when the birds have not much food, help us
   to remember them by putting out food and water so that they
   will not be hungry or thirsty. Teach us to look after all your
   creatures. *Amen*

6. Just as little birds must learn to fly or swim, so we have lots of
   things to learn. Help us, O God, to learn how to live as true
   children of our Father in heaven. *Amen*

7. O God, we are not always careful to do what is right. Some-times we do things that are silly and sometimes we say or do things that we know are wrong. Help us to know what you would have us to do and then to do it as best we can. *Amen*

8. Thank you, God, for all sorts of birds:
   For the birds we see around us every day,
   > *Thank you, God*;
   For birds which fill the world with cheerful song,
   > *Thank you, God*;
   For the birds we keep in our homes as pets,
   > *Thank you, God*;
   For chickens and ducks whose eggs we enjoy,
   > *Thank you, God*;
   For birds from other lands which we see in the zoo,
   > *Thank you, God*;
   Help us to remember that you made them all. *Amen*

9. We thank you, O God, that Jesus taught us how you know and care about the sparrows. Help us always to know that you care for us and love us because we are your children; and make us thankful that we can call you our Father. *Amen*

10. We think today, O God, of all the birds that you have given us to enjoy.
    For their cheerful songs which we love to hear;
    For colourful feathers that brighten our world;
    For the pleasure we get from watching them.
    Thank you, God. *Amen*

11. When we think of the birds and all your creatures, O God, we are reminded how wonderful you are. Thank you for our world and everything in it. *Amen*

12. You have given us a beautiful world, O God, full of lovely things. Help us always to look after it. *Amen*

All things bright and beautiful
All things which live below the sky
Hark! a hundred notes are swelling
I love God's tiny creatures
I love the sun
Little birds in wintertime
Morning has broken
The duck goes, 'Quack'
There are hundreds of sparrows

BIRDS IN THE BIBLE

| | |
|---|---|
| Noah sends out a raven and a dove | Genesis 8; 1–12 |
| Elijah fed by the ravens | 1 Kings 17; 1–7 |
| God sees the sparrows | Matthew 10; 29–30 |
| Don't worry! | Matthew 6; 24–26 |

INTEREST WORK AND ACTIVITIES

*Books*

Provide a selection of books with simple and colourful pictures of
birds and make them available for children to look at and handle. A
few suggestions are:

BIRDS *(Small World)*, Hamilton
I AM A BIRD *(Who am I?)*, Blackwell
BIG BIRDS AND LITTLE BIRDS *(Magpies)*, Hulton
WE DISCOVER BIRDS *(We discover)*, Arnold
BIRDS YOU CAN WATCH *(Starters Nature)*, Macdonald
OUR BIRD FRIENDS (6 books in slip-case), Chambers
SONG BIRDS *(Leaders)*, Ladybird
THE LITTLE CHICK *(Observing Nature)*, Wayland
BIRDS AND MIGRATION *(First Library)*, Macdonald

*Pictures*

Provide large pictures for display and small pictures for mounting. Some attractive pictures of birds may be found in magazines such as *BIRDS*, the magazine of the Royal Society for the Protection of Birds. Children can make their own pictures, too, painting, drawing, collage or sewing.

*Stories*

Tell any suitable stories about birds, e.g. *The Nighingale*, *The Ugly Duckling* (Hans Christian Andersen); and *The Fox and the Stork* (Aesop).

*Collections*

Encourage children to make their own collections of pictures and other items from magazines, periodicals and newspapers.
Make a collection of feathers.
It may be possible to find a nest (but ensure that children know not to touch a nest that is still being used).

*Listening and observing*

Make use of any tapes, cassettes or records that may be available of bird song. Encourage children to listen to sounds of birds and to note anything they see or hear on radio or television. Listen to simple songs about birds.
Observe and make notes about birds common to the environment. Give help in identification. Observe birds at bird table (see page 282).
Look for signs of nesting places, e.g. in gutters, eaves of houses, under porches, hedges, trees, on the ground, in holes. Notice twigs or tufts of grass that may give a clue. Someone may have a nesting box in the garden. Be aware of signs that birds are nesting there—birds going to and fro, carrying nesting material, feeding the young.

Older children could keep a bird diary and record simple day-to-day observations. Children with pet birds, budgerigars, canaries, parrots and others could make notes about these too.

## Visitors to school

Invite people in to talk to the children, especially local people with special interests—a bird-watcher, a pet-shop owner, a breeder, a pigeon fancier, a poultry keeper. Perhaps they could bring birds to show the children and talk about their care.

## Visits

Make visits to parks and other open spaces for observation. Note the different kinds of birds that are seen and obvious nests.

Visit a pond to see and feed the ducks, swans, waterfowl or gulls. Note any different species to be seen, size, colours, etc.

A visit to a zoo will provide added interest in birds from other countries.

Visit a farm to see chickens, ducks, or turkeys; or the harbour to observe gulls.

## Art and craft

Children's pictures of birds: painting, drawing, collage, sewing. Simple mobiles within the ability of small children are effective for display.

Make a template of a simple outline of a bird. Children draw and cut out the shape in stiff paper or card. Make a slit to take the wings. Colour shape both sides. Use finer paper such as tissue paper, oblong in shape for wings. Fold fanlike, pass through slit and open out both sides. Pierce a hole to take thread by which the bird is suspended.

Smaller birds can be made in the same way and suspended on threads of varying length from a metal clothes hanger which has first been painted or covered.

Similar shapes may be made in felt or other stiff material and decorated with feathers, sequins, beads, etc.

---

*Cookery (Birds' nests)*

While not suggested for everyday follow-up, could be used as a special event with a small group. An adult must, of course, deal with the heating and cooking but, with adequate supervision, this is an enjoyable activity.

You will need:

25g (or 1 oz) margarine or butter.
25g (or 1 oz) cooking chocolate.
25g (or 1 oz) sugar.
25g (or 1 oz) cornflakes or crispies.
1 tablespoon golden syrup.
Egg sweets, or home-made eggs.
Saucepan, tablespoon, dessert spoon and fork.
Greaseproof paper.

What you do:

1. Put the margarine, chocolate, sugar and syrup into the pan.
2. Place on a low heat and stir gently until the ingredients have just melted.
3. Turn off the heat and put the pan on a board to cool.
4. Add the cornflakes or crispies gradually, stirring until they are well coated with the chocolate mixture.
5. Using a spoon and fork, put six piles of the mixture on the greaseproof paper and shape into 'nests'.
6. Place one or two eggs in each nest and leave to harden.

If sweet eggs are not available, a substitute may be made with icing sugar and egg white, or with marzipan.

*Prayers*

Make up simple prayers to say thank you for the birds and to ask that people should care for them.

# 17 Creatures great and small

*All things bright and beautiful*
*All creatures great and small,*
*All things wise and wonderful,*
*The Lord God made them all.*

*The world is full of an abundance of wild life of which we cannot but
be aware. Through these stories, which are merely a very small
selection from the many that could have been used, children are made
aware of some of the creatures great and small, wise and wonderful,
which are part of creation. These are neither the cuddly pets they keep
in their homes nor the animals and birds they enjoy watching, but
rather the creatures that are not so popular yet nevertheless interesting
or those which are inaccessible.*

*Dinosaurs have been included partly as a matter of interest, since
most children are fascinated by 'monsters', but also as a link with the
last story which touches briefly on the subject of conservation. It is
important at an early age that children should learn the need for this
and a general care for the animal world. They may even learn that it is
not necessary to stamp on a spider just because it happens to be there!
It will certainly do **them** no harm.*

*Long ago an Old Testament writer advised 'Go to the ant thou
sluggard: consider her ways and be wise.' We can learn much from
the smaller creatures and their ways as is shown in a few stories.*

*Through thinking about these and other creatures and by some
consideration of the fascinating ways of even the smallest of them, the
children may be brought to an awareness of the wonders of creation
and begin to realize.*

**How great is God Almighty,**
**Who has made all things well.**

## 1  FLIES

Sit in the sunshine on a bright summer day and listen! You will soon
notice that there is a never ending hum made by insects of many
kinds. Lots of these are flies of all sorts, shapes and sizes. There are
over 75,000 different kinds of fly in the world, apart from other

insects such as greenfly (aphids) and dragonflies which are called flies but really belong to different insect families.

Some of these flies are so small that we can hardly see them. Others, like the bluebottles which buzz around our homes, can easily be recognized. Some flies are very pretty with brightly coloured bodies or wings that look as though they are made of fine lace.

They can be very interesting to look at, too. Have you ever watched a hover-fly keeping very still in mid-air? Or a swarm of midges 'dancing' in the air on a warm evening? If you have looked closely at a fly, you may have noticed what big eyes it has. They are really lots of eyes in one. A fly does not just look forward as we do. Its eyes can see all around, which is probably just as well, for this helps the fly to see danger approaching. Lots of birds like to eat flies.

Some flies are very troublesome to people and animals. They like sweet things to eat but they feed on dead things and on the mess left behind by animals. That is why we always try to keep flies off our food. They carry germs on their tongues and their feet and these can spread disease.

Flies are very important creatures. Think how much mess and filth there would be if there were not millions of flies to clear it up. So we must be thankful for flies—even though we may not like them.


2  BEES

Have you ever heard it said of someone that he is as busy as a bee? If you have ever watched a bee you will know why.

There are several different kinds of bee. One is the big, furry bumble bee, which seems too heavy ever to lift itself off the ground and fly. The commonest bee is the honey bee. We see lots of them flying from flower to flower collecting a sweet juice called nectar.

Bees gather nectar with their tongues and carry it in a special stomach called a *honey sac*. Back in the hive it will be made into honey. Bees also gather pollen, a powder from the flowers which the bees eat. They carry it in bags on their legs.

Bees do not collect all the nectar and pollen for themselves. They take it to the hive. In the hive is a queen bee, who lays eggs which will later hatch out and become bees. There are bees which spend all their time looking after the queen and the young bees. Some of the food is for them but a lot is stored up for the winter when there are no flowers.

Many of the bees will not need this winter food because they will have died. Most bees live only a few weeks in summer. Some, born late in the autumn, live all through the winter and are there to begin work as soon as the flowers first appear.

Bees are busy—busy working for the good of the colony with each one doing its job well. We could learn a lesson from the bees, remembering that we must work with others in our homes, our school, our country; and it is up to us to do our job as well as we can.

### 3  UNPOPULAR CREATURES

Have you ever sat in the garden on a warm summer day, enjoying the sunshine and something nice to eat, when an unwelcome visitor arrives? A small black and yellow creature flies around you and lands right on the food you are enjoying. It is a wasp. Wasps like sweet things just as much as you do!

Perhaps the first thing you want to do is to wave your hands to make it go away. Or maybe you know that the sensible thing to do is to keep quite still, even though the wasp may be crawling on you. Wasps usually sting only to protect themselves or if they are frightened. The more you hit out to shoo them away the more angry they become. Most people do not like wasps.

Also unpopular are insects that 'bite'. They do not really bite: they puncture a hole in your skin so that they can suck out some blood. Usually you do not know they are doing it until you feel a sharp jab—and then it is too late. You will soon have a small irritating bump. Gnats, mosquitoes and some flies are not very popular with people either.

Yet these and lots of other unpopular insects are all part of God's creation. They are very interesting and very useful—but we do not like them because they can hurt us.

There are people like that, too! They are all God's children but they are not liked because they do or say nasty things which are hurtful.

Do people sometimes want to have nothing to do with you? Have you wondered why? Is it because you do things which are unkind or unpleasant? If you are not popular with others, ask yourself why . . . and see if you can do something about it.

### 4  ST. FELIX AND THE SPIDER

Do you like spiders? Most people are not very fond of them. Perhaps they are not so bad when they do not come too close to you. There is a story about a man who was once very pleased with a spider. He was a good man named Felix, who lived long ago in the city of Rome, in Italy. Because Felix was a Christian, the Emperor was very angry with him and shut him up in a dark prison for a long, long time. He was given very little to eat and so he grew very thin.

One day, Felix escaped, and ran as hard as he could, but he knew the Emperor's soldiers on swift horses would soon catch him. He came to a valley between high mountains and thought that he must surely be caught.

Then, he saw a narrow crack in one of the rocks and he said to himself, 'As I am so thin, perhaps I could squeeze through there.' So he tried: he squeezed until he found he could just get through the crack. On the other side he found a deep, dry well, and he scrambled into it and felt he was safe. Presently he heard the sound of the soldiers close to his hiding place. One of them called out, 'Where can he have got to?' 'Look!' said another, 'Here is a crack in the rock, not really wide enough for a man to go through, but he was very thin, I am going to see.'

Felix was very frightened. Then he heard another soldier say, 'No, he can't be there—look, there is a spider's web right across it. No one has gone that way.' Then the soldiers rode away, still looking for Felix.

Felix knew then that in some wonderful way God must have sent a spider to spin a web across the crack and save his life. He was so glad and said a special 'Thank you' prayer to God. St. Felix always remembered the spider and how God saved him.

### 5  FROGS AND TOADS

When springtime comes and the weather becomes warmer than it has been during the winter, you may notice some frogs near the edge

230

of a pond. They enjoy the warm sunshine after the long winter, which they have spent asleep.

Very soon you will notice large lumps of jelly with lots of black spots in them. These are the eggs which the frog has laid and are called frog's spawn. One day some of them will be frogs. Perhaps, instead of lumps of jelly you may find strings of spawn. These are eggs laid by toads.

After a while the black spots in the jelly grow larger and change shape. Then they come out of the jelly and begin to move around the pond. We call them tadpoles. Have you seen tadpoles swimming? A tadpole has a round body and a tail that wiggles to make it swim.

As the tadpole gets older it grows legs. Its tail gets shorter until it has disappeared. It begins to breath air instead of taking air from the water. Then it is able to come out of the pond whenever it wants to. Grown-up frogs spend more time in the water than toads do. They must keep their skins wet. In summer you can often see a frog with just its head out of the water. Toads like a good soak too!

Frogs and toads wait for their dinner to come to them. They feed on flies, worms or other small creatures. The frog or toad sits very still until its dinner has come close. Then it flicks out its long, sticky tongue to catch the food. Frogs have their enemies, too. There are some animals and birds that like frogs for dinner! Frogs will sometimes dive for safety into the pond, where they can swim very well.

Perhaps you can get some spawn and watch it change into tadpoles and then into frogs. You may be able to find out more about frogs, toads, and other creatures. Our world is full of wonderful things that God has created—creatures for us to enjoy and to look after.

6 CROCODILES

Our world is full of lots of strange and interesting creatures. Some of these we enjoy. Others we may not like very much. Most of the creatures we come across are quite small. Larger animals live mainly in other countries, though we can see them in zoos or safari parks.

Imagine walking by a river and meeting a crocodile. You might not even have noticed it was there because crocodiles keep very still. Their tough, leathery skin can make them look something like a log by the river. A sleeping crocodile may look harmless enough but when it wakes up and opens its mouth you will see a lot of very sharp teeth. These teeth are set in very powerful jaws that can snap a heavy wooden board in two.

Crocodiles feed on fish, birds and small animals, which they seize in their teeth and swallow whole. The largest crocodiles are strong enough to kill an animal the size of a cow. They may pull the animal into the water and then twist and turn until it is torn to pieces. Crocodiles are ugly creatures which can be dangerous.

Would you like to meet a crocodile? Perhaps you would prefer to see one at a safe distance in a zoo where it cannot harm you.

Yet there is one small bird which is never afraid of a crocodile. It is called the crocodile bird and it can be seen sometimes on the crocodile's back where it feeds off certain insects which live on the crocodile. Sometimes it even pecks around the crocodile's teeth. And the crocodile does not mind one little bit. Perhaps it is just grateful that it has one little friend that is not afraid of it and helps it to be more comfortable.

There are some people who may seem rather like crocodiles. They may not be very pleasant to look at. They may be bad-tempered and snappy. Because of this, many people think they are not nice and keep right away from them. But it may be that they just need someone who will be a friend—someone to be kind and helpful, ready to do little things that will cheer them up. Perhaps we can be like the crocodile bird and be a good friend to someone.


7 ANIMALS WE HAVE LOST—DINOSAURS

Thousands and thousands of years ago, long before there were people in the world, a huge creature lived in a swamp. He had a huge body, a very long neck and a very long tail. From his nose to the tip of his tail was 22 m (*70 ft—nearly as long as 3 buses*) and he weighed about 31 tonnes (*about six times as much as an elephant*). He lived mostly in the water because his body was so heavy. We call him Brontosaurus, meaning 'thunder lizard', but he was not harmful. He fed on plants and spent a lot of his time asleep.

Allosaurus was different. He ran around on his two back legs. He had a small neck but a huge head and eighty long, sharp teeth. Allosaurus was one of the fiercest of these ancient creatures. He liked meat and hunted other creatures for food. Tyrannosaurus was even larger with longer teeth. He was the biggest meat eater that ever lived on land.

Many of the other creatures ran away from these fierce meat eaters, but not Stegosaurus. He had armour plates on his back and a tail with spikes on it. Any meat eater would not be able to get its teeth through the armour and could be badly hurt by that spiked tail.

These are just a few of the creatures which we call dinosaurs—a name meaning 'terrible lizard'. No one has ever seen a dinosaur and no one ever will. The last of them died long before there were people in the world. But we do know what they looked like because people found their bones and parts of their bodies buried in the ground.

And from what has been found we know that they were not all 'terrible lizards'. Some were. Others may have been large and ugly but were quite harmless and content to mind their own business.

We might remember not to judge people or things by their appearance. People who look similar may behave quite differently. An unpleasant looking person may have a heart of gold. A pretty person may be very bad-tempered or unkind.

What kind of person are you? Someone people enjoy being with? Or not very nice to know? And if not very nice, what are you doing to change that?

## 8  ANIMALS IN DANGER—WHALES

The largest animal that has ever lived is the whale. There are lots of different kinds of whale. Some are fairly small but the largest, the Blue Whale is much larger than the largest of the dinosaurs. A fully grown Blue Whale can weigh as much as 15 or 20 elephants.

Whales spend the whole of their lives in the sea but they are not fish: they are mammals. Fish breathe through gills which take air from the water. Whales have lungs and breathe air like we do. But, unlike us, they do not have a nose just above their mouth. They have nostrils, or a 'blow hole' in the top of their heads. Once a whale has taken a deep breath it can hold it for a long time, maybe as long as two hours. Then it must come up for air and it blows the old air out before taking another breath.

When a whale goes under water it closes the blow hole so that no water can get in. If water were to get into a whale's lungs it would drown, just as we would. For this reason a whale cannot breathe through its mouth because it has to open its mouth under water to catch its food.

Whales are very intelligent animals and most whales are harmless to people. But, a long time ago, men discovered that whales were useful to them, not alive but dead. The bones could be used for making a lot of things that nowadays are made of plastic. The flesh contained oil that could be used for lighting and heating. So men began to hunt and kill the whales.

Nowadays there are not many large whales left in the world. People still use whale products to make soap, paint, make-up, dyes, fertilizers, animals foods and lots of other things. Although it is now possible to make these things in other ways, many whales are still being killed. A lot of people want to stop the killing altogether. If we are not careful there will soon be no Blue Whales left, and perhaps some other kinds will be lost for ever too.

It would be a pity if, like the dinosaurs, there were no more ever to be seen.

**RELATED THEMES**

PRAYERS

1. Dear Father God,
   We like to think about the creatures you have made.
   We enjoy seeing them in zoos or wild-life parks.
   We like watching the smaller creatures in our gardens.
   We enjoy seeing pictures of huge animals of long ago,
   And of strange animals in the world today.
   Thank you for them all. *Amen*

2. Dear God, there are so many interesting things for us to see round about us. Help us to learn about them so that we can understand them better. *Amen*

3. Help me, dear Father God, to be as busy as a bee, not wasting my time but doing all the work that I should, so that I can grow up to live a useful life in your service. *Amen*

4. In your world, O God, there are lots of creatures we enjoy but there are others we do not like. Help us to remember that you had some reason for making them and that we should not harm those we may not like. *Amen*

5. O God, we are sorry that some kinds of animal will never be seen again.
   We are sorry that so many people want to kill some of the rare animals today.
   We are sorry that some people are unkind and wish to harm your creatures.
   Help us to look after every creature, large or small, and never harm or destroy. *Amen*

6. O God, when you made the world you put all sorts of living things into it. Help us to remember that you made them all and that we should be kind to them. *Amen*

7. Thank you, dear God for making this wonderful world with so many interesting animals and plants. And thank you for making us part of it. *Amen*

8. Thank you, dear God, for this wonderful world.
   For the great creatures that lived long ago;
   For large wild animals that live in far-off lands;
   For smaller creatures in fields, woods and gardens;
   And for those which share our homes;
   Thank you, God. *Amen*

9. Thank you, God our Father, for our world.
   For lots of tiny creatures which make the world interesting,
   > *Thank you, God our Father;*
   For pretty things—like butterflies, moths and ladybirds,
   > *Thank you, God our Father;*
   For busy little things—like bees and ants;
   > *Thank you, God our Father;*
   For useful things—like flies and earthworms,
   > *Thank you, God our Father;*
   And even for less pleasant things—like gnats and wasps,
   > *Thank you, God our Father;*
   Help us to remember that you made them all.
   > Thank you for everything. *Amen*

10. Thank you, O God, for all those creatures we like to see:
    For butterflies fluttering around the field or garden;
    For tadpoles that wiggle in the pond;
    For pretty little ladybirds and shiny black beetles;
    For [*add any of particular interest to the children*]:
    For all of these and many more, thank you, O God. *Amen*

11. We know, O God, that you care for the smallest of your
    creatures. We, too, are small and so we ask you to take care of
    us. *Amen*

12. When I look around me, O God,
    I see people and things I do not like.
    There are insects which may harm me:
    Teach me not to harm them.
    There are creatures that give me the shivers:
    Help me not to be afraid of them.
    There are children and grown-ups whom I don't like:
    Help me to try to be friendly towards them. *Amen*

HYMNS SUGGESTED

All things bright and beautiful
All things which live below the sky
God who made the earth
I love God's tiny creatures
Stand up, clap hands


BIBLE READINGS

| | |
|---|---|
| Creation of animal world | Genesis 1; 20–25 |
| Noah's Ark | Genesis 6; 13–7; 5 |
| Plagues in Egypt: | |
|     Frogs | Exodus 8; 1–15 |
|     Gnats | 16–19 |
|     Flies | 20–32 |
|     Locusts | 10; 1–20 |
| Jonah and the whale | Jonah 1 |
| Paul bitten by a snake | Acts 28; 1–6 |


INTEREST WORK AND ACTIVITIES

*Visits*

Visits can be made to zoos to see some of the larger animals. Any hedgerow, park or open space will provide opportunity to see many different insects and spiders. See how many different flies are there. Notice bees at work in the flowers.


*Visitors*

Visits to school from anyone who has responsibility for caring for animals to talk to the children. There may be a bee-keeper nearby who could talk about his work.

*Pictures*

Collect pictures of unusual animals.

*Books*

Provide a selection of books in the classroom for the children to look at and read for themselves. There are many from which to choose. Here is just a small selection:

BEES/FROGS/DINOSAURS/WHALES *(Starters)*,
  Macdonald
INSECTS THAT LIVE TOGETHER/FROGS AND
  TOADS/PREHISTORIC ANIMALS/VANISHING ANI-
  MALS *(First Library)*, Macdonald
BEES AND BEEKEEPING/SPIDERS AND SCORPIONS/
  AMPHIBIANS AND REPTILES/THE FIRST ANIMALS
  *(Blackwell's Learning Library)*, Blackwell
FLIES/BEES AND WASPS/SPIDERS *(Young Naturalist)*,
  Wayland
THE BEE *(Young Nature)*, Angus and Robertson
WATCH HONEYBEES WITH ME/BEES AND BEE
  LINES/WHY FROGS ARE WET/THE BLUE WHALE
  *(Let's read and find out)*, Black
INSECTS YOU CAN FIND *(Starters Nature)*, Macdonald
SMALL ANIMALS series, Hodder.
LETS FIND OUT ABOUT BEES/LET'S FIND OUT ABOUT
  FROGS, Watts.
FIRST LOOK AT CROCODILES AND ALLIGATORS *(First
  Look)*, Watts.

*Observation*

Some of the smaller creatures can be brought into the classroom. Frogs and toads can be put temporarily into a covered aquarium. Remember that frogs need to be kept wet. As both frogs and toads need live food, it is probably as well to keep them only for a day.
  At the appropriate time of year it may be possible to obtain some spawn and watch the tadpoles develop. The tadpoles will need some

pond weed for feeding. If kept long enough for them to grow into frogs or toads they will need an area on to which they can emerge from the water and the aquarium will have to be covered with muslin or a very fine mesh.

Children will also enjoy seeing any caterpillars that can be kept in the classroom. In summer the evolution from caterpillar to chrysalis to moth or butterfly is not too long. Caterpillars need the right kind of leaves for food. If possible gather some from the plant on which they were found and stand them in a small jar of water.

Perhaps a spider could be brought in a jar for observation—and information that it is harmless. Keep in a shady corner for just a short time.

*Art and Craft*

Paint pictures of strange or unusual animals to be put up in the class 'art gallery'.

Make a caterpillar:
A three-dimension 'picture' can be made by cutting out a number of discs. Paint the discs green or brown and stick on to a base to form a wiggling shape with the discs overlapping. Paint in the features for the head, six short black legs near the front of the body and suckers to match the body at the rear end.

. . . or a snake:
Fill a stocking with crumpled newspaper and decorate with scraps of all kinds—felt, coloured paper, materials, sequins, etc. Alternatively make a snake from cotton reels. Using a cork for the tail end, thread painted cotton reels on to thick string to the required length. An old rubber ball, also painted, can make the head with a cork for the 'nose'. Paint two eyes on the ball. Leave enough string in front of the 'nose' for the snake to be pulled along.

. . . or a crocodile:
Crocodiles can be made from egg boxes. Paint the cardboard egg boxes using the 'humped' part for the top. Starting with the tail er glue boxes together end to end then sideways to broaden the ' A hinged box, kept intact, can be used to form an open

239

For a wall decoration, the boxes can be cut, glued to the backing sheet and cut into the shape of a crocodile. The background can then be painted appropriately.

. . . or some dinosaurs:
Older children will enjoy making plasticine models of 'prehistoric monsters'.

. . . or a 'wild-life' park:
A park can be set up in a large tray such as a baker's tray. Line with sand and/or earth and set a mirror or small tray of water in one corner for a 'pond'. Add a few trees and a variety of small animals made from plasticine, clay, card or papier mâché.

*Music and poems*

Listen to any music or poems that may be available about wild creatures, e.g. a short excerpt from 'The Flight of the Bumble Bee'. Simple verses about reptiles or insects.

*Conservation*

Use any opportunity to bring into the classroom some aspect of conservation of wild life. Material is often sent into school by organizations such as the World Wild Life Fund.

# 18 Flowers and trees

*Wherever they live, in city, town or country, the children will have some access to flowers and trees, which frequently feature in school studies of one kind or another.*

*They will have opportunity to see at close quarters the unfolding of buds and leaves, the catkins and blossom, and the falling leaves in autumn. They will be able to admire the colours of flowers, whether in woods and fields, parks and gardens or perhaps only in the shops or on the barrows and stalls of the flower sellers.*

*They will discover that flowers and trees may be growing in the most unlikely places and we seek to encourage the children to look and look again at the wonder of nature and growing things, whether it be in the profusion of the countryside, in cracks between paving stones and walls, or on derelict sites in towns and cities.*

*Apart from the trees and flowers themselves there is the discovery of so many creatures dependent upon them.*

*It has been said that 'wonder is the beginning of worship'.*

1 SAY IT WITH FLOWERS

The Digby children stood outside the shop looking at the wonderful display in the window. This was a favourite place to visit while mother was in the butcher's shop a few yards away. They promised not to move and they really didn't want to anyway: there was so much to see.

The sign over the shop said 'FLORIST'. Another in the window said 'SAY IT WITH FLOWERS'. In the window and along the sides of the shop were lots of different flowers. Some were in baskets, some in tall vases and others were growing in pots. The flowers were so cleverly arranged that the colours looked brighter than ever. And the scent of the flowers, when the door was opened, was really lovely.

The arrangements the children liked best were the unusual ones, like the pretty cradle made of flowers for the mother of a newly born baby. They could remember seeing one once that was made in the shape of a dog and another a car, all made with flowers. On special occasions too, they had seen red, white and blue flowers, one made like the flag of Great Britain, the Union Flag. Of course the bouquets prepared for brides and bridesmaids were always very pretty.

They hadn't understood the meaning of the notice 'SAY IT WITH FLOWERS' until Mum explained it to them. It was a very nice way of saying things to other people if you sent them flowers—flowers which could mean 'Thank you', 'Welcome home', 'Happy Birthday', 'Happy Anniversary' or 'Glad you have had a new baby'. They can say 'I'm sorry' if we have upset someone, or they can show sympathy to someone who is sad.

Flowers can often show people that we love or care for them. We often send or take flowers to people in hospital to say that we hope they will soon be well again.

Long ago, mother told them, people sometimes used a 'flower language'. Different flowers had special meanings. If pansies were sent, they were for 'thoughts'. Red roses meant 'love'.

'We don't use flower language in quite the same way now,' said Mum, 'but we still send flowers as messages to people so that they know we are thinking about them. It is sometimes nice to be able to "say it with flowers".'

In this way we are able to share some of the lovely things of this world with others.

## 2 WILD FLOWERS

The children were busily arranging some flowers in jars before they settled down to their morning's work. They had gathered them on their way to school. The hedges and fields were full of the colour of early summer flowers, bright red poppies, golden buttercups and lots of others too.

Mrs. Bradshaw, their teacher, encouraged the children to keep the jars filled with fresh wild flowers and leaves they had gathered. As she did so, she thought of the children in her previous school. How nice it would be if they could see and enjoy all these beautiful flowers. But her previous school had been in a big city where there were no hills and fields, woods and hedgerows. Instead there were dusty roads, blocks of flats, brick buildings and factories. They were missing so much of this lovely country. They would not have seen the bluebells and primroses of springtime nor the sweet-scented honeysuckle just coming into bloom.

It just so happened that, whilst Mrs. Bradshaw was thinking about them, those same children in the city school were setting out to see what they could find. How many wild flowers were growing in those city streets? With their teacher and some parents they were going to explore. Each had a bag into which to put any 'treasures' they might find. They were told what to do. They must keep with the grown-ups; they mustn't step into the road; and they must listen to what they were told.

They were surprised at the number of flowers they could find. There was a dandelion between the paving stones and some willow-herb growing in the gutter which hadn't been swept lately. Some yellow ragwort was there at the foot of an old brick wall. In fact, wherever there was the tiniest patch of earth, there seemed to be a plant which had made it its home.

But the best find of all was on the patch which was known as 'the debris'. The building that had stood there was knocked down long ago, leaving old bricks and cement blocks which had become partly covered with earth. Grass had covered some of it, but among the grass and the rubble were ragwort, thistles, bindweed, daisies, buttercups and lots of other plants too. Soon the children were scrambling from place to place, gathering flowers to put in their bags.

Back in school, they put their finds in jars of water. What a lot there were! Some were plants they would not have noticed. Yet, there in the city streets, they were just waiting to be found.

What a wonderful world ours is, where, even in the most unlikely places, God is able to show us something of the beauty he has created!

3  GARDENS

Father was very busy in the garden. He liked to spend as much time as he could working there so that it was always neat and tidy with lovely flowers to enjoy. Sometimes the children helped him. Sarah and Paul did what they could but not as much as their big brother, John, who was much stronger than they were.

Mr. Digby was very proud of his garden. He had planned it so that there were lots of things to see. Each part of it was different. In one corner there was a fishpond with a rockery behind it. He could switch on an electric pump which made water run in three little waterfalls and back into the pond. The rockery was covered in small plants, many of them with white, yellow or purple flowers.

Nearby were the flower beds, with plants of different heights—large ones near the walls and smaller ones in front of them. Small plants with lots of flowers grew in the border. From Father the children began to learn a lot about flowers. Some grew best in sunny places; others preferred the shade. Some needed special care.

The children had their own patches of garden, where they could plant whatever kind of flowers they wished. Then they had to take care of them. They had to weed the garden and keep it watered. If it were not cared for it would spoil the look of the whole garden.

Mr. Digby stopped pulling up weeds, stretched himself because his back was aching a little, and stood still for a moment. Yes! His garden looked good and he was feeling very pleased with himself. There was so much colour and such a lovely scent. He was thankful that he had a garden to share with his family and any visitors who came to his home.

Father liked to share his garden in other ways too. It was very nice to be able to pick a bunch of flowers to take to old Mrs. Green up the road and to Miss Walker who was not very well and had no garden of her own. 'Gardens are for sharing,' he would often tell people. 'We mustn't keep God's lovely things to ourselves.'

Most people enjoy gardens and flowers, even though they cannot have a garden of their own. Mr. Digby often took the children to the local park where they had some lovely gardens. Whole beds of the same kind of flower were a blaze of colour and were changed by the gardeners as soon as the flowers began to die. There was a large flower bed made to look like the town's coat-of-arms (badge) all in flowers. There was even a clock made from flowers and its hands moved.

Those gardeners were always busy, giving pleasure to lots and lots of people.

## 4   GARDENS OF ALL KINDS

Not everyone has a garden but lots of those who do not have one still like growing plants and flowers. So we find 'gardens' in all sorts of places. Even in the middle of a city there are often little gardens which are ablaze with colour.

Many of these 'gardens' are not even on the ground. They are set on window ledges high above the ground where the flowers can be enjoyed by people in offices who see them through the window and by people in the streets who look up at them.

Many people who live in blocks of flats also have window boxes or tubs standing on the verandas of their flats. Some of them, no doubt, had gardens of their own once upon a time and enjoyed the flowers. Now they have no garden, they want to do the best they can to brighten their home. Hanging baskets, fastened to the balcony above, look very pretty and climbing plants can grow up a trellis or brighten up some old railings.

Nowadays people in many towns like to make their streets as bright as possible and plant flowers in flower beds by the roadside or even in old horse troughs. These were put there many years ago to provide water for the horses that pulled heavy carts. Now there are few horses the troughs have been filled with earth and are full of blossom in gay colours.

Sometimes we find that gardens have been planted on railway stations to make them more colourful. The men who work at the station, porters and ticket collectors, look after the gardens, which are enjoyed, not only by people using the station, but by passengers on the trains which pass through.

Some schools are lucky enough to have gardens. They may not be very big but they can be very enjoyable. The children like making their own gardens, planting the seeds or the plants which they may have been able to bring from home.

In one city a school had no garden at all. Then some old houses were knocked down and large blocks of flats built in their place. These children had no gardens of their own but a piece of the old street next to the school was left empty. The Head teacher thought it would be nice if the children could have a garden. Permission was given to use the street. Some earth was brought and tipped there. Soon the children were growing not only flowers but vegetables as well. That garden gave lots of pleasure to lots and lots of children.

That, after all, is what gardens are for—to give pleasure to people as they enjoy the beauties of the world and especially those beauties they have helped to make themselves.

## 5  UNUSUAL PLANTS

One day Mr. Digby called Sarah to him and gave her a lovely posy of sweet peas, carefully wrapped in a piece of coloured paper.

'Be a dear and take these along the road to old Mrs. Green: she will enjoy a few flowers,' he told her.

Sarah did not need asking twice. She liked to take flowers to Mrs. Green because the old lady always seemed so pleased to have them. Soon she was standing outside Mrs. Green's house.

'Do come in,' said Mrs. Green. 'Sweet peas! Aren't they lovely? My favourite flowers. Now you *must* come and see my own special flower.'

She took Sarah into her living room and there, on the window ledge, was one of the brightest of flowers. It was brilliant red with white things hanging inside and it was growing on one of the oddest plants Sarah had ever seen.

'What is it?' Sarah asked.

'It's a cactus,' Mrs. Green told her. 'Some of them are ugly plants but have such pretty flowers. Look! I have lots of different kinds!'

Sarah reached out to touch one of them—and wished she hadn't done so. It had sharp prickles, one of which stuck in her finger and made a drop of blood appear. She wasn't sure that a cactus was a very nice plant.

Mrs. Green told her to look closely at the cactus plants. There were lots of different ones. They come from hot countries and have to be kept indoors. They grow very slowly in dry sandy soil and do not need watering too much. Some cactus plants grow very tall. Perhaps you have seen pictures of them in cowboy films.

Sarah was interested in some of Mrs. Green's other plants too. They were all indoor plants which came originally from hot lands. 'One of these days you must go to visit those special gardens where they have a lot of strange plants that grow only in hot lands. Some are very interesting. There is one that catches and eats flies.'

Sarah wasn't sure that she liked plants that ate insects and she was still thinking about it on the way home when she thought she had been attacked by a plant. She had rubbed against a stinging nettle and soon her leg had a patch of white blisters. She wasn't very happy when she arrived home but Dad had the answer. He found a dock leaf which he rubbed on the blisters. Soon all was well. Dock plants often grow near nettles. There are lots of other plants, too, which can be used to help make us well and some of them grow in our own gardens. How wonderfully God made our world.

What a lot of interesting things we can learn about some of the unusual plants around us.

6  BLOSSOM

By the roadside a sign read 'Blossom Trail' and there was an arrow to show which way to go. This was in Kent in springtime, when the fruit trees are covered with blossom and look so beautiful. There are many people who will travel a long way to take this 'Blossom Trail' and see hundreds and hundreds of trees, all a mass of pink or white blossom.

In springtime, the blossom on the fruit trees can be seen in many parts of the country. Cherry, apple and pear trees are found in orchards and gardens. Many people have flowering almond trees which they grow just so they can enjoy the blossom. It is not on the tree for long. Soon the petals fall to make a colourful carpet under the tree. As the wind blows the white cherry or pear blossom away, it looks almost like a snowstorm.

Once the blossom has fallen not much remains. There is just the small centre of the flower, but that is the beginnings of the fruit and, later in the year, the tree will be laden with apples, pears or cherries.

The blossom is one of the signs of spring, reminding us of the bright, warm weather we shall soon have. Soon there is blossom on other trees too. Laburnum trees with their bright yellow flowers look very colourful.

One tree which can easily be recognized is the Horse Chestnut. Big candle-like clusters of blossom grow very quickly until the tree has lots and lots of them. In time the blossom drops and the fruit begins to grow. It is not a fruit like an apple or pear that you can eat but it is one that is of especial interest to boys. It is a shiny green fruit with spikes on it and it is one you would not like to eat. But, when it falls from the tree, this green case bursts open and inside are the shiny brown conkers that we love to play with.

Many smaller trees and shrubs have beautiful flowers too. In gardens and parks we can often see beautiful azaleas and rhododendrons, with flowers that are so lovely. Even with the largest paint box in the world we should find it difficult to copy all the colours.

What a wonderful plan there must have been for the world. Often when we make pictures the colours do not seem to go well together. Yet in the world of nature all the greens of the leaves and the colours of the flowers seem to fit together so perfectly that we can always enjoy the sight.

## 7  TREES

What would you say is the largest or tallest living thing in the world? An elephant? A giraffe? A whale?

You would be wrong. These may be the largest or tallest animals but the largest and tallest living thing is a tree. Not only are some trees the biggest things alive, they are also the oldest. There are trees which are hundreds of years old and they will probably continue to grow for many years more unless they are cut down by people who want to use the wood of the tree for making something they need. We use wood to make lots of things for our homes.

But trees are useful in other ways too. A tree in blossom is something beautiful to enjoy. The fruit or nuts of the tree give us food. On a hot day the leaves of the tree give us some welcome shade. When the wind blows cold we can find protection against the trunk of the tree.

They are good for games too. How many of you have played hide-and-seek among the trees? Or have used a tree as a wicket when playing ball games? Maybe you have used two trees as goal posts.

Lots of people have enjoyed climbing trees too. They like to get up into the branches to hide there or perhaps get a better view of what is happening below. In the Bible we read of a little man called Zacchaeus, who climbed a tree so that he could get a better view of Jesus when he passed. Some children have even had a tree house in their gardens. A platform built in the branches gave them somewhere to play or have a picnic.

It is not only boys who climb trees. Lots of animals do too. Perhaps you have watched a cat climb a tree. What other animals do? (Squirrels, monkeys, etc.) Some of these do not just climb the trees for fun. They do so because it is their home. They like the shelter of the leaves, the holes in the trunk and the food it provides. Squirrels not only eat nuts and acorns but chew at the bark as well.

Birds also like the trees. They build nests in the branches and sing their songs from the highest branches. Take a close look at a tree and you will be surprised how many smaller creatures have also made it home.

You can have lots of fun too in finding out all you can about trees—the shapes of the leaves, the different kinds of bark and those trees which give us some of things we need—rubber, cork, maple syrup, dates, figs.

Trees are very important to people!

## 8 FORESTS

'Come on, children.' Mr. Digby called out. 'It's time we were going or the day will be half gone.'

'Where are we going?' Paul asked.

'That's my surprise,' his father replied.

Soon they were driving away from home, through busy streets and out into the country. After half-an-hour they came to a notice which said 'PICNIC AREA'. Mr. Digby drove into the entrance, pulled up close to a table and seats made from tree branches. Soon they were enjoying the sandwiches and cakes that Mum had packed into their picnic basket. Sarah threw some of her bread crumbs to some cheeky little sparrows that had learned to expect food from · visitors to the forest.

'Come on.' Mr. Digby said. 'Let's go exploring!'

So they put all their things in the car and set off. Soon they were deep in the forest. Above them the leaves of the trees blocked off the sunlight and made the forest dark. Below their feet a thick carpet of dead leaves was soft and springy. Here and there small trees were growing. There were ferns and mosses and some toadstools which interested the children. 'Don't touch them'. Dad said. 'Some toadstools, like those, are poisonous.'

They were startled by a rustling noise nearby. It turned out to be a bird on the ground. Soon the children were watching out for all sorts of wild animals, birds and insects in the forest. It was a day that they enjoyed.

On the way home they were talking about forests. Mum explained that they were not all the same. Some forests were like the one they had been in with lots of different trees. Some were of one kind of tree, like pine or spruce, which had been specially planted so that one day they would give people the wood they needed.

In some cold parts of the world there are lots of these forests. In hot lands, jungles of big trees stretch for miles and miles and miles. The plants beneath the trees grow so thickly that people have to cut their way through them.

There are many stories told of adventures in forests. Some of these tales are very old, but nowhere near as old as the forests which have covered the world right from the beginning.

Forests, like so many other wonders of our world are places to be explored . . . and enjoyed.

RELATED THEMES

PRAYERS

1. All around us, our Father, we see so many flowers;
   Wild flowers growing in fields and hedgerows;
   Beautiful blooms in greenhouse and garden;
   Flowers that grow indoors or in window boxes;
   And even some we think of only as weeds.
   Thank you for their beauty;
   And thank you for letting us have it to enjoy. *Amen*

2. As the trees lift up their branches towards the sun, O God, help us to reach upward to receive the sunshine of your love. *Amen*

3. Dear God, we enjoy all the flowers and trees, which you have given us to make our world more lovely. Help us to look after them and all your gifts to us. *Amen*.

4. Dear God, we thank you for parks and gardens with so many beautiful flowers. Thank you, too, for all the gardeners who work so hard to bring us such pleasure. *Amen*

5. For the beauty around us, in the flowers and the whole world of creation, we praise your name, O God. *Amen*

6. Help us, O God, to remember those who are sad or lonely and to cheer them up by bringing some brightness into their lives. *Amen*

7. O God, our Father, thank you for trees:
   For all the enjoyment they give us;
   For their lovely shapes, their leaves and flowers;
   For great forests and woods that we can explore;
   For all the wild creatures that live in them:
   Thank you for all these things. *Amen*

8. Teach us, O God, how to enjoy our world;
   To keep our eyes open for lovely things;
   To look for beauty in unexpected places;
   And to know that these are your gifts to us. *Amen*

9. Thank you, dear God, for all the beautiful flowers that surround us. Keep us thankful for all your good gifts. *Amen*

10. Thank you, dear God, for gardens of all kinds, and for all those odd corners where we can find beautiful flowers. Teach us how to enjoy them all. *Amen*

11. We praise and thank you, God:
    For all the lovely flowers we can enjoy,
        *We praise and thank you, God;*
    For the wild flowers of the countryside,
        *We praise and thank you, God;*
    For the gorgeous flowers that grow in gardens,
        *We praise and thank you, God;*
    For the blossom of trees and bushes,
        *We praise and thank you, God;*
    For all you have given us, we praise you. *Amen*

12. When we think of all the lovely things you have given us, dear Father God, we ask that you will help us to share them with others. *Amen*

HYMNS SUGGESTED

A little child may know
All the flowers are waking
All things bright and beautiful
Daisies are our silver
God who made the earth
I have seen the golden sunshine
I love God's tiny creatures
I love my little garden
I love to play among the flowers
In our dear Lord's garden
Morning has broken
The flowers that grow in the garden
There are hundreds of sparrows
Think of a world without any people
'Tis good to see our Father's world

*Books*

FLOWERS/TREES *(Starters)*, Macdonald
LOOK AT FLOWERS/LOOK AT SEEDS AND WEEDS/
    LOOK AT TREES *(Starters Nature)*, Macdonald
WILD FLOWERS IN BRITAIN/TREES AND FORESTS
    *(Blackwell's Learning Library)*, Blackwell
GARDEN FLOWERS *(Nature Table)*, Evans
GARDENS AND FLOWERS *(Our World)*, Burke
HOW FLOWERS LIVE *(First Library)*, Macdonald
WE DISCOVER PLANTS *(We discover)*, Arnold
TREES *(Young Nature)*, Angus and Robertson
I AM A TREE *(Who am I?)*, Blackwell

*Stories*

Tell stories about gardens, flowers, forests and trees, e.g. Rumer
Godden: *An Episode of Sparrows.*

*Pictures*

Encourage the children to collect pictures of flowers. Seed
catalogues are a good source. Make a 'Flower Book' for the
classroom or a frieze cut from these pictures. Similar activities with
pictures of trees.

*Collecting*

Collections for the classroom: wild flowers for pressing; leaves;
skeleton leaves; pieces of bark; seeds.

*Rubbing*

Make leaf rubbings. Place leaf on table, vein side up. Hold paper firmly over it and rub with wax crayons. Bark rubbings with special wax rubbing sticks on paper held against tree trunk.

*Leaf art*

Leaves can be used in many ways for art forms.
1.. Draw round leaves, colour, cut out and mount.
2. Leaf prints. Paint vein side of leaf and press on paper.
3. Spatter prints (with older children), using paints and an old toothbrush to spatter round leaf.

*Growing things*

Work in school garden, planting and tending. Plant fruit stones and pips. Dates and acorns to be soaked for two days before planting, other pips one day. Keep moist. Put glass over pot and leave in a sunny place. Pips in damp cotton wool and refrigerated for two days sometimes get better results.

*Visits and visitors*

Arrange visits to parks and gardens. Look for any unusual gardens, window boxes, etc. Excursions into school environment to look for wild flowers and plant life. Visit to a forest or wood. Visitors to talk to children, e.g. gardener, park keeper, florist, forester.

# 19 Autumn

Seasonal themes are important ones in any primary school, where the natural world forms a basis of so much of the classroom work. The nature table is filled with all sorts of interesting exhibits and talk is about those things which can be observed especially at that time of year.

Autumn is the most colourful of the seasons, and the first in the school year. The changing colours of the leaves and the bright berries are easily observed. It is suggested that the theme might best be taken towards the end of October but this will vary a little from year to year and from one part of the country to another to get the fullest advantage from nature.

Certainly there will be lots of opportunities to observe the natural world in the school grounds, the neighbourhood and any local open spaces. It will be an opportunity to introduce the cycle of nature in this wonderful world of creation.

Preparations are also being made for winter—fires at home, stocking up on winter fuel, getting out the winter clothes and digging over the garden. The wild creatures too are preparing in all sorts of different ways.

The bonfires of fallen leaves and other plant refuse lead naturally to the bonfires of 5th November and the annual warnings of dangers from fire and fireworks which need to be given.

## 1 AUTUMN LEAVES AND COLOURS

The school caretaker was very busy in the playground sweeping lots of leaves into a pile in the corner. Just then there was a sudden gust of wind which blew them across the playground again. He stood with his hands on his hips, looked at all the leaves and sighed. Now he would have to do it all again. He would be glad when there were no more leaves to be swept up. It took such a lot of his time.

Just then Julie saw one very pretty leaf. 'Can I have that one, please?' she asked. 'You can have as many as you like,' she was told. 'I don't want them.'

So Julie clutched her leaf and took it into the classroom to show her teacher. 'Isn't this pretty,' she said. It had so many different colours in it. There were still touches of green here and there but most of it was a golden brown with deep red patches.

Her teacher took the leaf. 'It is such a pretty one that I think we should put it on our nature table so that we can all have a look at it.'

During the next few days the other children began to look for leaves too. There were all sorts of interesting leaves, some red, some brown, some golden, some yellow, and some that were still green.

'Why do the leaves fall off the trees when they are so pretty?' Julie asked her teacher.

She was told that autumn had come and that winter was on its way. During the winter the tree goes to sleep and does not need its leaves. After the winter it will grow new ones ready for the next summer. The leaves change colour because the sap, which is the tree's life-blood, has gone down into the roots and there is nothing to keep them alive. After they have changed colour, they drop off the tree.

Later that week the children went for a walk to the park, where they could see lots of trees that were no longer green but golden-brown and yellow and red. How lovely they looked.

Beneath the trees were the leaves that had already fallen. Some were picked up to be taken back to school. The others would form a carpet under the tree which would slowly rot away and put new goodness into the ground.

God's world is a wonderful world, in which everything has its use, even dead leaves.

## 2 SEEDS

As George sat at his desk in the classroom, he saw a little ball of fluff blow in through the open window. Slowly it drifted towards his desk. Suddenly George grabbed at the ball of fluff but he missed it. His hand had moved the air and made it dance out of his way. It was just as though it said, 'You can't catch me!'

This time George watched. Slowly it dropped until it landed right on his desk. He looked at it carefully. It was a little brown object in the middle of a ball of whiskers. His teacher told him that it was a seed from a flower. It had all those whiskers so that the wind would carry it away to find a place where it would grow. Of course it wouldn't grow on George's desk. It had gone the wrong way. It should have landed somewhere in the earth. Then it would have stayed in the earth through the winter ready to grow next year.

Teacher explained that lots of plants had ways of sending their seeds far enough away from them to have room to grow. The children went outside to look at the plants that were in the school garden. During the summer it had looked very beautiful. There had been some giant sunflowers, some pretty-coloured lupins and lots of other bright flowers. Now the sunflower had no petals, the lupins had only black seed-pods and the pretty flowers were all dead.

The children could see all the seeds in the 'face' of the sunflowers and they looked carefully when teacher showed them the lupins. Some of the seed-pods were empty but she nipped the end of one that still had the seeds in. Suddenly it burst open, twisted and threw the seeds out as it did so. 'That is another way plants scatter their seeds,' she told them.

During the next few days the children collected lots of different seeds for the nature table. There were several kinds that were carried by the wind, some of them having a little hairy parachute. There were big oval seeds from the sunflowers, curly ones from the marigolds and hollyhocks, tiny little round ones from the poppies and bigger ones from the sweet-peas.

Some they could not recognize. The children who brought them did not know which plants they had come from.

'The only way we could find out what they are is to plant them next year and see what grows,' teacher said. 'All these seeds are God's way of making sure there will always be plenty of plants and lovely flowers for us to enjoy. We must remember to say Thank you to God for the flowers we have enjoyed this year and the seeds to give us more next year.'

3 FRUITS AND NUTS

On their way to school, Betty and Tony stopped to watch some older boys playing conkers. They each had a conker on the end of a piece of string and were taking it in turn to swing their conker to see if they could hit the other person's conker and break it. Each time a conker was broken, they took another one out of their pocket, threaded the string through a hole they had made in the middle of it and started another game. 'Mine's a niner,' said one of the boys, meaning that his conker had broken nine others.

There were some conkers on the nature table in the classroom. Some of the children had found them under the horse-chestnut tree. Near them were some acorns, some of them still in their little cups. These are the seeds of the oak tree. The sycamore seeds were also interesting. They had wings so that the wind would carry them away. Trees and bushes have seeds just as the flowers do and they are all different.

Some of them have very hard cases. Do you like nuts? Perhaps you have them at Christmas. Dad may get out the nut crackers and crack the shells so that you can eat the soft nut inside. Some of these nuts, like Brazil nuts, come from other countries but there are trees in Britain which have smaller nuts. Perhaps you can find some beech nuts or hazel nuts.

Another thing you will expect to see at Christmas is some holly with its bright red berries. These berries are the holly seeds. There are lots of bushes that have bright red berries and you will see some bushes in autumn that are covered with red berries—small ones on the hawthorn and larger ones on the wild roses. There are bunches of round black berries on the elder and larger bluish sloes on the blackthorn. If you squash these berries you will find seeds inside.

Perhaps the berries you like best are the ones you can eat. Don't try eating *any* kind of berry. Some are not very nice and could harm you. But beneath the trees and in the hedgerows, late in the summer, you have probably found some nice juicy blackberries to eat or to take home for Mum to use in a pie. And don't forget, too, that the birds enjoy all sorts of berries. You will often see them having a feast in autumn. They also help to carry the seeds to where they will grow.

So we say thank God for fruit and nuts to eat, for feeding the birds and even for the fun we can have with conkers—all part of the great world of nature that he has given us.

4 PREPARING FOR WINTER

Before you came to school this morning you probably had a good breakfast. No doubt you will have lunch, tea and supper as well before you go to bed at night. There is always enough in the pantry, and the freezer, and plenty more in the shops.

Suppose someone were to tell you that there would be no food in a few weeks' time! What would you do? Most people would go to buy all they could so that they would not go hungry. There are some animals that spend the autumn gathering and storing food so that they will not go hungry in winter. Squirrels do this. No one tells them that there will be no food in winter. They just know. That is the way they are made.

Squirrels are fond of nuts and there are lots of these in the woods in autumn. So, if you live anywhere where there are squirrels, perhaps you will see them busily looking for nuts and other things which they like to eat, then picking them up and carrying them to a little hidey-hole, where they will be safely stored for the days when there are no nuts to be found.

There are lots of birds, too, that know there will be no food in winter. They feed on insects, which will either have died or hidden themselves away. So, in autumn, you will see these birds gathering for a long flight across the sea to warmer countries, where there are plenty of insects still to be found.

Some insects, of course, also store for the winter. Bees are very busy during the summer collecting nectar from the flowers to take back to the hives. A lot of this is eaten by other bees but some of it is stored away.

Autumn, then, is a time when lots of creatures work hard to prepare for the future. I wonder how much we do that? You can probably think of preparations that are being made at home. Is Mum busy knitting, getting out the winter woollies or finding extra blankets? Has Dad built up the woodpile or got in a stock of fuel to warm the house?

But there is another way in which we all have to prepare, not just for winter, but for our whole lives. Are we storing up all the knowledge we can so that we shall be able to live full and useful lives?

5 HIBERNATION

Do you like the cold wintry weather? Or do you sometimes wish you could go to bed when the weather gets cold and stay there until the springtime, when you could wake up to enjoy the warm sunshine again? There are lots of living creatures that do go to sleep for the winter.

If you keep a tortoise as a pet, you will be able to watch what it does. During the summer months it spends its days basking in the sun or wandering around looking for food. As the days get shorter and the sun is not so hot, you will find that it does not move around as much as it did and it does not seem very interested in food. If it has the run of the garden, you may find that it begins to bury itself in the earth for the night. Tortoises can bury themselves completely in the earth so that they cannot be seen and are protected from the winter frosts.

Most people who keep tortoises as pets keep an eye on them in autumn. When tortoises look as though they are ready to go to sleep they are put into boxes of straw and kept in a shed or a cellar, where they will be protected from the cold.

There are lots of other animals which go to sleep for the winter. Dormice curl up in cosy little nests that they make for themselves. Toads hide themselves away in odd corners and frogs will not be seen in the ponds until spring comes again. Some insects, the bees and flies that we see early in springtime, have also slept all through the winter so that they are ready to visit the first spring flowers.

There are many insects which never see the winter at all. They live through the warm summer and die before winter comes. Those that do go to sleep make sure that the world of nature carries on next year. God has made lots of different creatures to share our world and it is very interesting to learn about the way they live.

6  AFTER THE HARVEST

If you live in the country or visit the country you will know that it is always changing. In springtime many of the fields are green with growing crops. In summer the corn turns from green to a golden brown and large machines move into the fields to harvest the grain. All that is left is the stubble—the short stalks that still stand up in the earth. You may have seen black smoke rising from these fields as the farmers set fire to the stubble. The ashes that are left behind will be ploughed into the ground to help next year's crops grow.

At harvest time the farmer is kept very busy from early morning until late at night. It is very important to gather in the harvest at the right time or the crop may be spoilt. But, once the harvest is in, he cannot just sit back and take it easy. There is much to be done to make sure that there is another crop next year.

Soon the farmer is ploughing the fields. In days gone by he used one or two horses to pull his plough. Nowadays he uses a tractor, which is much stronger and can pull a much larger plough. A plough has one or more blades which cut into the earth and turn it over. Each row of earth that is turned over is called a furrow. Most ploughs cut several furrows at once.

As the farmer ploughs his fields he is usually followed by a lot of birds. Gulls are often there in large numbers. They enjoy the farmer doing his work because as he turns over the earth, they can find lots of worms and insects that they like to eat. You will see how quickly they swoop on anything that will make a tasty meal.

For the rest of autumn and through the winter many of the fields will be brown. Nothing is growing. Much of the seed for the new crops has not been planted. But that does not mean nothing is happening. The remains of old crop that were ploughed in are rotting away to make the soil richer. The broken ground is left for the frost to get into it and this helps prepare it for the next year's crops.

Those brown fields, which look so uninteresting in autumn, will one day be green again as the new crops begin to grow. God's world of nature is always changing.


## 7  HALLOWEEN

It is a good thing sometimes to remember men and women who have done very good things to help others or to make our world a better place. Some of these are people whom we call saints. In the church each of these saints is remembered on one special day. So St. Peter is remembered each year on 29th June, St. Matthew on 21st September and St. Luke on 18th October.

But there is one day in the year when *all* saints are remembered and that is 1st November. It is called All Saints' Day or All Hallows and it has always been considered a very holy day.

Long ago, people used to believe that there were all sorts of evil spirits in the world. They believed in witches who could cast spells on people and animals. They believed in fairies and goblins, some of which did bad things. Because All Saints' Day was so holy, no one believed that these bad people and spirits would dare to do anything on that day. They would, therefore, be especially busy on the evening before All Hallows, known as Hallowe'en.

So Hallowe'en became a night to be feared by some people. They would light bonfires in their farmyards to keep evil spirits away from their animals. Sometimes they would march round those brown fields shouting, singing, stamping and making all the noise they could to drive away evil spirits. As they walked they carried blazing torches of fire.

But there were lots of other things to do on Hallowe'en which were much more fun. In some places people made lanterns, called Punkies, out of large turnips. The inside was cut away and a face cut in the turnip. A candle inside shone through the holes.

Children in some parts of the country still make punkies today. People enjoy Hallowe'en parties, when they decorate their halls and rooms with witches and cats, spiders and bats, and all sorts of other things which remind them of those old beliefs.

It is nice to know that we do not need to be afraid of evil spirits. It is also a good thing to remember people who have done so much to help us to know about God and to make our world a better place.

## 8  BONFIRES AND FIREWORKS

At the beginning of November, lots of children get excited about the things that will be happening on 5th November. No doubt most children know what we call that evening. (Bonfire Night . . . Guy Fawkes Night . . .)

It is the night when many people build bonfires and enjoy themselves by letting off fireworks. Nowadays there are some people who have their fireworks on other days near 5th November instead of on the actual day. The nearest Saturday is sometimes chosen.

But why 5th November? It was on that date, in the year 1605, that a group of men plotted to blow up the Houses of Parliament when the King was there. They put some barrels of gunpowder in the cellars and one of them, a man named Guy Fawkes, stayed there so that he could light the fuse that would explode the gunpowder. But someone told of the plan and Guy Fawkes was discovered before he could light the fuse. He was taken prisoner and the King was safe.

From that year people wanted to show how pleased they were that the King and Parliament had been saved. So they lit bonfires and made a lot of noise by making small explosions with fireworks.

Nowadays we have lots of different kinds of firework. Which are your favourites? Those you can hold in your hand, that give out a shower of sparkling lights? Jumping crackers that hop from place to place? Bangers? Roman candles that shoot coloured lights into the air? Catherine wheels that sparkle as they turn? Rockets that burst high in the sky? There are so many to choose from.

Whichever kind we have can be dangerous if they are not handled properly and so it is very important to read the instructions on the firework and to do only what is written there. Every year, lots of children have to go to hospital on Bonfire Night because they have not been sensible with their fireworks or their bonfires.

It is very nice to be able to enjoy ourselves but we have to take care that we do nothing that could harm us or hurt anyone or anything else.

OTHER AUTUMN CELEBRATIONS

Fairs. Michaelmas, 29th September
Nottingham Goose Fair, first Thursday in October.
All Saints' Day, 1st November.
State Opening of Parliament, early November.
London: Lord Mayor's Show, on or near 9th November.
Remembrance Sunday, second Sunday in November.
St. Andrew's Day (Patron Saint of Scotland), 30th November.
St. Nicholas (Santa Claus), feast day, 6th December.
Nobel Prize Day, 10th December.

AUTUMN DAYS

Harvest's gathered; fields are bare;
Nuts and berries here and there;
Squirrels nutting; swallows fly;
Smoky bonfires; misty sky;
Autumn colours—browns and gold;
Warmer clothing—days grow cold;
Leaves are falling; frosts appear;
Put the clocks back! Winter's near.                    R.P.

**PRAYERS**

1. At Hallowe'en, dear God, we think about all sorts of spooky and nasty things. Thank you that we need never be afraid of them because you, our Father, care for us and watch over us. *Amen*

2. Dear Father God, we thank you for all the beauties of autumn, for the lovely colours of the trees and the bright red berries. Help us to enjoy your beautiful world. *Amen*

3. Dear God, I enjoy bonfires and fireworks.
   I like the warmth that comes from the fire
   on a chilly autumn night.
   I like the colours of the fireworks;
   The rockets that burst high in the sky;
   Spinning Catherine wheels and jumping crackers;
   And those that make a loud bang.
   Thank you for fires, fireworks and fun. *Amen*

4. Dear God, when I come to school, I like kicking the leaves that are lying on the ground. I like to hear them rustling round my feet. I like to pick up a handful and throw them in the air, too! I like leaves. Thank you for letting me enjoy them. *Amen*

5. For the season of autumn,
   *We thank you, God our Father;*
   For pale sunshine and misty mornings,
   *We thank you, God our Father;*
   For ripening fruits and falling leaves,
   *We thank you, God our Father;*
   For golden leaves and bright red berries,
   *We thank you, God our Father;*
   For giving us such a lovely world,
   *We thank you, God our Father;*
   As we remember your goodness, give us grateful hearts. *Amen*

6. O God, the days are getting a bit colder now that summer has passed. We need to put on warmer clothes to keep out the chill. Thank you for warm clothes and for those who bought them for us. *Amen*

7. On these chilly days, dear Father God, we say thank you for the warmth of our homes and the care of our parents. *Amen*

8. Thank you, God our Father
   For all that we can enjoy in autumn;
   For the lovely colouring of the trees;
   For acorns, conkers and nuts of different kinds;
   For fruits and berries on brambles and bushes;
   For falling leaves that rustle as we walk;
   For the birds we like to watch
   And animals getting ready for winter.
   For all these things and all your blessings
   Thank you, God, our Father. *Amen*

9. Thank you, Lord, for fruits, berries and nuts—food for our friends the animals and birds; and thank you for your care for them and us. *Amen*

10. We are thinking today, O God, of lots of animals that are getting ready for winter. Thank you for teaching them how to look after themselves when the cold weather comes and there is not much food for them to find. Thank you, too, for teaching us what we should do and how we should live. *Amen*

11. When we look at the bare fields and the leafless trees, help us to remember, dear God, that they are not dead but storing up new life that we shall see when winter is past. *Amen*

12. When we look at tiny seeds, O God, it is hard to understand how these can become lovely flowers or large trees but we do know that they are part of the wonderful world you have made and we say thank you for all the marvellous things you have put into it. *Amen*

Autumn leaves are falling down
Blackberries in the hedges
For the golden corn
Frost and snow
Look for signs that summer's done
O lovely world of colour
We praise thee for the sun

[*see also the hymns suggested in the 'Harvest' section*]

INTEREST WORK AND ACTIVITIES

*Books*

Here is a small selection of books suitable for the classroom book corner.

AUTUMN DAYS *(First Stories)*, Macdonald
A BOOK FOR AUTUMN, Wheaton
MY AUTUMN BOOK, Chatto
AUTUMN *(Nature Table)*, Evans
OBSERVE AND DISCOVER IN AUTUMN *(Observe and Discover)*, Macmillan
LEAVES *(Leaders)*, Ladybird
THE SQUIRREL/THE HEDGEHOG *(Animal World)*, Macdonald
SQUIRRELS/HEDGEHOGS *(Young Naturalist)*, Wayland
THE SQUIRREL/THE HEDGEHOG *(Eye View)*, Angus & Robertson
FARMER BARNES' GUY FAWKES DAY, Deutsch

*Songs and poems*

Find and learn some simple songs and poems about autumn.

266

*Collecting*

Collect leaves of all colours, shapes and sizes for display on the nature table or for mounting.

Make a collage of leaves.

Press some of the most colourful leaves and later mount in a book with names of leaves.

Collect seeds, ears of corn, grains of corn, burrs, seed cases, nuts and other 'finds' which can be displayed or used for craft work. Interesting designs and pictures can be made by gluing such things to stiff paper and spraying with gold paint.

Collect such things as poppy-heads, teasels and reed-mace that can be used for decoration when dry.

Encourage children to bring in acorns and conkers, which can be used for craft activities and also for weighing and counting.

*Acorn and conker craft*

Make acorn men. A large acorn for the body and a smaller one with cap for head. Join with piece of matchstick. Matchstick arms and legs. Make animals too.

A conker spider in web. Choose small round flat conker. Push about six long pins, evenly spaced, into conker. Wind white cotton, twisting round each pin in turn until web is complete. Put two small pins for the eyes of the spider in her web.

Conker furniture. A small flat conker with four pins for legs will make a chair or stool. Pins with woven cotton or wool for back of chair. A large flat conker for a table.

*Hallowe'en*

Make decorations of witches, cats, bats and spiders to be suspended on black thread or as mobiles.

Make masks and witches' hats.

Hollow out a large turnip, cut face and put candle inside for a 'punkie'.

*Guy Fawkes Night*

Make a frieze or collage of bonfire and fireworks.

Pictures with crayon and paint. Make a Guy Fawkes Night picture with wax crayons, particularly of bonfire and fireworks. Wash over with thin black paint so that whole paper is covered. The wax will not hold the paint and will stand out giving a night scene.

# 20 Winter

*In the cycle of nature winter is the time when the world is asleep yet developing in readiness for the coming of spring. Yet in many ways it is an exhilarating season, with lots of excitement for children, especially at Christmastime but also with the first falls of snow.*

*Whilst this theme may be taken before Christmas, it is anticipated that it is more likely to be appropriate in the early part of the year when frost and snow are most usually experienced and warm homes most welcome. Christmas itself is not a part of this theme: it appears later in the book.*

*We attempt here to bring to the attention of the children the wonder and beauty of the season. Glittering frost and snow do indeed present a winter wonderland. There is plenty of fun to be had outdoors and in. Warm homes and clothing are all part of the winter scene. So, too, are thoughts for the elderly, who face hardship in winter and for the birds which need feeding.*

*All seasons demand thoughtfulness but perhaps winter more than most.*

## 1 SNOW AND SNOWFLAKES

When the two boys awoke one winter morning there was a strange kind of quiet: everything seemed still and hushed. Roger slipped out of bed and peeped out through the curtains.

'Look!' he exclaimed excitedly. 'Snow!'

In no time at all, Colin had joined him at the window. Overnight, it seemed, the whole world had changed. It was a world of dazzling whiteness in the pale morning sunshine. Snow covered the road, the hedges and the trees. Roofs, telephone wires, cars, and the pillar box along the road, all wore a cap of white snow.

They could hardly wait to get outside. There was no difficulty or fuss about getting up, washing and dressing. As soon as breakfast was over, they put on warm clothing and boots, then rushed out into the snow.

They loved the crunchy feel of their boots in the crisp snow and were glad they were making the first footprints. Well! Not quite. Some birds had already left their tiny footprints here and there but, apart from that, the snow was untouched.

The boys were pleased it was Saturday. They had plenty of time to enjoy the snow. They made snowballs and threw them at each other. Then they made a snowman and dressed him in an old hat and scarf of Dad's. He had two pieces of coal for eyes and a bright orange carrot for a nose.

As they sat indoors later that morning having a nice hot drink, they asked about the snow. Where had it come from and why had it come so suddenly in the night?

Mum explained that the cold wind from the north had brought the snow. She told them about the snowflakes—millions of them carried by the wind and every one different from all the others. Just imagine all those different shapes. 'If you were to look at them under a microscope,' Mum told them, 'you would see that each one is a complete pattern, very beautifully shaped.'

Later that day the snow did not look as attractive as it had in the morning. Traffic on the roads had churned it into a dirty brown slush. People on the pavements had trodden it down so that it was icy and slippery. In the country, snowdrifts make travelling difficult but the snow remains white, marked mainly by the footprints of wild creatures looking for food or shelter.

Snow can be beautiful and enjoyable but it does bring hardship. We remember that some of our friends may have come from hot lands and they find it cold and uncomfortable. We may have fun with the snow and enjoy our snowballs, but there are children who are made unhappy when snow is thrown at them.

We need always to be thoughtful and considerate towards others.

## 2  FROST AND ICE

Jack Frost had been very busy during the night. When Roger and Colin woke up, they found patterns in frost on their windows. These were much more beautiful than any patterns we make ourselves.

It was very, very cold and the boys lost no time in getting their clothes on, after having been nice and warm in bed. Jack Frost gets busy when it is too cold for snow. Wherever there is any water, even tiny drops of moisture, it becomes frozen and changes into ice. The patterns on the window are made from moisture that has formed there from inside. If you breathe on a cold window, you can see for yourself how it makes a kind of mist on the glass.

The boys went to school that morning well wrapped up in their warm clothing and scarves. They had to walk very carefully because the path was very, very slippery. When they passed the pond, they noticed that it was completely covered in ice. The ducks were standing on the ice and unable to get at their food. A man was there already, with some bread that he threw so that they would not go hungry.

'Let's go on the pond!' Colin exclaimed.

'No!' said Roger. 'You remember what Mum has said. Never go on the ice unless she says so. You can never be sure how thick the ice is and thin ice can be dangerous. Lots of people have been drowned when the ice has given way beneath them.'

When they reached school, Roger and Colin discovered that some boys had made a slide in the playground. It was very slippery. They ran to the slippery part and then slid as far as they could. Roger tried it and slid quite a long way. Then Colin had a go but fell over and banged his head. He wasn't very happy.

Just then the caretaker came out and put some salt on the slide to melt the ice. Slides can be fun but they can also be dangerous. Anyone treading unexpectedly on the ice can hurt himself badly if he slips. It is especially important to think of old people, who cannot keep their balance as we can. Motorists, too, do not like ice because it makes their cars skid on the roads and perhaps cause an accident.

The patterns made by the frost, and the icicles that hang from the gutters, can be very beautiful. Sliding on the ice can be great fun. But always we need to remember those who face hardship because of the ice and we must think of them more than we think of our own fun and games.

### 3 WINTER GAMES

Roger and Colin had been playing with their friends on the way home from school. It had been lots of fun throwing snowballs at each other and they had made one very large snowball by rolling it along in the snow until it was larger than a football. By the time they reached home their fingers were tingling with the cold, which had gone right through their gloves. Roger was feeling rather uncomfortable too. One of the other boys had put some snow down his neck. The other boy thought it was funny but Roger didn't. '*He* wouldn't have liked it if I had done it to *him*!' he complained.

Mum made them a nice hot drink to warm them up and told them not to put their hands where it was hot or they would ache. It was far better that they should warm up slowly.

They had a special visitor at home. Whilst they had been at school, Great-grandmother had arrived to spend a few days. She was their mother's grandmother and she seemed very, very old. In fact they liked listening to some of the things she would tell them about the time when she was their age—back in 'the olden days'.

Great-gran had been one of a very large family. She had eight brothers and three sisters, so there were plenty of things to do together. 'We didn't have some of the games that you play,' she told them. 'We did have Draughts, Ludo, Snakes and Ladders and Happy Families. We played Snap and we enjoyed doing jig-saw puzzles. But we didn't have much money and so lots of the games we played were ones we made for ourselves. There were lots of things we could play indoors on cold evenings.'

'We had outdoor games, too, to keep us warm in winter. We played some games like you do and some that children do not play now. We enjoyed bowling hoops along the road and controlling them with a hook. We used to skip, sometimes with our own ropes and some-times with a long rope. We used to take it in turn to turn the rope for others to skip and we had rhymes and chants to go with it. One we often said, as the rope turned, was "Salt, mustard, vinegar, pepper". We had lots of fun playing "He" and other running games.'

'But on days like this,' Great-gran said as she looked out of the window, 'my brothers made a sledge and we went sliding down the hills. It was grand to rush down the slope on it.'

The boys looked at Dad. 'All right,' he said with a smile, 'I'll see if I can make you one tomorrow.'

Great-gran went to the door to see them off next afternoon. She smiled. 'Just the kind of sledge my brothers made for us in the olden days,' she muttered. 'Some things don't change!'

## 4 WARM HOMES

Roger and Colin were sitting at the table playing games when Dad came home from work.

'Hello, Dad,' they called out to him.

'Hello, boys,' he replied. 'You're in the right place tonight.'

It was a cold blustery night. The north wind was howling round the trees and chimney pots. It seemed to find every little crack round the doors and windows as though it were trying to say, 'You can't keep me out!'

Dad took off his big coat and scarf, changed his jacket for a comfortable jumper, and sat in his favourite armchair by the fire, where he took off his outdoor shoes and put on some warm slippers. Then he rubbed his hands together, lay back in the chair and said, 'Ee! There's nothing like a nice blazing fire on a cold winter's night!'

The blazing fire was something the family enjoyed on the really cold evenings. Usually they had an electric fire to warm their living room but, as winter approached, Dad always made sure that he had a good supply of logs in the woodpile outside the back door. There was something rather pleasant about the warmth of the fire, with its flames curling round the logs and the smoke rising up the chimney. Sometimes the family would look into the fire to see whether it made any interesting shapes or pictures as it burned.

'I'm glad I'm not an animal or a bird,' Roger remarked. 'I wouldn't like to have to be outside tonight. How do they keep warm?'

Dad explained that they had to find what shelter they could. Many animals make snug little nests in which they can snuggle down and some of them sleep right through the cold winter. Birds try to find a sheltered place to roost and fluff up their feathers, which helps keep them warmer.

'Man is much more fortunate,' Dad went on. 'He has learned how to make warm homes. He learned how to chop down trees to burn; he found coal under the ground and dug it out; and he discovered how to make electricity. Nowadays many homes have central heating so that the whole house is always warm.'

'We are fortunate,' Dad told them. 'Heating the home costs a lot of money but I have a good job and can pay the bills. There are lots of people, especially old people, who do not have much money, and they are the ones who really need to keep warm. Think about them on these cold nights.'

The boys did—and they began to wonder whether there was some way they could help old people to keep warm.

## 5 EVERGREENS

Colin came into his bedroom just as Mum was tidying up. She had put a few of his books in a neat pile and was clearing up some bits and pieces that had been left lying here and there. She picked up the remains of a sprig of holly that had been left after Christmas.

'It's a wonder you haven't had the goblins after you,' she said with a smile.

'I don't believe in goblins.' Colin replied.

'You probably would have done if you had lived in the olden days,' Mother told him. 'People used to believe in all sorts of things like that. They believed that the goblins would be after anyone who still had Christmas greenery in the house after 2nd February. In those days people did not have coloured chains and other Christmas decorations like the ones we have today. They used to decorate their homes with green leaves, which looked nice until they began to die and turn brown.'

Colin thought of the greenery they had used in their home. There was the Christmas tree, which had been decorated with pretty lights and lots of other colourful things. There was the holly, with its bright red berries, which they had hung round the pictures. They had stuck a little piece in the Christmas pudding, too. There was the mistletoe that Dad had hung in the middle of the room. There were some green leaves, too, that had been put with flowers and candles to make special decorations.

Some of the greenery they had bought in the shops but some they had cut from the bushes in their garden. It was rather nice to be able to see those trees and bushes that were still green in winter after the other trees had lost their leaves.

It is not that evergreens never lose their leaves. Unlike other trees, they lose them a few at a time so that there are always some left. Most of them are hard shiny leaves or needle-like leaves such as those on the Christmas tree.

In the cold, dark winter months, the evergreens have their own special place but, all the year round, we can enjoy their soft greenness. There is something particularly nice about the evergreen forests with their soft carpet of needles on the ground and their very pleasant scent.

Evergreens are there all the year to remind us of the wonder of nature.

6 FEEDING THE BIRDS.

*The North wind doth blow, and we shall have snow,*
  *And what will the robin do then, poor thing?*
*He'll sit in a barn, and keep himself warm,*
  *And hide his head under his wing, poor thing.*

Poor little robin! He has no nice warm home such as we have. Whatever the weather the robins, and other birds too, must do the best they can to look after themselves in the cold outdoors.

We may envy the birds in summertime when they can fly around in the sunshine, enjoying the gardens or the open country but we would not wish to change places with them in winter. It is difficult, often to find food. They cannot go to the shops as we can. They have to search for their food when the trees are bare, insects have disappeared and the frozen ground is too hard for them to peck it to find worms or other food. Sometimes they cannot find water to drink because everywhere the water has frozen into ice.

Sometimes the birds are fortunate to find a farmer who is ploughing his fields or a gardener digging his garden. They are able then to look for food in the earth that has been turned over.

But we need not leave things to a few people. We can all help the birds in winter, whether we live in the town or the country. There are many people who have, in their gardens, bird tables on which they can put food and water. Robins and tits are happy to feed from a table but some other birds, such as blackbirds and thrushes prefer to feed on the ground.

Pieces of fat, bread and seeds all make food for the birds. A special treat could be nuts which they love. Hang a bag or container of nuts on a tree and watch the birds. Blue tits are very amusing to watch. They will cling with their claws and hang upside down as they eat. It would be interesting to see how many different kinds of bird come for the food.

Feeding the birds in winter is something we can all do. It costs us nothing to give them our crusts and scraps of food and, by doing so, we are helping to look after some of the little creatures which give us so much pleasure.

### 7 SNOWDROPS AND WINTER FLOWERS

One day a lady, who lived in a big city where the buildings were very high and close together, decided to go to visit some friends who lived in the country. The winter had seemed long and cold and she thought it would be rather nice to go into the country for a breath of fresh air and to see what was happening in the world of nature. She remembered a verse that she had learned long ago when she was at school:

> 'February brings the rain;
> Thaws the frozen ponds again.'

It was quite true. The ponds had thawed; the ditches were full of water; raindrops sparkled on the grass; and everywhere seemed so fresh and sweet-smelling.

Suddenly she saw a lovely sight. All around the bottom of a tree, a mass of green and white showed that snowdrops, the first flowers of the year, had bravely grown up and were showing their flowers with the pure white centre and the smaller petals tinged with a tiny patch of green. They looked so frail and tender, yet they had pushed their way through the earth to be the first of all the flowers. They make such a lovely picture and seem to suggest that spring, with its nicer weather and warm sunshine, cannot be far away.

In the woods, other flowers begin to appear. Small celandines and aconites bring their own touch of colour but, of course, there are very few flowers to be seen until spring has really arrived.

Years ago, people were especially pleased to see the spring flowers because there were none to be seen in winter. Nowadays we can have flowers all the year round. People have learned how to grow plants in heated greenhouses so that they bloom even in the coldest weather.

Some people like to have flowering plants growing in pots in their homes. Some like to buy cut flowers to put in vases. Chrysanthemums are very popular and there are lots of different sizes and colours. It is nice, too, to have spring flowers, such as daffodils, long before they bloom outdoors.

In many ways, winter is not the pleasantest of the seasons but the lovely flowers help to cheer it up and bring a little brightness into our lives.

8 PREPARING FOR SPRING

Roger and Colin wrapped themselves up nice and warm. Dad was taking them for a walk through the countryside. It was a sunny morning but there was still a nip in the air which brought the colour to their faces and made their eyes water a little.

The earth seemed very still, as though it was having a long rest before the time came for it to wake up again and send new life spreading in all directions. Most of the trees held up their bare brown branches towards the sky: their leaves had fallen long ago and were lying·on the ground, rotting away. Many of the animals were asleep for the winter, some waking to take food before snuggling down again in their warm beds.

As they clambered over the banks of earth the boys noticed how hard they seemed. In summer they had been springy beneath their feet but now they were rock hard as the moisture in the earth had frozen solid.

But beneath the surface, where the boys could not see, something was happening. Sometimes the sun was a little warmer than it was that morning. Moisture had gradually made its way through the earth to reach the seeds, the bulbs and the roots that were there.

Away below their feet the little seeds and bulbs began to grow. Roots were sent downwards and shoots were sent upwards, ready to break through into the spring sunshine.

Above their heads the rooks were flying, cawing noisily as they flew. Soon they would be building their nests in the branches, looking for mates and laying eggs. Other birds were beginning to think it was time to sing their songs of welcome to spring.

In the fields beside the road were sheep with the little lambs, which had been born whilst the snow was covering the ground. The farmers had made special shelters to give them some protection from the cold.

Dad and the boys stood by the gate watching the lambs.

'Lovely aren't they?' he remarked. 'One of the first signs of spring. Soon the whole countryside will be full of life once more. Our world is a wonderful place and we should be thankful even in winter for all God has given us.'

SOME WINTER CELEBRATIONS

New Year, 1st January.
Epiphany/Twelfth Night, 6th January.
Chinese New Year, Mid January to Mid February (variable).
Candlemas, 2nd February.
St. Valentine's Day, 14th February.
Shrovetide, weekend before Lent (variable).
Mardi Gras/Shrove Tuesday/Pancake Day (variable).
Ash Wednesday and Lent (variable).
St. David's Day (Patron Saint of Wales), 1st March.
St. Patrick's Day (Patron Saint of Ireland), 17th March.
Mothering (Mid Lent) Sunday (variable).

PRAYERS

1. Dear Father God, we say thank you for this lovely world, especially for those green trees and red berries which brighten the wintry scene. Make us thankful for all your gifts. *Amen*

2. On these cold wintry mornings, we say thank you, O God, for the warmth of our homes and our school. Give us thankful hearts, we pray. *Amen*

3. Thank you, dear God, for all that brightens our winter days;
   For pretty, gently-falling snowflakes;
   For trees and houses capped with snow;
   For the pale light of winter sunshine;
   For frost pictures on our window panes;
   For icicles that sparkle in the sun;
   And for the brightness of the sky at night.
   Thank you for all these things. *Amen*

4. Thank you, dear God, for the flowers and all the lovely things which help to brighten the dark winter days. *Amen*

5. Thank you, God our Father, for all the games we can play in winter; for the fun we can have outdoors; and for the games we enjoy indoors. Help us to play well and fairly, and teach us, when we lose, to do so cheerfully. *Amen*

6. Thank you, O God, for signs that winter is nearly over:
   For the first flowers peeping from the ground;
   For birds thinking of building their nests;
   For animals gradually awakening from their sleep;
   For new-born lambs in the fields and on the hills;
   And for all that reminds us of new life.
   Thank you, O God, for all these things. *Amen*

7. Today, O God, we think of the birds. We like watching them in summer and we feel sorry for them in winter when it is difficult for them to find food or shelter. Show us how we can care for them. *Amen*

8. We remember, today, O Lord God, all those who do not like the winter cold, especially those who are old or ill. Help them to keep themselves warm and show us ways in which we can help them. *Amen*

9. We thank you, O God:
   For all the things we can enjoy in winter,
   > *We thank you, O God;*
   For snow, and snowballs and snowmen,
   > *We thank you, O God;*
   For frost, and ice, and icicles,
   > *We thank you, O God;*
   For frozen ponds, and slides and sledges,
   > *We thank you, O God;*
   For steaming hot drinks and blazing fires,
   > *We thank you, O God;*
   For comfortable homes and cosy beds,
   > *We thank you, O God;*
   Thank you, O God, for all you give us. *Amen*

10. When Jack Frost paints his pictures on the window panes and icicles hang from the gutters, keep us thankful, dear God, for the warmth and comfort of our homes. *Amen*

11. When skies are grey and cold winds blow we are thankful for our homes where we can keep warm and snug. Help us to remember those less fortunate than ourselves, and particularly the old people who may be very cold. *Amen*

12. Winter is nearly over, O God, and we see signs that spring is on its way. Thank you for all the new life in the countryside and the promise that brighter, warmer days will soon be here. *Amen*

Frost and snow
In the winter birds need food
Little birds in winter time
See how the snowflakes are falling
To God, who makes all lovely things
Water in the snow
We thank you, loving Father God
When the world is dark and dreary

INTEREST WORK AND ACTIVITIES

*Books for the book corner*

A BOOK FOR WINTER, Wheaton
WE DISCOVER WINTER *(We discover)*, Arnold
OBSERVE AND DISCOVER IN WINTER AND SPRING
    *(Observe and Discover)*, Macmillan
WINTER *(Nature table)*, Evans
SNOW *(Starters)*, Macdonald
A DAY IN THE SNOW *(First stories)*, Macdonald

*Things to collect*

Winter pictures: snow; clearing roads; digging out sheep; frozen
lakes; icicles. Make a winter collage.
    Evergreen leaves and berries. Try to identify.
    Any winter specimens for the nature table, e.g. skeleton leaves,
pieces of bark.

*Things to make*

Snowmen: Toilet roll centres covered in cottonwool. Ball of
cottonwool for a head (pushed into the top of the cylinder). Make a
hat. A scrap of cloth or wool will make a scarf.
    Mobile of snowflakes: Draw and cut out hexagonal shapes. Paint
white. Spray with glitter. Suspend on white cotton.

---

Wind chimes: Cut a foil pie plate from rim to centre and fold to make a cone, then fasten. Wash and flatten milk bottle tops, thread and fasten to cone. Suspend the whole. Wind will blow bottle tops together to make chimes.

An indoor garden: Fill a deep tray with earth. 'Plant' twigs, bits of evergreen, etc. Fill with any finds such as acorns.

### A bird table

Obtain or make a simple bird table. A flat piece of wood or hardboard can be nailed to the top of a wooden stand or suspended from a branch of a tree. Have a dish for water.

Encourage children to bring suitable food to put on the table.

Thread peanuts on a thread or string and suspend from the edge.

### Help!

Find out about any organizations or associations which help old people in winter and those which help birds. See if any practical help can be given.

# 21 Spring

*We have in mind the fact that this material will be used with children from widely differing environments. The seasons of nature are part and parcel of everyday life for country-bred children, but this is not so for children of the cities and towns, including children from overseas, many of whom may be quite unaware of the great changes taking place each season. This theme—Spring—is presented as it might be seen through the eyes of a group of town-bred children who, for the first time, are experiencing the advent of spring at first hand.*

*We make no apology for this: the wonder of spring and the new life of the world at this time is so familiar to children in rural areas and it may interest them too to appreciate what the commonplace could mean to their peers living in a city environment.*

## 1 NEW BEGINNINGS

There was an air of great excitement in the home of the Lawrence family, living in Maryport Road in the centre of a large city. Their father's work made it necessary for them to leave their home and move to a house a long way from the city where they had always lived, into the country. Of course, they *did* feel a little sad at leaving their friends, but were so excited at the prospect of living away from the city, they didn't feel sad for long. The furniture and all their possessions having been loaded into the huge pantechnicon, off they all went—to a new adventure.

It seemed very strange at first, but with their familiar belongings, their own beds and other furniture finally in place, they soon settled down. There was so much to see and do—interesting things they had never seen or done before. When they had first seen their new home it was winter time, cold, wet, and with the trees so bare. Now it was spring, and so different!

It felt just as though the whole earth was waking from a deep sleep. All around there was a kind of movement: things were happening. Birds began to sing as though they were calling, 'Wake up, everyone! Spring is here!'

It seemed that nature, in waking, had decided to dress the earth in a new dress of the palest green. Tiny buds were bursting to show the green of leaves ready to unfold. Green shoots and blades of fresh grass were pushing up through the hard soil. Spikes of the spring flowers showed promise of the beauty soon to come. People were busy in the fields preparing the soil and sowing the seeds. There was so much to be done so that food would be produced.

People were busy in the gardens: others were caring for the animals. Lambs were bleating, birds calling, and small animals coming out of hibernation—their long winter rest now ended. They found frog spawn in the ponds and so many things to learn and discover. A whole new world was there at their very feet. And it *was* a new world, for in spring, the first season of the year, the world is new, fresh and making a new beginning.

## 2 BABY ANIMALS

There was so much that was new to the Lawrence family in their new home. They made friends and learned from them so many things they hadn't known before. Robert, Jill and David were very happy in their new life. They were becoming aware of many things going on all around them and learning more and more each day.

One day they saw young lambs in a field. Some had black faces, or black ears, and black patches on their faces. One or two were quite black and the children laughed as they all sang together, 'Baa, baa, black sheep, have you any wool?' They were told that some of the lambs had been born earlier in the year, when snow drifts had piled up burying some of the sheep, and babies had been born in the snow. The lambs had been dug out with their mothers just in time to save their lives.

They noticed that the young lambs stayed quite close to their mothers, to be fed, and perhaps, too, because it made them feel safe.

One lamb strayed too close to the road and the ewe quickly followed, nudging her young back to safety in such a manner that Jill was sure she was scolding her lamb. The young lambs could jump quite high. The children laughed at the way a lamb could jump and kick out its hind legs as if to show the world how happy it was to be alive.

There were other young animals, too. It seemed to the children that so many babies were being born at this time of the year. They had never been aware of so many tiny creatures. There were calves in the cowsheds and yellow fluffy chicks in the henhouses; baby rabbits flopped across a grassy patch to disappear behind a tree; and tiny hedgehogs scurried for shelter. In the farmyard a huge tabby cat was proudly displaying her kittens in the spring sunshine.

All the baby creatures seemed so full of life. They played and had fun with each other 'Just like us.' said Robert. 'We like to play, too.'

'And we like to feel that Mum is close to us, just like the baby animals do,' said David.

The children learned later that animal parents quickly prepared their young to fend for themselves and the young ones did not stay young for very long. But they noted how the parents cared for them while they were young, seeing that they were fed and protected, then showed them by example how and where to find their food.

In that springtime, when they first learned about the new life all around them, they understood how God showed his love for all and made the parents careful for their young.

### 3  BUILDING NESTS

The children were having breakfast in the kitchen. From time to time Jill glanced out of the window, looking at the garden with its trees and bushes, and thinking how much she enjoyed living here. She watched the antics of a robin and was sure it was the same cheeky robin which came close to the kitchen door in search of stray crumbs. Now the robin was busily engaged on some mission, carrying scraps of material in its beak. Back and forth it went. 'Must be building a nest,' thought Jill.

She had been watching the birds and noticed their behaviour this springtime—how they seemed to be interested only in one other bird of their own kind. They were engaged in the important business of finding a mate with whom they could build a nest where the hen bird could lay eggs. They looked for the right place first and then began to build.

Robert was watching the birds, too, and noticed how they planned and made their nests. Different birds had different methods of building. Until now the children, if they thought very much about it, had thought all nests were much the same.

Now they watched the robin, which was making lots of journeys into their shed! There was a small space where a pane of glass had been broken and removed and Dad had not yet found time to replace it. This was the way in for the robin. All sorts of building materials were carried in—pieces of wool, bunches of grass and small twigs. Sure enough, in time the children found the nest tucked away at the back of a shelf in their shed and inside they found six little eggs. They had been told not to remove the eggs so they looked at them and left them in the nest.

As time went by, they discovered more nests and eggs. They saw the blackbirds' nest made of grass and horsehair and some roots, mixed with mud, and with a soft lining of grass, to make it nice and cosy. Inside they saw the brown spotted bluish eggs.

Again the children were filled with wonder as they came to see how the birds worked to provide homes for their families—all part of God's wonderful world.

### 4 BABY BIRDS

The Lawrence children were enjoying their experiences this spring-time and kept a close watch on the nests in which the different birds had laid their eggs.

They soon discovered that springtime is a very busy time for most birds. Not only do they have to find food for themselves but also for the young birds that have hatched out of the eggs in their nests. A few weeks before, the mother bird laid those eggs and sat on them to keep them warm. Then, one by one, the baby birds broke out of the shells. Ugly little creatures they were, too, with no feathers, a large head and eyes not yet opened.

Soon their mouths were open and expecting food. The nest became a noisy place with all the babies squeaking for food. Both parents flew to and fro finding food for their growing family. Each time they returned with food, all the little beaks opened wide. Each little bird wanted as much as it could get. Baby birds do not think of fair shares!

Within a few weeks the baby birds grow up until at last the day comes for them to try out their wings and see if they can fly. Sometimes they flutter to the ground and find it difficult to get up again.

Maybe you have seen a baby bird like this and have picked it up to take it home or into school. It is something you should never do.

You cannot look after it properly and it is quite likely to die without proper care. If ever you do see a baby bird that is in difficulty, you may also see one of its parents too, wanting to help as soon as you have gone and it seems safe for it to do so.

Baby birds can be very interesting to watch but you should always do so from a distance. Birds in their nests should not be touched and young birds should never be picked up and taken away.

## 5  FLOWERS IN SPRINGTIME

On a sunny spring afternoon the Lawrence family set off for a walk to explore more of the land where they lived. The birds were singing, lambs bleating, cows softly mooing—and the sun was shining!

Raindrops from a recent shower were sparkling on grass and leaves. 'Just like tiny jewels,' thought Mother, who stopped to look at a spider's web festooned with raindrops. The world was fresh and cool and green.

When the family went out in this way they played a game—a kind of 'I spy'—when they looked for something they had not seen before. They soon had their first 'spy'—a clump of primroses, fresh and creamy yellow, looking out from a bank. A raindrop had settled right in the centre of one of the flowers: others shone on the petals in the sun. Close by they discovered some violets, shyly hiding, almost out of sight. Soon they had noticed more and more primroses, violets, and celandines.

Jill's first thought was to pick as many as she could see and take them all back home with her, but Mum and Dad explained that this was not a good idea. They would take *some* home to put in water so that they could enjoy them there, but it was much better to leave the rest for others to see and enjoy and make sure that more would grow next year. The children were shown how to pick the blooms carefully so as not to damage them or pull up the roots. The primroses and violets made a pretty posy for them to take home. The flowers smelt fresh and earthy and the ground was warm and damp.

A few weeks later, enjoying another walk, they visited the woods. Again the sun was shining and they grew warm walking, so, as they came nearer to the woods, everyone thought how nice it would be to enjoy for a while the shadiness of the trees and the damp wood and leaf smell they expected.

As they came to the edge of the wood, they stopped and stared. The picture they saw before them was the most beautiful they had seen yet. 'Ooh!' gasped Jill. 'It's just as if someone has laid a blue carpet all over the wood.' The blueness spread as far as they could see.

The bluebells held their heads proudly as though they knew what a lovely sight they made. How beautiful was the world at springtime.

### 6  BUDS, CATKINS AND BLOSSOM

One very important discovery the children made, as soon as they moved into their new house, was a horse chestnut tree in their own garden. They had seen these in the park near their old home, and there was always a scramble in the autumn to gather the conkers before anyone else came along. Quite often they were disappointed. Now, to have one which was all their own . . . They looked forward to the day when the large shiny conkers would be theirs.

In the meantime, there was much to interest them. Dad cut some of the sticky buds so that they could grow in water and they watched the buds gradually open to reveal the delicate green leaves. The tree produced large 'candles' of blossom, standing straight and balanced, and, when these dropped from the tree, the petals around looked like snow.

Trees, bushes and shrubs were so much more than just branches and leaves, the children discovered. Some produced blossom or catkins before leaves. In a hedge they found a hazel. They noticed it first because of the long graceful catkins hanging from the twigs. Their friends called these 'lambs' tails' for they did resemble the tails of lambs. They also noticed the catkins of the willows, which were not long and hanging as the hazel, but soft and round and fluffy, 'Pussy willow' they heard it called—like tiny cats.

The pink almond blossom was a pretty sight and so was the bright yellow forsythia, its blossom making a brave bright show for a time before it dropped and the tiny leaves were seen growing. Blossom on fruit trees was beautiful. Each small flower had inside it the possibility of fruit. Apple, pear, plum and cherry were all to be seen—so much blossom and so lovely to look at.

288

Until now the children had not understood that all trees bore fruit of some kind—not just fruit to be eaten, but fruit of many kinds, all containing seeds to grow into more trees if planted and nourished.

Catkins and blossom all have the beginning of life of the tree inside them. The wind blows the pollen and insects help spread it too. Later the wind and the birds spread the seeds so the life of trees and plants is continued year after year.

He is a great and wonderful God, who has planned that this world would always have in it so much of beauty and wonder.

## 7 MARCH WINDS AND APRIL SHOWERS

> *'March winds and April showers*
> *Bring forth May flowers.'*

This is a very old saying. There is another which says:
*March comes in like a lion and goes out like a lamb.*

In the Lawrence house it was warm and snug. The wind howled and blew: it rattled the tiniest loose fitting and found every possible space to blow into. It really did sound like a roaring lion . . . sometimes, blowing down the chimney and making such a noise they were glad to have strong walls which protected them from the wind and the cold. It seemed rather sad that sometimes the wind blew so fiercely that some flowers and trees were buffeted and beaten. On windy days the cat seemed to be extra frisky and playful as though the wind excited her. The children in school, too, were excited by the wind. It made them want to run and shout and jump. I wonder why? Perhaps it was so that they could be heard above the noise. In the playground they ran here and there just for the fun of it. They were battling against something stronger than themselves and wanted to prove their own strength.

Jill, David and Robert enjoyed battling with the wind. They put their heads down and walked into the wind, feeling its strength and feeling their cheeks being whipped to a rosy red.

At this time it is too cold for many of the insects which fly around carrying pollen from blossom to blossom. Instead the wind helps by blowing it around. The wind gradually dies away and the soft April breezes blow. The flowers and plants, responding to the increasing warmth and passing of time, unfold and develop, but unfortunately, in the month of April, there are often sudden spells of cold weather with frost which can destroy blossom and other growing plants.

This year, as April brought its usual showers, the children saw the unfolding of so many buds and things growing all around. The soft April rain and the sun worked together so that soon the fruit trees around the house, as well as those lining the roads and bordering the fields, were alive with promise. The branches and new leaves of many trees gave shelter to birds and young animals.

All around them were the signs that summer would soon be here, reminding them of God's wonderful world.

8 TURN A STONE OVER . . .

Mr. Lawrence was planning the garden in their new home. He had promised the children they could have a patch of garden for themselves. So, plans were made and a part of the garden marked off for Robert, David and Jill.

'Now, what shall we plant?' asked David.

Dad laughed. 'Before you think about what to grow, you must prepare the ground.' he said.

The children were not quite so keen about this, but if they were to have a garden they had to do the work needed. Spade, fork and rake were borrowed from Dad and they set to work. Lots of stones needed to be dug up and taken from the patch. They were amazed at the many creatures they discovered underneath them.

'Ugh!' exclaimed Jill, 'Just look at this huge worm.'

She didn't know what to do with it, so Father explained the important work worms do in a garden. They watched it slowly work its way back into the soil.

As they cleared the patch, they tackled a pile of large stones which seemed to be firmly embedded in the ground. The stones were almost rocks; they were so large and took some effort to lift. Jill gave another squeal as they moved the stones and she watched the scurrying of the creatures exposed, that had suddenly lost their shelter. Woodlice, a spider, and beetles of different sizes, shapes and colours were there. 'Nasty,' thought Jill.

But Robert and David were fascinated and interested to hear of the special work some creatures do in the soil. Their interest was aroused and they made a habit of lifting stones whenever they saw them just to see what was underneath. Slugs, snails, and centipedes were all there. There are lots of strange creatures which all have their part to play in the world of nature.

That first springtime in their new home was an important time in their lives. It was a really important new beginning for them as they learned about the first season of the year.

RELATED THEMES

SOME SPRING CELEBRATIONS

Mothering (Mid-Lent) Sunday may fall in springtime.
Maundy Thursday: Distribution of the Royal Maundy.
Baisakhi (Sikh New Year), about 13th April.
The Easter Parade, Easter Sunday.
All Fools' Day, 1st April.
St. George's Day (Patron Saint of England), 23rd April.
May Day, 1st May.
Cornish Furry Dance (Flora Day), 8th May.
Morris Dancing.
Blessing the Sea: Local customs in various ports.

*(There may be other colourful local spring festivals.)*

1. As we look around us in springtime, dear Father God, we see so many signs of new life in the world. Open our eyes to enjoy all these things and help us to remember that you have made them all. *Amen*

2. Dear Father God, we thank you for the spring and all the beauty and freshness of this time of year, which makes us feel glad to be alive. Give us thankful hearts for all your gifts to us. *Amen*

3. For springtime, with all its beauty and colour,
   *We give you thanks, O God;*
   For golden daffodils in fields and gardens,
   *We give you thanks, O God;*
   For banks of primroses, and violets in the woods,
   *We give you thanks, O God;*
   For the blue carpet of the bluebell woods,
   *We give you thanks, O God;*
   For the fresh green of leaves and catkins,
   *We give you thanks, O God;*
   For the sweet singing of all the birds,
   *We give you thanks, O God;*
   For all the new life we see around us,
   *We give you thanks, O God;*
   Help us always to enjoy this wonderful world which you have given us. *Amen*

4. I like the springtime, dear God;
   There are so many lovely things to see and hear.
   It is nice to hear the song of the birds again
   And to watch them building their nests;
   The lambs in the fields are fun to watch
   And some of the other baby animals are so cuddly;
   I enjoy the pretty flowers
   And the greenery of the fields and trees:
   Thank you, God, for springtime
   And for health to enjoy it. *Amen*

5. In springtime, dear God, when everything is coming back to life, we say thank you for watching over us in the dark winter days and we ask you to bless us in the days to come. *Amen*

6. In the countryside or the garden we see lots of interesting creatures, O God. Some of them we like but some are not so nice. Help us to know how important they all are in our world and to do nothing to harm them. *Amen*

7. So often, O God, I am so busy doing what *I* want to do that I do not take time to look around me and I miss so many lovely things. Help me to make time to enjoy this special season of the year. *Amen*

8. Thank you, dear God, for the new life in the countryside and on the farm; and thank you that I can enjoy all these things. *Amen*

9. Thank you, Father God,
   For flowers in the fields and gardens;
   For waving catkins and opening buds;
   And for the lovely blossom on the fruit trees.
   For all beautiful things we say thank you. *Amen*

10. We remember, dear Father God, that Jesus taught us how you care for the birds. Help us, too, to care for the birds and do nothing to harm them or their young ones. *Amen*

11. When the wind blows and the rain falls, making us feel rather uncomfortable, help us to remember that these things are needed by the growing plants if we are to enjoy their lovely flowers. Teach us how all these things are needed in our world. *Amen*

12. You have given us so much to enjoy at this time of year, dear God. Help us to show our thanks by taking care of all the good gifts we have received. *Amen*

---

All the flowers are waking
Daisies are our silver
Frost and snow
Glad that I live am I
Hark! a hundred notes are swelling
In the early morning
Praised be our Lord
See the farmer sow the seed
Seeds and bulbs
Sing a song of May-time (Spring-time)
The farmer comes to scatter the seed
We praise thee for the sun
We thank thee, Heavenly Father
What do we see on a warm spring day?
What is the west wind singing?
When the corn is planted

INTEREST WORK AND ACTIVITIES

*Books*

Just a few that could be put into the book corner:

> FIRST DAY OF SPRING *(First Stories)*, Macdonald
> SPRING/BULBS *(Nature Table)*, Evans
> OBSERVE AND DISCOVER IN WINTER AND SPRING
> *(Observe and Discover)*, Macmillan

*Songs and poems*

Find a few simple songs and poems which the children can learn or enjoy hearing.

*Display*

Have a theme of springtime for display in the hall and throughout the school. The bright greens and yellows will make a colourful show.

*Collections*

If possible, have spring flowers of various kinds in the classroom for display. Some pictures of flowers, blossom and woodland scenes could be mounted also.

Have a number of twigs with buds in jars of water to see how they develop. Sticky buds of the horse chestnut are always a favourite. Forsythia will demonstrate the order of development of such plants, with leaves following the flowers. If possible have catkins on display too.

*Art*

Make a spring collage. Egg boxes, cut and painted yellow, make good daffodil trumpets. Templates of lambs and rabbits will enable children to draw these for painting and cutting out.

*Nests*

If possible, have a nest available. It may be one of last year's or one that has been deserted. Sometimes deserted nests still containing eggs can be found.

Visit the park, wood, hedgerow or other suitable place to see what nests are there to be discovered.

Ask if any children have birds nesting in boxes in their gardens or elsewhere, such as under the eaves of the house. Keep a record of any observations.

*Observation*

Make a wormery. An old aquarium will do. Put in layers of soil, sand, decayed leaves, etc. Put in some worms. Note how the soil becomes mixed by the movement of the worms.

Take the children out to look under any large stones and note what is seen.

*Conservation*

Talk about the preservation and conservation of the countryside. Warn about removing roots of plants and anything which would spoil the countryside for others. The Country Code could be introduced. The need for keeping the countryside clean and free from litter can be discussed. Relate to the school environment.

*Help*

It may be possible to make posies of spring flowers to take to people who are housebound and no longer able to see flowers in their natural setting.

# 22 Summer

*Summer is a popular time of the year with the promise of warmer and longer days, allowing children to spend more time out of doors. The long holiday break from school is anticipated and plans are being made for holidays—maybe by the sea, or in the country, caravanning or camping. Probably this season ranks as second only to Christmastime in the child's calendar.*

*There is another important aspect to be considered at this time and we think it important to include this. The summer term also brings the end of a school year and the children are faced with the situation of change in their school life. They have come to the end of a year spent in a class with their own teacher and now anticipate a new class, probably with a new teacher after the holiday.*

*Even greater is the change faced by those leaving the Infants' school or department and meeting the challenge of entering Junior School with all that entails. This may not seem very important to older people, but to a child it can be viewed with some trepidation, and, we hope, with pleasant anticipation, too. This subject has therefore been included in this theme.*

## 1 LONG DAYS

The children living in Park Close were very fortunate. This was part of a new estate and they were living in nice new houses with gardens. They were close to the park too, so there was plenty of space where they could play. Better still, there were other children to play with most of the time. Many of the families moved into their new homes about the same time and the children quickly made friends. The Mitchell family, with Jean and Brian, lived next door to the Brown family with Sarah, Tony and Jane. Just along the road and around them lived other families with children.

Summer was here and the children of Park Close were enjoying the pleasures that the long days brought. Early in the morning they woke to the sound of birds singing their morning song, and they went to bed whilst it was still daylight. 'Why must we go to bed when it is still daytime?' Brian asked Mum.

Brian would soon be nine years old, and felt quite grown up. Certainly he felt too old to go to bed in the daytime.

'If you stayed up until dark in the summertime you would go to bed *very* late indeed,' replied Mum, 'and you need just as much sleep in summer as at any other time of the year.'

'Well, it seems all wrong to me.' Brian was in the mood to argue. 'We go to bed in daylight in summer, and in winter we have to get up while it is still dark, when we would rather stay in bed!'

Dad came in just then and heard the conversation. He explained about the sun and the movement of the earth and the seasons.

He explained how the days were longer in the summer, each day having more and more time of daylight until 21st June, which is the longest day of the year. Then each day is just a little shorter than the one before, until mid-winter, when we have the shortest day of the year.

'And we sneak an extra hour of daylight, too,' said Dad. 'In the spring we put our clock forward one hour so we have that extra hour of daylight to use, and then, in the autumn, we put them back to get back to normal. Although there is still the same number of hours in a day we make sure we have the daylight when we are able to make good use of it. So, stop grumbling, and use all the time you have to enjoy the summer days.'

The children did enjoy the summer days, too. This was a time when all the flowers, trees and grass seemed at their very best. There was always so much to do and see and they were happy to make use of the long days of summer, to play and explore, so that, when they went to bed, even though they could still see a chink of light peeping through the curtains in the bedroom, they were glad to rest and sleep, preparing for yet another busy day tomorrow.


2 PLAYING OUTDOORS

The Mitchell family, the Brown family and all their friends, found there were many discoveries to be made. They had so much to learn—about the park, the roads where they lived, and about each other.

In these long days of summer there were happy hours to be spent in the garden, in the park or in the fields and woods further afield. The younger children, Tony, Jane and Jean loved to play on the slide in the park. They liked to feel the 'wooo-oosh' as they slid from top to bottom, and feel the wind rushing past their ears. They never tired: as soon as they jumped off the bottom of the slide, they ran as fast as they could to the steps to do it again.

On the swings Sarah and Brian were able to work themselves up quite high. Up and down, up and down they went. As they went up, they looked across the park to their houses and for just a second could see what was happening in their gardens.

The summer days went happily by, playing in the park, helping in the garden, exploring, finding more and more things to do and learn about. The big park provided lots of hiding places and corners in which to play. The younger children, with their friends, stayed mostly near home, playing the 'make-believe' games which they enjoyed.

The older children went further afield, to the woods and the fields, where they could run, jump and play to their hearts' content. It was lovely to be able to shout and make a noise without being told to be quiet, or to have to think about disturbing people! This was one of the best things about being able to play outdoors: so much could be done and enjoyed without being a nuisance to others.

After playing outside for a long time, it was good to go home for tea and finally to settle down at night in their nice comfortable beds. As they drifted off to sleep, even though the light from outside came peeping round the curtains, the children of Park Close were glad they had comfortable beds and safe homes to rest in after all the busyness of the long day.

### 3 KEEPING THE OUTDOORS NICE

Before school broke up for the long summer holiday, the children were reminded about keeping the outdoors tidy. Their teachers talked to them about the part they could play in making sure that litter and rubbish would not spoil the enjoyment of everyone. They had a special *Keep Britain Tidy* campaign and they saw pictures of the way people sometimes made really beautiful places look ugly by leaving litter behind. They sang the song about the milk bottle tops [*see page 364*] and rubbish being left in all kinds of place and were told that it was not enough just to sing about it—something must be done.

The Mitchell children and the Brown children were full of all they had seen and heard and went home to tell their parents about it.

'What a pity so many places are made ugly and uncomfortable for others by people being thoughtless and selfish!' said Mrs. Mitchell. 'Just think. If everyone left places clean and tidy and with no litter, we would have a very clean and tidy land, and could be proud of it.'

'Now,' said Mr. Brown, 'the best way of encouraging others to be careful is to set an example yourself. If no bins are available, take the rubbish home with you and put it in the dustbin.'

They all went for a walk one day and came to a place they enjoyed visiting. There was a big green space with a small wood, and they had good fun there. It was rather spoilt for them, though, when they saw that some people seemed to have been camping there, or having a picnic of some kind. There was orange peel, food wrappers, cans and bottles, some of these broken, left lying in the open. It would be so easy for an animal or small child to step on the glass and be badly injured. So, as well as being very ugly, it was very dangerous.

They stopped to have a drink of orange juice and some biscuits. When they had finished, their parents collected the containers and papers, then put them carefully into a bag to be taken home again. Some other children nearby had been eating their picnic and were about to screw up their wrappings and throw them, with their cans, into a hedge. Instead, having seen the Browns and the Mitchells put their rubbish away to take back home, they did the same. 'You see,' said Mr. Mitchell, 'you have set a good example to others.'

'I hope they will always remember to do that,' said Mrs. Brown. 'People would not dream of leaving rubbish in the middle of the floor at home, so they should not do so when they are outdoors.'

#### 4 IN THE GARDEN

What a special place a garden is! The children in Park Close thought so. Each family had a garden, though they liked to share it with their friends and neighbours. When visitors came, it was nice to be able to show what they had done and tell what they were planning to do.

Each family had plans for laying out their garden and they were all different. Of course they all had certain things in them. Mum needed somewhere to hang the washing. Some had children's swings or sandpits.

The Mitchells had some garden furniture so that they could sit in comfort and enjoy the garden. Sometimes they had tea outdoors. It was fun on a bright day.

Each family wanted to grow things. Most of them decided upon some vegetables—potatoes, beans, cabbages, lettuces or onions; and some planted fruit bushes or trees—gooseberries, currants, raspberries, apples or pears.

Most of the mothers and fathers had favourite flowers that they liked to grow. They helped each other by sharing seeds, exchanging roots or cuttings, and offering advice.

There were some bad moments at first, especially when the children were wanting to help with the garden. Brian and Jean offered to help their father one day and he said they could do some weeding.

After school, before Father came home, they thought they would start and give him a lovely surprise. They weren't quite sure what Dad meant by weeding, but they thought it meant picking out the plants which were not too good. They found some that looked a bit sad, so they worked hard and soon had pulled them all out. Dad was really very surprised when he saw their handiwork. They were proud of the way they had worked and so were taken aback to see that father looked a bit strange. Well! How were they to know that they had pulled out the plants he had been struggling to grow and had been carefully tending for the past week?

Dad told them it was more sensible to wait until he or Mum could show them exactly what to do. They could be so much more helpful if they pulled out weeds instead of plants and he would show them which were weeds as they went along and worked together.

All was well, but it was a lesson that Brian and Jean never forgot—to make sure that they were *really* helping.

The gardens were a great joy to the people in Park Close. They brought the families together into what we call a 'community' and helped them all to be good friends—the parents as well as the children.

## 5 SUNSHINE AND WARM DAYS

Brian and his friend Jim lay on their backs in the long grass. Jim, who lived at the other end of Park Close, was in the same class at school as Brian.

The sun was shining and it was a warm day. The boys had been out most of the day, just going home for lunch and then out again as soon as possible. They had climbed trees, chased butterflies and made a collection of beetles which were now in a container in the shed in Jim's garden.

As they lay in the grass now, the boys did not speak. Each was occupied with his own thoughts.

Brian was gazing towards the sky. What was up there he wondered? He watched a 'plane come into view, trailing a white streak from its engines. He could hear the drone of the engines as it gradually disappeared from view.

Just then he heard another drone—almost in his ear. Hardly moving his head he could see a bee taking off from a clover head. Brian noticed that on its legs the bee had some little bags in which it carried pollen back to the hive.

'This is fine,' Brian thought. 'If Jim and I were the only people in the world, we could have such a wonderful time. We could do what we like, when we like. We could eat what we like and go where we like. . . . Must remember to let out those beetles when we go home.'

Jim had been watching the 'plane, too. 'I wonder where it is going? When I grow up, I'd like to be a pilot and fly all over the world. I'd visit every country I can think of . . .'

He rolled over and spread out his hand in the warm grass. What was that he felt? Something moved. A grasshopper had not been quick enough to get out of his way. He watched it jump on to a small plant and sit there rubbing its legs to make a chirping noise. How nice it was to be able to lie there doing nothing but enjoy the sunshine and the world of nature. There was no one to disturb them . . .

'Brian! Jim! Where are you? It's tea time!'

Both boys sat up. It had been a grand day. They had really enjoyed themselves. It had been fun to think of having the world to themselves . . . but it was nice to have someone to get tea for them.

'Coming!' Brian called. He was feeling decidedly hungry.

'Thank you, God, for a lovely world,' he thought. 'And thank you, too, for all those people who help me enjoy it.'

6  OUTINGS AND PICNICS

During the school holiday, an outing was arranged for the children from the estate to a Wild Life Park where there was also a very good place to picnic. A coach was ordered and the children met in the school playground with packed lunch bags or boxes of one kind or another.

There was a scramble on the coach as they all sorted out where they would sit and who they would sit with, but in time everyone was seated. Children and helpers set off on their adventure.

At the Wild Life Park, the children, in small groups in charge of an adult, went off to see the animals. In part of the park were animals they could handle, stroke and play with—a lamb, some rabbits and guinea pigs.

Then it was time for their picnic. They sat on the grass and set out their food—sandwiches, sausage rolls, crisps, fruit . . . (What do you like best to take to eat on a picnic?) Everyone had a nice cold drink, which was very welcome after so much excitement and games. The food seemed to taste better when it was eaten outdoors, but perhaps it was because they were all so hungry and had so much fresh air to breathe that it just seemed to taste better. Children shared their food with each other and made sure everyone had enough.

All the rubbish and litter had to be collected and put into one of the bins that stood around the picnic area. The crumbs were left on the grass for the birds. Then some games were organized—races and competitions. The sun shone so that everyone was happy, feeling good and friendly towards each other.

The journey back was much quieter than when they set out earlier. Everyone was tired and glad to rest, talking quietly about all they had done and what they could see from the windows of the coach. It had been a lovely day. They came near to the school at last, to find their parents waiting for them, glad to welcome them home and to hear all about the happenings of the day.

Outings and picnics with others do more than enable us to enjoy ourselves. At these times we help each other to be happy and we remember the comfort and pleasure of others as much as our own. Summer time gives us more opportunities to enjoy doing things together. God has made us to be people who are able to work and play together and we have to learn never to be selfish but share things happily with each other.

### 7  ON THE BEACH

The Brown family were setting off for a holiday. They had been talking about it for months and now the day was really here! A great sense of excitement gripped the children—Sarah, Tony and Jane—and their dog Butch, too.

Everything was packed in the car or on the roof-rack—suitcases, games, a beach ball and one or two things for the journey. For two whole weeks they would be living in a bungalow by the sea.

The Mitchell family came to their gate to wave good-bye and off they went. Along the roads they drove for a while and then towards the coast. Suddenly, the cry went up, 'There's the sea!' And there it was, with little white flecks on the waves.

Quickly they unpacked and settled into the bungalow. Dad took them to the beach for a while so that Mum could get what she called 'organized' and prepare tea. The children couldn't walk: they hopped, skipped and ran to the beach. On the sand they waved their arms, jumped about and felt fine. Butch joined them in their glee. It was the beginning of a wonderful holiday.

Each new day brought more time to dig in the sand, make sand pies and build sandcastles. This they did with Dad's help, making a moat and digging channels to fill the moat with water from the sea. They bathed and paddled and played. Jane, who was the smallest, was a little nervous of the sea at first—it was so big—but after a while she loved it, though she kept near to Sarah or Mum or Dad.

As the sea went out it left little puddles and these gave great pleasure. The water in the puddles was warm and in it were tiny creatures—shrimps, little crabs and others. On the sands the children found larger crabs and lots of seaweed. On the rocks were winkles and limpets, which they tried to move but could not, so tightly did they hold on to the rocks.

Dad fished from the jetty once or twice and caught some fish for their supper. They visited the little harbour to see the boats at anchor there, some with white sails, some with red, and others with no sails but an engine which made a 'zhoo-ming' noise when it took off.

The days were long and sunny and happy. At night the family slept soundly, tired out with fresh sea air and exercise. All too soon, it seemed, they had to return home, but for a while they had been able to see another part of the wonderful world God had created—and they loved every moment.

## 8 AFTER THE HOLIDAYS

The long summer holiday would soon be over. The children of Park Close and the rest of the estate had spent the holiday in different ways. Some had been to the seaside, others to the countryside. One family had been to Ireland; some others to Scotland; and Jim's family went to Spain. Winston had an exciting holiday adventure this year. His family had visited Jamaica to see his Great-grandma. They had saved for this holiday for a long time. There were others who stayed at home but went on visits, outings and picnics. It had been a good holiday, warm, sunny and very happy.

As the beginning of the new term and new year at school came nearer, the children began to think and talk of school. Little ones who had been in Nursery class or Nursery school would be joining the Infants. Some Infants would be going to Junior school. Everyone would be going up to a new class and maybe a new teacher. They all looked forward to being more grown up and doing harder work, but felt a little funny feeling in their tummies when they thought about it. They were sorry to leave the teachers they knew so well. Mums and Dads talked to them about it.

Brian and Jim were already in the Juniors; Sarah and her friends would be leaving the Infants. There, they had been the oldest in the school and had been very helpful, taking messages and doing jobs. In the Juniors they would be the youngest and smallest—big people of ten years of age and over would be there. Sarah and her friends would find things different for a while.

Nursery children would have to be in school with a larger number of children than they had in Nursery, and would learn to do different kinds of work. Soon they would be reading and doing number. What a big step they would all be taking—meeting different people, learning new things, growing up and becoming more independent.

The new school year is another new beginning. It is like starting a new book with lots of clean pages ready to be filled. Some pages we fill with good work, others are not so good. In the school year we will do some things well and get on well, sometimes we may not do so well, or behave as well as we should. The important thing is that we do the very best we can and try as hard as we can. We may make mistakes but this helps us to learn how to do things well and in the right way.

On the first day of term the children of the estate were up bright and early. They looked fresh and clean and sun tanned. They wore clean clothes, some of them new for the new school term. Some little children were starting school for the first time: others were going to new classes and departments.

It was a new beginning for *everyone*.

RELATED THEMES

SOME SUMMER CELEBRATIONS

Ascension Day: Fortieth day after Easter.
The Longest Day, 21st June.
Midsummer Day, 24th June.
Well dressing in several Derbyshire villages.
Tynwald Day, Isle of Man, 5th July.
St. Swithin's Day, 15th July.
The Royal Show and county agricultural shows.
Rush-bearing at Ambleside, about 26th July.
Lammas Day, 1st August.

PRAYERS

1. As we look around us, O Lord God, we see so many beautiful things which you have given us. Thank you for all these things. *Amen*

2. Dear Father God, be with us today. Help us to enjoy this lovely world and to do nothing that would spoil it for others. *Amen*

3. Dear God, the holidays are nearly here and we shall be able to enjoy outings and holidays in the country or by the sea. Help us to enjoy ourselves without hurting or annoying others. *Amen*

4. During the summer months, O God, we enjoy the warmth of the sunshine and the beauties of the world of nature. Thank you for all these good things. *Amen*

5. For parks, gardens and places where we can enjoy the sunshine, praise be to you, O God. *Amen*

6. Help me to remember, dear God,
   That I have a lovely world to live in
   And that I mustn't spoil it for others.
   Make me thoughtful for others
   And thankful to you. *Amen*

7. I like the summertime, Lord,
   I enjoy the warm days and fine evenings;
   I like to see the flowers and listen to the birds;
   It is fun playing with my friends,
   Or going on outings and picnics,
   And especially going away for holidays,
   Thank you, Lord, for summertime. *Amen*

8. Lord God, as the sunshine brings warmth to our world, let the sunshine of your love bring warmth to our hearts. *Amen*

9. Thank you, God our Father, for all you give.
For summer sunshine and cooling breezes,
              *Thank you, God our Father;*
For outings and picnics on moors and hills,
              *Thank you, God our Father;*
For holidays in the country or by the sea,
              *Thank you, God our Father;*
For times to play and enjoy ourselves,
              *Thank you, God our Father;*
And for friends with whom we do these things,
              *Thank you, God our Father. Amen*

10. We thank you, God our Father, for all we can enjoy in summer.
Give us grateful hearts. *Amen*

11. We think today, dear God, of people who cannot enjoy the
summer as we can, the ill, the elderly, the housebound, the
blind. Help us to share our pleasures with them. *Amen*

12. When we come to the end of our school term, O God, help us to
remember what we have learned, and to look forward to all we
shall do next year. *Amen*

SUGGESTED HYMNS

All things bright and beautiful
All things which live below the sky
Daisies are our silver
Frost and snow
Glad that I live am I
God made the shore
Let us sing our song of praise
Milk bottle tops and paper bags
We praise thee for the sun
We wake up with the sun
What fun it is beside the sea
What makes the day-time

308

INTEREST WORK AND ACTIVITIES

*Books*

Provide a selection of books on summertime pursuits and activities. Here are some suggestions

> SUMMER/GARDEN FLOWERS/THE WAYSIDE *(Nature Table)*, Evans
> OBSERVE AND DISCOVER IN SUMMER *(Observe and Discover)*, Macmillan
> DISCOVERING OUT OF DOORS, Lion
> PLAYING OUTDOORS/SEASIDE AND COUNTRY *(Our World)*, Burke
> IN THE GARDEN *(Zero)*, Macdonald
> A BOOK FOR SUMMER, Wheaton
> THE SEASHORE *(Blackwell's Learning Library)*, Blackwell
> SEASHORE *(Starters)*, Macdonald
> BY THE SHORE *(Starters Nature)*
> A DAY AT THE BEACH *(First Stories)*, Macdonald.
> A DAY BY THE SEA, Hamilton

*Decor*

Use themes of summer for the general decor of hall, corridors and classrooms. Collages and pictures on specific aspects. Alcoves or display areas could be used for different themes such as Holidays, The Beach, Flowers, The Park.

*Collections*

Make collections of wild flowers and grasses. Attractive vases of garden flowers. Garden flowers, brought to school, could also be made into posies and taken to housebound or elderly people without gardens.

Items can be displayed that have been brought back from visits or holidays.

*Holiday pictures*

Encourage children who go on holiday in term time to send a post card of the place they visit. Mount as a wall display of 'Our Holiday'. Children could bring in postcards or holiday snaps of previous holidays to make a display in the classroom.

*Help*

Collect to provide a picnic or outing for one or two local elderly or handicapped people. If there is an outing arranged locally for such people, it may be possible to provide cash for each member to have a treat.

*'Keep Britain Tidy'*

Run an anti-litter campaign through the summer term. Keep school and playgrounds free from litter. Emphasize when going on school visits. Stress need to observe the litter rules whilst on holiday or outings.

*Safety*

A few words and warnings would be appropriate concerning safety when playing outdoors or near water.

*Moving up*

If not already the practice, arrange some kind of function for children transferring to a different department or school. Visit the new school and meet the teachers. Ensure some form of recognition of the importance of the progression from Infants to Juniors or from class to class.

# 23 Harvest

*Harvest is a happy time, celebrated by people all over the world in their own fashion. Often there are thank-offerings to their God or gods to show their appreciation for their food and other blessings. Perhaps, with some, there has been a superstitious element, with the hope that such thank-offerings would ensure future harvests. Some of our present customs date back to the ancient practices: others are more modern, in keeping with the changing world in which we live. Harvest thanksgiving will vary, too, according to the locality. Traditional services are held in farming communities, whilst 'sea harvest' or 'industrial harvest' services are not uncommon today.*

*Harvest celebrations naturally centre upon a sense of thankfulness for all the things which we are able to enjoy and upon thoughtfulness for others who have few of these things. With the younger children there will be much to be learned about the cycle of nature, the wonders of fruit and flower, the provision of God and our dependence upon many people who bring us the harvest.*

*No doubt opportunities will be found to stress the need to share the good things of this world and to make individual contributions by giving something for someone who is in need.*

### 1 EAT AND BE THANKFUL

Peter wasn't feeling very happy. He sat at the table picking at his food, pushing it to the side of his plate and turning up his nose as he did so. 'For goodness' sake get on with your dinner!' said Mother. 'Don't like it!' he said sullenly. 'Well, just eat it,' he was told. 'I don't like to see good food wasted. You ought to think yourself lucky that you have such a nice dinner. Think of all the people who won't have a dinner today.' Peter did not know of any. All his friends had dinner. And he said so.

'I mean people in other countries,' his mother said, 'people who *never* have a good dinner; boys and girls who are always hungry . . . very, very hungry. Many of them live in countries where there are poor harvests because there has been no rain. Many are so poor that their families cannot afford to buy food. They would love to have a dinner like yours.'

Peter hadn't thought about people like that. He wondered what it would be like to be hungry.

'And think of all the people who gave you your dinner,' Mother went on.

'You gave it to me,' Peter said.

'Yes, I did,' Mother replied, 'but think of all the people who helped to get it for you. There was the fisherman who spent all night in a rough sea to catch the fish you have. There were the farmers who worked hard in the fields to grow and harvest the potatoes and the greens. Then there were the drivers who took the food to market, the market people who sold them to the shopkeepers and the shopkeepers who sold them to us.'

Peter thought for a moment. 'And there was Daddy who worked to get the money so we could buy the food,' he said.

'Yes,' replied his mother, 'and lots of other people too. We ought to be thankful to all these people who have given us our food, and to God who sent the sun and the rain to make it grow. And one way of saying thank you is by not wasting the good food we have.'

## 2  GREW IT MYSELF!

Alwyn was very excited about his piece of garden. It was not a large piece but it was *his* piece. His family had been living in a flat where there was no garden at all. Now they had moved into a house with a garden and Dad had said he could have a part if he promised to look after it.

'Dig it up well,' he said. 'Here is some money to go and buy yourself some seeds to plant in it.'

So Alwyn dug his garden and went out to buy the seeds. What should he get? He thought it would be nice to have some pretty flowers, so he bought several packets of flower seed. Maybe he could grow a few vegetables, too. He bought some carrot seed and some marrow seed. Wouldn't it be fun if he could grow a really large marrow?

After a while things began to grow. He couldn't wait to see what they were. He soon discovered what grew best—the weeds that needed to be pulled up if his plants were not to be choked.

One day his neighbour looked over the fence. 'What are you growing?' he asked. Alwyn told him. 'Marrow, eh!' he said. 'You need some muck if you are going to get any marrows on it. Horse manure is good for marrows.'

So Alwyn took a bucket to the stables and got some horse manure. It didn't smell very nice but if it would make his marrow grow it would be worth it. As the weeks passed, the marrow plant grew and had bright orange flowers on it. After the flowers came the marrows, and one of them was a real beauty!

It was about that time that a Harvest service was being held in Alwyn's school and the children were asked if they could all bring something, no matter how small, as a way of saying thank you to God for the harvest. Some went to the shops to buy things. Others asked their mums and dads to give them something.

Alwyn took his marrow. 'I grew it myself,' he proudly told his teacher. It was a lovely feeling to have done so.

But he wasn't quite right was he? He had dug the ground, planted the seed and pulled up the weeds. But Dad had paid for the seeds. And the man next door had helped. So had the horse! And, of course, God had sent the sun and rain. Harvests are made by lots of people together. We can never say, 'I did it all by myself.'

3 THANK YOU, GOD

Prakesh is a little Indian boy. His family are Hindus. In one of the rooms in his house there is a shelf on which there is a picture of one of the Hindu gods. Sometimes his father places some food or flowers in front of the picture and says some prayers to this god. He knows that in his sacred book, the Gita, the Lord Krishna says that if even a leaf, a flower, or fruit or water is offered to him he will enjoy the gift.

Rachel belongs to a Jewish family. For eight days in the autumn her family have their meals in the garden under a shelter or booth. This is the festival called Sukkoth and it has been kept by Jewish people for nearly four thousand years. It is one of the festivals when Jewish people say thank you for the harvest. Shevuoth (in June) was when they said thank you for the corn. Sukkoth was when they said thank you for the grape harvest. At both of these there are special services in the synagogue.

A long, long time ago, Moses had told people that, when they had gathered their harvest, they were to put some of it into a basket and take it to the priest to be offered to God. This would be a way to say thank you to God for a good harvest but also for God's goodness in giving them the Promised Land.

Robert and Sarah come from a Christian home. Their parents attend the church near their home and the children go to the Sunday School. Each year at the end of September, they have a special Harvest Festival Sunday, when the church is decorated with flowers, fruit and vegetables. They sing hymns about harvest-time and thank God for all the good food and lovely flowers.

Thanksgiving services like these are held by people in many lands in churches, synagogues, temples, schools and other places. People of many religions like to remember that God is good and to say thank you for all his good gifts—the food and the flowers and the sun and rain that makes them grow.

We should always remember to say, 'Thank you, God.'

## 4  SAINT CADOC

Long ago, in the mountains of Wales there lived a boy named Cadoc. He loved God and wanted others to know him too. So he went to a village in the valley to learn from a holy man how he could teach them.

He found that the people of the village were very sad. Bad weather had meant a bad harvest. When Cadoc asked if he could stay in the village and learn to be a teacher, the holy man shook his head sadly. 'I am sorry, there is not enough food for you. We are praying to God to help us so that we may not all starve this winter.'

Cadoc was so disappointed. He went away and sat under a tree to think what he could do next. Then he heard a rustling sound. A little mouse had come out of a hole carrying a grain of wheat in its mouth. Presently it came back without the wheat, went into the hole and came out again with another grain of wheat. This happened again and again and again.

'Where is the mouse getting all the grain?' thought Cadoc. 'Is there a store under the ground?' So he went to the village and returned with a group of men who had spades. They dug into the hillside and there, to their surprise, they found a cellar which had once been part of an old house. The house had fallen into ruins long before and earth had covered the cellar. There, in the old cellar, were sacks of wheat, enough to feed the people through the winter and leave some to sow in the fields in spring.

So Cadoc was able to stay in the village and learn from the holy man. Then he returned to his mountains where people loved him and learned to love God too. Cadoc was such a good man that he became known as Saint Cadoc.

## 5   SAM SAYS, 'THANK YOU'

Many years ago people went to Canada to make new homes for themselves and their families. Small groups of people found places where they could build their homes, they cut down trees and cleared land so that they could grow food to eat.

In one of these settlements, named Moose Creek, there was one store where people could buy things they needed. They often used to stop there to talk to each other because their farms were far apart. They even used it as a church, because there was no church building in Moose Creek.

One day, as they talked, one of the older men said, 'We ought to have a church. God has been very good to us since we came here five years ago.' The others agreed. Building a church would be one way of saying thank you to God.

Sam was one of the men. As he rode home, he was thinking about the church. Then he thought about those huge fields of wheat growing around his cabin. God had been very good to him. He could give a quarter of his crop for the new church. Perhaps the money would pay for some lovely coloured windows to make the church beautiful.

So Sam worked hard and harvested his wheat. A few weeks later he set off with a wagon loaded with grain to travel about thirty miles to Moose Creek. He was thinking about the church and the windows when suddenly his horses refused to go any further. Sam soon knew why. He could smell burning and he could see smoke rising from blackened fields.

Leaving his wagon, Sam rode over to the sad-looking people who stood nearby. It was all they had. They had spent all their money last year to buy the grain. Now the harvest was all gone. They had no money to buy food or more grain.

Sam sat for a moment. He thought of the windows and he thought of these poor people. 'I'll be back,' he said and rode away. Soon he was back with his wagon of grain.

'We can't afford to buy that!' the farmer said.

'I'm not asking you to *buy* it,' Sam replied. 'I'm *giving* it to you. It was going to buy windows for a church in Moose Creek but I'm sure this is a better way to say thank you to God.

## 6 HARVEST FOR SHARING

Once upon a time there was a lady who lived in a lovely cottage in the country. Behind her cottage was a garden with pretty flowers, rose bushes and a few vegetables that she had grown herself. In the corner was a small apple tree. It did not have many apples but they were really delicious, a lovely golden colour, sweet and juicy.

All through the summer she watched her apples growing. She counted them too—one, two, three . . . eighteen lovely apples. If she had one each day they would last her more than two weeks. Then, one day, about the beginning of October, she picked all her apples, polished them carefully and put them in a bowl on the sideboard in her living room. Perhaps she would have the first one after she had eaten her lunch!

Just then a coach drew up beside the common opposite her house. Some city children had been brought for an outing to the country. As they came out of the coach, she noticed that they all had something wrong with them. Some walked with sticks: some were in wheelchairs, helped out by the welfare ladies. They all seemed glad to be there.

She counted them as they got out of the coach—eighteen—just the number of apples in her bowl. She looked longingly at her apples, then looked at the children; she knew what to do: She took her apples and asked the teacher if the children would like one each. How the children enjoyed those delicious apples!

Back indoors she looked at her empty bowl. Not one apple had she eaten herself. Then she thought, 'If I had eaten them myself I would have made one person happy: now I have made eighteen . . . No! twenty three—because the teacher, the welfare ladies and the coach driver are happy as well.'

Perhaps it should be twenty-four for no doubt God was happy too!

7 WEST INDIAN HARVEST

On many of the islands of the West Indies the people enjoy the special Harvest Sunday services. On the day before, they make their way to the church with all sorts of interesting fruits, nuts and roots. There are mangoes and guavas, melons, yams, and peppers, sweet potatoes, bread, fruit and lots of other things as well. Some people travel long distances along uneven roads, carrying their produce in baskets on their heads or slung across the backs of their animals.

On one of the smaller islands there were two chapels, one near the harbour and one on the hill. For many years they held their harvest services on different days so they could enjoy each other's harvest. But something went wrong and the happy sharing at harvest time was forgotten. They even had their services on the same Sunday.

Then, one year, just as the harvest was about to be gathered, a fierce storm blew across the island. The folk on the hill lost nearly all they had. Their houses were damaged, their crops were flattened and all the trees were stripped of the fruit. For them there was no harvest: they were just thankful to be alive.

Down by the harbour it was a very different picture. The storm had passed by. The people decorated their church as usual without giving much thought to the folk on the hill. They would see if the poor folk needed help *after* they had thanked God for their harvest.

Imagine their surprise when the minister stood up to take the service. No harvest hymns were sung and neither the prayers nor the Bible reading were usual harvest thanksgiving ones. And when the minister spoke they knew why. They had done wrong to think only of themselves and not of the poor folk on the hill.

When the service was over, they decided what to do. Everyone gave a hand to take down their display and carry it to the chapel on the hill, where they carefully rearranged it to make one of the finest displays ever. And that evening they had a *real* harvest service with harbour folk and hill folk joining together to praise God for the harvest they were sharing and for the important lesson they had been taught.

8 THE GREAT HARVEST

Long before harvest time many of the apples will have fallen off the trees. We call them windfalls because they have been blown off by the wind.

If we look closely at a windfall we may find a small brownish hole in the apple. Cut the apple open and there is a tunnel leading from that hole to the centre of the apple which has been partly eaten away. It is that which weakened the apple and caused it to fall.

The story of that apple began a long time before, when the tree was in blossom. An insect laid its egg in the flower so that when the blossom changed into an apple the egg was right inside. This egg then hatched out and the grub that came out of it really enjoyed eating that apple. When it was big enough the insect ate its way through to the outside and left the apple—or what was left of it, for it was not much use to anyone. It was rotten inside and badly bruised where it had fallen on the ground.

Jesus sometimes spoke to people about God's harvest, when he would gather into his kingdom those people who had been true to him and lived good lives. It would be rather like the harvest that we know with the good fruits being gathered in. Many would not be included because they had fallen away from God.

People can be likened to the apples on the tree. Just as maggots can spoil the apples, so evil things can spoil people. And unless we can get rid of evil ways we shall never be near to God.

The man who owns the apple tree knows that he can keep many of the apples from being destroyed by spraying the blossom and killing the insects. So we can ask God to protect us from all evil and make us fit for his Kingdom

RELATED THEMES

---

1. Dear God, teach us to take care of all the good things you have given us, and to use them in the right way. *Amen*

2. Dear God, thank you for things that grow:
   For golden fields of grain to make bread, biscuits and cakes,
   >*Thank you, God our Father;*
   For potatoes, carrots and all sorts of other vegetables,
   >*Thank you, God our Father;*
   For apples, oranges and lots of lovely fruits,
   >*Thank you, God our Father;*
   For lovely flowers in the garden and hedgerow,
   >*Thank you, God our Father;*
   For things that we can grow ourselves,
   >*Thank you, God our Father;*
   Dear God, accept our thanks for all your gifts. *Amen*

3. Dear God, we remember the people who have helped to give us the harvest:
   Farmers, who ploughed the land, planted the seed, looked after the growing plants and reaped the harvest;
   Lorry drivers, sailors and lots of other people, who brought the food from where it grew;
   Market owners, buyers and sellers, who got the food that is sold in the shops;
   People in factories, who prepared some foods and put them into tins or packets;
   Shopkeepers who have so many kinds of food that we can buy to eat and enjoy.
   For these and many others we say thank you, God. *Amen*

4. O God our Father, we remember how food that is growing can be destroyed by harmful insects or disease and we ask that, as we grow, you will keep us free from evil things which can harm our lives. *Amen*

5. Take us, O God, into your care; protect us from evil; help us to grow good; and receive us into your kingdom. *Amen*

6. Teach us, O God, that harvests are for sharing and that the good food you give should give life to all people. Help us to be thoughtful of the needs of others and not waste those things we have. *Amen*

7. Teach us, O God, to share the good things we have and so bring happiness to other folk. *Amen*

8. Thank you, O God,
   For seeds to plant in the ground;
   For the rain that makes them grow;
   For the sun that makes them ripen for harvest;
   And for people who gather the harvest for our food. *Amen*

9. Thank you, God our Father, for looking after us, for providing us with food, and for giving us so many other good things. Give us thankful hearts. *Amen*

10. This is your world, O God. Help us to look after it and all that is in it, to know what you would have us to do, and to try our best to please you. *Amen*

11. We remember all the good things you have given us, O God, and we say thank you for them all. *Amen*

12. We thank you, God, for plants which give us food:
    For wheat and oats to make bread and breakfast foods;
    For green vegetables and roots which we eat for dinner;
    For apples and pears which grow in the orchard;
    For melons and guavas that grow overseas;
    For sugar cane and the sugar that makes things sweet;
    For spices and herbs to make our meals tasty;
    For so many interesting foods, we say thank you, God. *Amen*

*For other suitable prayers see under 'Food' pp. 96–7 and 'Bread' pp. 109–110*

Blackberries in the hedges
Ears of corn are waving
First the seed
For the golden corn
O lovely world of colour
See, here are red apples
See the farmer sow the seed
The farmer comes to scatter the seed
We plough the fields
When oats and corn have ripened
When the corn is planted

### HARVEST IN THE BIBLE

| | |
|---|---|
| Jewish festivals | Exodus 23; 14–19 |
| Share with the poor | Leviticus 19; 9–10 and |
| | Deuteronomy 24; 19–21 |
| An offering to God | Deuteronomy 26; 7–13 |
| Praise for the harvest | Psalm 65; 9–13 |
| Ruth in the harvest fields | Ruth 2; 1–9 |
| Parable of the sower | Matthew 13; 1–9 and 18–23 |
| Parable of the weeds | Matthew 13; 24–30 and 36–43 |
| The growing seed | Mark 4; 26–29 |

### INTEREST WORK AND ACTIVITIES

*Books*

Have available some books on various aspects of harvest so that the children can enjoy reading them or browsing. In addition to those listed here, some of the books in the sections on 'Bread', 'Food', and 'Autumn' could be useful.

FARMS AND FARMING *(Blackwell's Learning Library)*, Blackwell
FARMS AND FARMERS *(First Library)*, Macdonald

THE FARMER *(Easy Reading)*, Ladybird
ON THE FARM *(Zero)*, Macdonald
THE FARM/VEGETABLES/FRUIT *(Nature Table)*, Evans
WE DISCOVER CROPS WE GROW *(We discover)*, Arnold
SEEDS AND WEEDS *(Starters Nature)*, Macdonald

*Harvest decor*

Harvest time is a season that provides a fine opportunity to provide a theme for decoration and display throughout the school. In the country there will be opportunity to obtain plenty of natural materials—stems and ears of grain left behind after the harvest, grasses, sedges, bullrushes, reed-mace, teazels, the colourful hips and haws of the hedgerow, beech nuts, acorns, fir cones and anything else that will give an atmosphere of the season.

Town schools, with little opportunity for obtaining some of these things may be able to enlist the aid of local churches. Most churches hold Harvest Festival services towards the end of September or beginning of October. Whilst they have outlets for distribution of fruit and vegetables, they often have greenery, berries, small sheaves of corn, or perhaps a harvest loaf, that they would be only too pleased to pass on if they can prove useful. School harvest services would probably be held in most schools early in October, giving time to learn the harvest hymns.

Perhaps different classes could be responsible for the decoration of one alcove or part of the corridor, each having a particular emphasis, e.g. Cereals, Fruit, Berries, Seed pods, or Nuts.

Harvest pictures are usually easy to find and can provide good background display material.

The harvest need not be just a traditional 'farm' harvest. A harvest of the sea is probably more relevant to some children. There is also the 'harvest' of the mine or the factory.

*A harvest service*

Organize a Harvest Festival. Encourage the children to bring something for the service. It is good if everyone can bring something, however small, so that each has taken a part in the preparation.

Arrange for the produce to be distributed afterwards to elderly, ill or housebound people. There may be a local branch of the Red Cross or a similar organization with contacts through which distribution could be made, perhaps by a few children from the school at one of the day centres. A knowledge of the kind of people to whom distribution will be made can help in the guidance offered to the children as to what they should bring.

Classes may like to prepare their own part of the display, arranging any harvest gifts in boxes, baskets or trays.

The Harvest Festival may be an opportunity to invite a visiting speaker . . . if one can be found who is able to speak well to young children. Ask the visitor to keep the talk simple and brief.

A Harvest Festival can demonstrate practically how we give to God by giving to other people.

## Visitors

A visitor to a Harvest Festival may be only one of several visitors to come to school. Other suggestions are:

A Jewish minister or Rabbi to talk about Sukkoth.

A Christian church leader to talk about Christian services.

A farmer to tell what harvest time is like.

A fisherman or miner to talk of other harvests.

## Visits

For country children harvest time is part of life. Town children are somewhat removed from this reality. Perhaps they could be taken in small groups to see end products in the shops of the greengrocer and the fishmonger or in the market.

## Other aspects

Farm machinery, past and present, could be introduced as an added interest.

If a corn dolly can be obtained, it would provide an introduction to harvest beliefs and customs.

Interesting art work can be produced by sticking grain, seeds and other natural matter on to a dark background paper to make pictures or patterns.

*Help*

Practical help in connection with the harvest can be offered to organizations, such as Oxfam or Christian Aid, which offer help or relief to those who have no harvest.

# 24 Christmas

*Christmas has sometimes been described as 'the children's festival'. Certainly it is a time of year with so much that is exciting and wonderful in children's eyes.*

*As a Christian religious festival it is naturally centred around the birth of Jesus Christ. Some of the traditions are symbolic: others go far back into history to the Roman Saturnalia and the Norse Yule. The intertwining of these traditions and customs has given us the Christmas we know and enjoy. It is also a time of goodwill and benevolence, demonstrated in so many different ways.*

*But for the children it is the season of Santa Claus, Christmas trees, fairy lights, Christmas puddings and presents. It is a time of wonder and happiness . . . with a lovely story of a very special baby in a stable.*

## 1 SANTA CLAUS

A story is told that, many years ago, in the part of the world we now call Turkey, there was a good bishop named Nicholas. There was also a very poor man who had three daughters, all of whom would have liked to get married.

But in those days the girls needed some money, called a dowry, before they could marry and their father did not have any to give them. They were all very sad. The good Saint Nicholas heard about it and went quietly to the house one night, leaving gold in the shoes of the eldest daughter. She was delighted. Now she could be married.

Twice more Saint Nicholas called at the house, leaving gold each time for the other girls. But on the third time the poor man was waiting and the secret was out. He soon told other people about the good Saint Nicholas and his kindness.

The story of Saint Nicholas spread to many other countries. He is remembered especially on 6th December. In Holland, he sails into Amsterdam, wearing his bishop's robes, on the evening before with his servant Black Peter. He is met by the Queen and there is a big parade. That night the children leave their shoes by the fireside in the hope that Sinter Nicholas, or Sinter Klaas, as he is known, will leave something for them.

Years ago, when Dutch people went to America, they took this old custom with them. Sinter Klaas became Santa Claus. Nowadays we expect Santa Claus, not on the eve of St. Nicholas's Day, but on Christmas Eve. Children in many lands look forward to a visit from Santa Claus or Father Christmas, as he is often called.

On Christmas Eve we hang up our stockings or pillow cases or some other kind of bag which we hope will hold all the things we would like to receive.

Then, on Christmas morning, we find that it has indeed been filled with all sorts of goodies. Was it Santa Claus who filled it? Or was it someone else? What does it matter? We love the custom. It is part of the magic of Christmas and Santa Claus, or Father Christmas is part of our special celebration at this time of festival.

## 2 CHRISTMAS TREES

Over 100 years ago, Queen Victoria, who was the Queen of England, married Prince Albert and they had a big family of boys and girls. Prince Albert had come from Germany, where, for hundreds of years, it had been the custom for people to have an evergreen tree, which was taken indoors and decorated for Christmas.

In German families, the Christmas tree was an important part of Christmas Eve celebrations, when the family gathered together to exchange gifts and be happy together. After the telling of the Christmas story and the singing of carols, the children would be expected to say a poem or perhaps sing a song in front of the tree before receiving a gift from the tree.

Prince Albert thought it would be nice for his own children to enjoy the kind of Christmas that he enjoyed at home in Germany, so he arranged for a small fir tree to be brought to Windsor Castle. In this way the first Christmas tree was introduced to England.

At first the twinkling lights on the Christmas tree came from candles, which were clipped on to the branches. This, of course, could be dangerous because the candles sometimes set the tree alight. Nowadays our trees are decorated with bright electric fairy lights, with tinsel, coloured baubles, toys and packages. They make a lovely sight.

Today we see lots of different kinds of Christmas tree. Some are

326

real trees but some are made by man, not grown. They may be gold or silver or made of plastic to look like a real tree. But the real Christmas trees are ones which have been grown and brought in especially for Christmas.

Many Christmas trees grow in cold lands such as Norway. There, each year, they cut down one of the finest trees and put it on a ship bound for London. Then it is unloaded and taken by road to Trafalgar Square, where it is lit with lots of coloured lights. It is a way in which the people of Norway like to say thank you to the people of Britain for helping them during the war years, over forty years ago.

Christmas is a time for remembering in many ways. We remember old friends and send them greetings or presents. We remember God's great gift to us when he sent Jesus Christ, whose birth we celebrate each Christmas Day.

## 3 CAROL SINGING

It was such a lovely Christmas card. The whole family thought so. It was a picture of a group of people, grown-ups and children, standing together in the light which came from a lantern on the end of a long pole, held by one of the men in the group. They were all dressed very warmly in their winter coats, with woollen scarves, hats, gloves and with boots on their feet. The light from the lantern fell on their faces, rosy with the cold, and on the snow which covered the ground. From the picture it could be seen that they were singing, their mouths open wide to give full strength to the words and tune.

The group stood outside a large door, which was just being opened to show the inside of the house, all gay and alive with light—lights from the rooms and from the huge Christmas tree standing in the hall.

Just looking at the picture the children felt that they were there with the carol singers, feeling the cold of winter in their tingling fingers and toes, and on their cheeks, but feeling very warm in their scarves and hats and with the kind of warmth which comes from feeling happy—happy in doing something with other people and for other people. This kind of happiness comes especially at Christmas time.

Father explained to them that the picture was telling a story of the kind of life which people lived a long time ago. The people living in the very large house would be some of the important people in the neighbourhood. The singers, when they had finished, would probably be invited into the house to enjoy some mince pies and a hot drink before going on their way.

Carol singing is another very happy and enjoyable part of the celebration of Christmas. We learn to sing carols when we are quite small. Usually the carols are about the birth of the baby Jesus and all the wonderful happenings of Christmas. Not all carols have been about Christmas. Carols are happy songs, which people have made up about all kinds of happenings, but we usually associate them with Christmas time, for it is then that we learn the special songs which we only sing at Christmas time.

We hear the sounds of carols ring out in our busy shopping streets while people are hurrying to get all their Christmas shopping in time for the great day. We sing carols in school and in church: we hear them from all sides and they give us a warm glow. Many of them are songs or hymns which are so well known that we can join in and sing them ourselves.

Like the carol singers in the Christmas card picture which the children saw, people use this way of singing for the enjoyment of others and also to collect money for all kinds of reasons, to help other people and make people happy, because it is Christmastime. Carol singers today, if properly organized, can bring a breath of Christmas to others.

For just a short time in the year we make the most of these happy songs. We sing them and love them. It is just another part of the magic of Christmas.

4 THE CHRISTMAS STORY

In the little town of Nazareth lived Mary, and Joseph the carpenter, who worked hard to make things out of wood for the people of the town. A notice came from the important people who ruled the land that every man must go to be registered in the place where his family came from. So it meant that Joseph had to travel to another town—Bethlehem—his family home and take Mary with him. Mary was soon to have a baby.

They set off on their journey which would take quite a long time.

There were no trains, cars, 'planes, or buses. Everyone had to walk, or, if they were very fortunate, they may have had a little donkey to help them, to give them a ride for part of the way and to carry their belongings.

It was a rather weary journey for them and took a long time, so that when they came to Bethlehem it was already late in the day. People were all settled down, perhaps staying with relatives or having found a place to sleep.

Mary was very tired and Joseph tried to find somewhere for them to stay for the night. He called at one or two places where he thought there may be shelter, but they were already full: so many people had been looking for a place to stay.

He saw an inn, where he hoped there might be some room for them, and went to ask if there was. The innkeeper was very sorry; every part of his inn was full; he had no more room. So Joseph and Mary turned wearily away. The innkeeper saw that Mary needed somewhere to sleep and he probably felt rather sorry for them. Then he remembered the stable where the animals slept. At least it was dry and warm and would give shelter for the night. It was not really a very nice place to stay, but better than being out in the open. So he called to Joseph and offered him the stable as a shelter.

Joseph was very glad of *any* shelter for Mary and himself and gladly accepted the offer. They went to the stable. It was rather dark, but it was a shelter where they could stay for the time being. There was straw to make a soft bed and so they prepared to stay there for the night.

Perhaps they could hear the sounds of the animals: we don't really know, but we do know that something very special happened that night. A little baby was born to Mary there in the stable. He was a very special little baby, because all kinds of people came to visit him. Some shepherds came to see the baby and worship him. They had been told the news by an angel.

Later, some wise men from a long way off came too. They said they had followed a special star which had led them all the way until it stopped over the very place where Jesus was. These are some of the stories we remember each year at Christmas. It is that Baby at Bethlehem who has made it all so special for us.

## 5 CHRISTINGLES

Christmas is a time when we enjoy lots of bright, cheerful lights and decorations. It would hardly seem like Christmas if there were no cribs, or stars, or angels, or lights.

These things are more than just decorations. They may look pretty but they also remind us of parts of the Christmas story. The cribs remind us of the manger in the stable where the baby Jesus was laid. The angels once gave that special message to the shepherds. Stars remind us of the one that led the wise men to Jesus and twinkling lights recall the stars in the sky at Bethlehem that night. Tinsel and other bright things bring their own happiness to this season.

In Moravia, which is part of the country we call Czechoslovakia, there is a special service for children known as a Christingle Service, which has been held at Christmastime for over two hundred years.

A Christingle is a specially decorated orange, which reminds people of what Christmas is all about. A hole is made in the top of the orange and a candle pushed into it. Around the candle four goose feathers are stuck into the orange, each of which has a jelly or sweet attached to it. A red ribbon may be tied round the orange.

The round orange is a reminder of the world. The candle represents Jesus, the Light of the World, and the four feathers tell how the Light of the World goes in all directions, north, south, east and west. The sweets represent the good things that come to us through knowing Jesus and the red ribbon is a reminder of the blood of Jesus.

As the children gather for their service the Christingles are lit. The children hear the familiar Christmas stories and sing their carols by the light of the candles. Then they take their Christingles home . . . and no doubt many of them later eat the orange, remembering God's good gifts.

Often the Christingles were given to children after they had done something to help poorer children. It is a custom which has spread to other countries including our own. A Christingle is a reminder of God's care for the world and of our care for others who are less fortunate than we are.

That is a very important part of Christmas. In fact it is really what Christmas is all about.

CHRISTMAS ROUND THE WORLD

It might be interesting to the children to tell them how children in other parts of the world may be celebrating Christmas. Perhaps some may have relatives overseas. There are many interesting customs of which the following are but a few:

*Australasia*

Children 'down under', in Australia and New Zealand, will have started their long summer holiday. Christmas will be celebrated by many out of doors, perhaps having their Christmas dinner on the beach or in the country. Those staying at home may visit each other's homes in the morning and go for a picnic after Church and lunch.

*Scandinavia*

Christmas is associated with the old festival of Yule and the lighting of the Yule Log is sometimes part of the celebrations. In Sweden it is the custom in some villages to keep the largest sheaf of grain after the harvest. On Christmas Eve, perhaps helped by the children, father hangs the sheaf from the roof of the house to provide the birds with their Christmas dinner. In Finland, children may sleep on straw, instead of in their beds, as a reminder of the stable in which the baby Jesus lay.

*Sarawak*

In Sarawak, where the 'streets' are water and the houses stand on poles, young people on Christmas Eve go in their boats to sing carols outside the houses of their Christian friends. To welcome them, the friends set off fire crackers . . . so Christmas Eve is noisy until, as Christmas Day comes, they return to their homes.

## CHRISTMAS CUSTOMS

There are lots of interesting customs at Christmastide and these could provide extra material for telling if so desired. Most books of festivals give some information about these.

*Christmas cards:* An important part of Christmas, started last century, bringing a lot of happiness.

*Holly and ivy:* The subject of a well-known carol with quite a lot of symbolism. Both were believed to have special powers.

*Mistletoe:* Dating back a long way to Celtic Britain. Sacred to the Druid priests. Never used to decorate churches.

*Feasting:* Associated with the old Roman seven-day mid-winter festival of Saturnalia. Feasting is still a part of most Christmas family celebrations.

*Christmas pudding:* Originated as plum porridge, into which all sorts of things were put. The setting alight of brandy dates back to sun and fire worship.

*Mince pies:* Originally savoury minced meat in a pie in the shape of a cradle. The 'baby' was taken out before the pie was eaten.

*Wassailing:* Christmas singing took its name from Wassail, a spiced drink. Wassail means 'Good health', the message passed on by the wassailers.

*Christmas boxes:* Gifts made at Christmastide to show appreciation of services rendered. Also used to help the poor and needy.

*Christmas charity:* Help for the poor, sometimes given on St. Thomas's Day, 21st December. Nowadays there are appeals by most charitable organizations.

*Christmas presents:* Gifts to relatives and friends, perhaps reminiscent of the gifts of the wise men or of God's great gift.

PRAYERS

1. Be with us, dear Father God, during this happy Christmas season. We remember that we have Christmas because you sent Jesus to teach us about you. Help us to learn all that he taught us. *Amen*

2. Dear Father God, I like Christmas:
   The decorations and lights are so pretty,
   And I can't wait to open my presents.
   I enjoy the Christmas music and carols;
   And there are such lovely things to eat.
   It is nice to send and receive greeting cards
   And to know I have so many good friends.
   I know I am fortunate to have all these things:
   Help me to remember all those who do not. *Amen*

3. In the rush and bustle of Christmas, O God, when I have so many exciting things to do, please help me not to forget you. *Amen*

4. Keep me mindful, dear God, that we have our Christmas because you sent your Son, Jesus, into the world; and make me thankful for all that you have given to me. *Amen*

5. Lord Jesus, I shall have lots of good things to enjoy this Christmas. You had none of these things when you were born in that stable so long ago. Help me to remember other children today who will have very little to enjoy. *Amen*

6. Lord Jesus, Son of God,
   You have given me so much:
   Help me to give what I can—
   A special gift of my life
   To be used for your glory. *Amen*

7. Loving Father, help me to know that you sent your Son, Jesus, to teach me what I should know about you. Show me how to live so that I can be all that you would want me to be. *Amen*

8. Thank you, God, for Christmas:
   For all the things we can enjoy,
             *Thank you, God;*
   For music and carols, fun and enjoyment,
             *Thank you, God;*
   For Christmas trees and pretty lights,
             *Thank you, God;*
   For Father Christmas, presents and toys,
             *Thank you, God;*
   For lots of lovely food to eat,
             *Thank you, God;*
   But especially for sending Jesus
   To bring your light into our world, we say
             *Thank you, God. Amen*

9. Thank you, O God, for all I shall have this Christmas. Help me
   to remember all those who will not enjoy Christmas as much as
   I shall: some sad and lonely; some old or ill; and the very poor,
   hungry people in many parts of the world. Be with them, O
   God, and make me thankful for all that I have. *Amen*

10. You have given me so many things, O God. Help me this
    Christmas to use your gifts to bring happiness to others. *Amen*

SOME CHRISTMAS HYMNS

A little Child on the earth has been born
Away in a manger
Bring the Christmas in
Child Jesus, Child Jesus
God takes good care of me
In Bethlehem so long ago
Jesus, baby Jesus
Little Jesus, sweetly sleep
On Christmas Day, what do we see?
Softly sleeping, softly sleeping
Wise men seeking Jesus

THE BIBLE STORY

| | |
|---|---|
| Promise of the Messiah | Isaiah 9; 6–7 and 40; 1–11 |
| The Annunciation | Matthew 1; 18–25: Luke 1; 26–38 |
| The Birth Story | Luke 2; 1–20 |
| Wise Men from the East | Matthew 2; 1–12 |
| The Word | John 1; 1–14 |

INTEREST WORK AND ACTIVITIES

*Books*

Have a few Christmas books available for the children to enjoy. Here are some:

CHRISTMAS *(Starters Facts)*, Macdonald
THE CHRISTMAS BOOK, Macdonald
LET'S FIND OUT ABOUT CHRISTMAS *(Let's find out)* Watts
LONG AGO IN BETHLEHEM, Black
A BABY CALLED JESUS/THE WISE MEN FROM MORN-ING LAND *(Little Lions)*, Lion
THE CHRISTMAS STORY *(Bible Stories)*, Hart-Davis
CHRISTMAS CUSTOMS *(Our Customs)*, Ladybird

For teachers, TOGETHER FOR CHRISTMAS and TOGETHER AGAIN FOR CHRISTMAS are resource anthologies, published by Church Information Office, Dean's Yard, Westminster SW1P 3NZ.

So much is always planned for the Christmas season in school that there is little perhaps, to add, but one or two ideas are offered, which may be used or adapted to continue thoughts about the story and message of Christmas.

Most schools have a post box to receive cards, etc., to be delivered in the school. Classes or groups may like to make a Father Christmas Wishing Box. For this you will need: a fairly small cardboard box or container; fine card; felt-tip pens, crayons or paints and scissors. Draw an outline of Father Christmas, slightly larger than one side of the box, so that the head and shoulders stand up above the top of the box. Cut out, leaving sections each side to be wrapped round the box and glued. Colour the figure and glue it to the side of the box with the side flaps folded round and glued in place. The box should be painted red and the top flanges cut off.

Children may write lists of things they would like and post them in the box.

*Mobiles*

As well as using wire clothes hangers, try making a mobile using a small rod (Garden cane cut down to size would do). Use a cotton reel for centre point, with two stars drawn, cut out and stuck one on each side. Pass the stick through the cotton reel. Draw and cut out two 'Christmas' shapes. Using wool, fine string, or fine elastic, suspend a figure from each end.

*A Christingle service.*

One Christingle for each child may not be practical but some could be made.

In the top of the orange, cut a hole just large enough to take the base of a small candle and sufficiently deep to hold it steady. Wooden cocktail sticks could be used in place of goose feathers, with sweets (jellies or chocolates) on the end of the sticks, which are pushed firmly into the orange. Decorate with a scrap of tinsel or other glitter-type decoration.

With candles finally lit, the Christingles could be held by children as they process round the room to the singing of a carol.

# 25 Easter

*Easter is the most important of the Christian festivals, being the hub of Christian belief in the death and resurrection of Jesus Christ. At one time it was celebrated to a greater degree than Christmas but its commercial pull is smaller.*

*As with Christmas, the Easter festival has become entwined with customs which date back long before the Christian era. The name itself comes from Eostre, the Anglo-Saxon goddess of Spring. The egg has long been a symbol of new life and resurrection.*

*The concept of the Easter Story is difficult for many adults, yet it is important that it should be told to children. We have therefore told it simply and in such a way that it will not be too stark or unpleasant for the young listener.*

## 1 PALM SUNDAY

It was all so exciting: Rachel and Samuel were looking forward to the visit they were to make into the city. Everyone, it seemed, was planning such a visit. It was near the time of Passover and relatives were coming to see their families, to spend the holiday with them and with friends. For the Jewish people, the time of Passover was very special.

Many exciting things had been happening lately. Samuel and Rachel were finding life was full of wonderful things. Their parents were interested in the work of the new teacher who had been helping people. They heard how he had made sick people well again, just by talking to them and putting his hand upon them. Blind people had been made to see and cripples able to walk again. He talked to people and told them important things to remember. Their mother and father had actually seen him and heard him as he went among the people. Mother and father said what a kind and loving person he was. He was very brave, too, and not afraid to stand up for what he thought was right.

Now, they were ready to go into the city with Mother, Father, and baby brother John, to join in the festivities. In the centre of the city crowds and crowds of people thronged the roadway. There was such a buzz of voices and people seemed to be gathering along the main street as though they expected something to happen.

The crowds grew larger and people were pushed against each other. Rachel and Samuel felt rather squashed, but they didn't want to miss anything. Mother held on to their hands and told them to stay close. They craned their necks and stood on tiptoe. Father put little John up on to his shoulder.

A hush fell on the crowd and then a cry went up 'He is coming! He is here!' Other voices called 'Hosanna' (which is like saying 'Hooray'). The cheers grew louder and people pushed forward to get a better view. In the distance the voices were heard, getting louder and louder, 'Hosanna! Blessed is he who comes in the name of the Lord!'

Then, into view came a man riding on a donkey. 'Why, it is Jesus,' said Father. 'Look, children, this is Jesus, the leader we told you about.' And Jesus it was, riding into Jerusalem on a donkey!

People became more and more excited, so excited that they took off their cloaks and laid them down on the ground to make a carpet for Jesus to ride over. They reached up and broke off palm branches to wave and to put down on the ground too.

The children looked at the figure coming nearer and nearer. Jesus seemed quite calm, looking round at the people clamouring on all sides. He looked rather sad—not at all excited as they would expect him to be. 'Isn't he glad all the people are happy to see him?' asked Samuel. Mother and Father couldn't answer this question. They were glad that Jesus was being welcomed, not knowing that Jesus was probably sad because he knew that soon he would be in danger and people would be against him.

After a most exciting time the family went home. As the children settled down to sleep that night, they thought over all the happenings of the day. And they remembered how sad Jesus looked.


2 THE PASSOVER

Great preparations were taking place in the home of Rachel, Samuel and John. Passover time was almost here and all the Jewish people looked forward to this time of festival which they spent with families and friends. The Passover feast had been held each year since the time when Moses led the people away from Egypt, where they had been slaves, to the land where they had settled down.

In the house, Mother had been busy for many days, cleaning,

polishing and cooking. The house was now clean, with everything in its right place and special food was prepared.

All was ready, and the family gathered together to eat, to say prayers and remember special times of the past when God had taken care of the people of Israel.

Jesus was spending Passover with some friends, too. They met together in an upstairs room where they all sat round the table to eat and to pray. Jesus was sad as he looked round at his friends. He knew that very soon he would be in great danger, that people would say all sorts of unkind things about him and that he would be hurt very badly, even killed.

He knew, but his friends did not know, that this would be the last time they would meet and eat supper together in this way.

Although Passover time was a happy time of festival, it was a very sad time for Jesus.

### 3 SAD DAYS

Samuel and Rachel did not know what was wrong, but they felt a kind of unhappiness in their home. Baby John was too small to understand, but *they* knew that their parents were very troubled about something. People were coming and going and talking to their parents. They heard snatches of conversation among the grown-ups, though they couldn't really understand them. Certainly it seemed as though dreadful things were happening and they were to do with Jesus, the leader whom they had seen in Jerusalem a short while ago. Mother and Father were unhappy and didn't talk very much: they just looked very troubled.

The children heard talk of Jesus going before the council where people turned against him and accused him of all kinds of things. They heard a crowd noise as though people were yelling and shouting. They thought of the happy day when Jesus rode in triumph into Jerusalem. People had been so glad to see him and treated him as a hero. Now the shouting was different; it was ugly and unkind; and people shouted, 'Crucify him! Crucify him!'

They were very sad when they heard from people who came to the house that Jesus had been taken out of the city, up to a hill, and there he was killed, put upon a cross to die. It was such a sad day for all the people who had followed him and thought he had come to lead them in a way that would make the world better for everyone. The friends of Jesus gathered in each other's homes. Some came to the home of Samuel and Rachel. They talked in whispers about how Jesus had been left to die on the cross and then had been taken away.

It was now the Sabbath, but they didn't feel very happy about it, because of what had taken place the day before. Everything they had hoped for was finished and they wondered what would happen next.

That night, the children were a little fearful as they went to bed. They didn't understand it all, but because the grown-ups were unhappy and fearful, they felt it, too. They went to sleep to try to forget all about the unhappiness around them.

## 4 EASTER MORNING

The children were still asleep when someone came running to their house and seemed very excited about something. It was one of the friends of their parents who was so excited at what had happened, he couldn't wait until everyone was up to tell them all about it.

From the friend the children and their parents heard a strange story. One of Jesus' friends, Mary, thought she would go along to the garden where the body of Jesus had been placed in a kind of cave. She wanted to go to see that all was well. As she came to the place of the cave, she was amazed to see that the big stone in front of the opening had been moved away. This made Mary feel worried and sad because she thought someone had taken away the body of Jesus. She was so sad that she began to cry and put her face in her hands. So she didn't see someone come along and stand near her: she just heard a voice asking her why she was crying. She thought it was a gardener and asked him why Jesus had been taken away.

The person behind her just spoke her name, 'Mary,' and she knew that voice. She turned and saw that it was Jesus standing behind her. Other friends of Jesus also saw him and Jesus told them to let all their friends know what had happened.

Jesus had come back to them, not as a person who would live among them any more, but to let them know that in a very special way he would always be with them, even when they could no longer see him.

340

It was such a wonderful day for the friends of Jesus, and it is a wonderful message for all the friends of Jesus even today. Indeed, it is a message for everyone. Jesus can be with us always, though we cannot see him. If he had gone on living with the people he could be with only a few, but now he can be with everyone, all the time.

It is the very special message of Easter which has made people ever since shout for joy, 'Hallelujah—Praise be to God'.


EASTER CUSTOMS

There are many customs associated with Easter and these could be used as extra material if so desired. Further details are readily available in books about festivals.

*Easter eggs:* Nowadays usually chocolate. The eating of eggs used to be forbidden during Lent but at the end of Lent they were coloured and given as presents.

*Pace (Paschal) eggs:* Hard boiled eggs with a dyed shell. It was customary for children to beg for pace eggs. Pace-egg plays are still performed. A game called 'Shackling' or 'Jarping' is played with hard-boiled eggs—rather like conkers but with eggs held in the hand. Egg-rolling is a related custom, the winner being the person whose egg rolls farthest down the hill before breaking.

*Hot-cross buns:* Spicy buns with the symbol of the cross are made to be eaten on Good Friday.

*Easter cakes (biscuits):* Flat, round, currant shortbreads, tied in threes to represent the Holy Trinity, are given to members of the family on Easter Day.

*Simnel cakes:* Spicy fruit cakes with almond paste on top. Eleven almond eggs represent the eleven apostles (leaving out Judas). Given to mothers on Mothering Sunday and kept to be eaten at Easter.

*Easter bunny:* A modern error! It was the hare that was an animal sacred to Eostre.

*Sports:* Many local customs, including Heaving, Lifting, and Bottle-kicking, take place on Easter Monday. Others, including Orange Rolling and the Marbles Championship are held on Good Friday.

*Royal Maundy:* Coins distributed by the Monarch on Maundy Thursday (the day before Good Friday).

*Church Services:* Special services are held during Holy Week, notably on Maundy Thursday, Good Friday and Easter Day.

PRAYERS

1.  We remember, dear God, how the people of Jerusalem welcomed Jesus into their city. Help us to welcome him into our hearts and our homes so that we may learn to live in the ways that he taught us. *Amen*

2.  O God, sometimes people let us down and we get upset. We remember how Jesus was let down, even by his best friends, yet carried on with the things he knew he should do. Help us to be like him. *Amen*

3.  We think, dear God, of that sad day long ago when your Son, Jesus, died, and we know it was so that people could know of your great love. Help us to love you and to know you as our dear heavenly Father. *Amen*

4.  Thank you, dear God, for that lovely Easter story of how Jesus came back to his friends and made them so happy. May Easter be a very happy time for us, because we know that Jesus can live in our hearts today. *Amen*

5.  For all that makes Easter such a happy time, we give you thanks, O God, in Jesu's Name. *Amen*

---

HYMNS FOR PALM SUNDAY AND EASTER

At Easter time the lilies fair
Coming from the winter
Hurray for Jesus
Jesus comes riding on a donkey
Jesus, good above all other
Jesus is alive
Jesus was the son of God
Morning in the garden
Praise King Jesus
The children were praising, praising, praising
There is a green hill
Very early in the morning
We have a king who rides a donkey

THE BIBLE STORY

| | |
|---|---|
| Palm Sunday | Matthew 21; 1–11 |
| The Last Supper | Matthew 26; 17–30 |
| The Betrayal | Mark 14; 10–11 and 43–50 |
| The Trial | Luke 23; 1–25 |
| The Crucifixion | Luke 23; 26–56 |
| The Resurrection | John 20; 1–30 |

INTEREST WORK AND ACTIVITIES

*Books for the book corner*

THE EASTER BOOK, Macdonald
EGGS *(Starters)*, Macdonald
WE DISCOVER EGGS *(We discover)*, Arnold

*A 'Palm Sunday' procession*

Cut large palm-shaped leaves from sugar paper and paint green.
Make banners to carry, with simple wording such as 'Hosanna' and

'Praise to the Lord'. Process from playground to hall, singing a suitable hymn, e.g. *We have a king who rides a donkey.*

Older children could make palm crosses from dried rushes, but this is too intricate for young fingers.

### Decorated eggs

Have a decorated egg competition or display. Each child to make as interesting an egg as possible. Hard-boiled eggs can be painted or have 'additions' made from plasticine, paper or card.

### Easter chicks

Make a basic structure of wire or pipe cleaners. Cover with yellow cotton wool balls or ordinary cotton wool painted or dyed yellow. Cut a tiny beak from card or sticky paper and put black specks for eyes. Feet made from wire are fastened to the pipe cleaner or wire frame.

### An Easter Garden

Make an Easter Garden, as is displayed in many Christian churches at Easter. Fill a tray with earth. Make a mound in one corner with three crosses and another mound with a round stone pressed into the front. Decorate with mosses and small plants to make it bright and cheerful. Keep moist.

### Easter Cards

Make Easter Cards to take home to parents at the end of term.

# Prayers and Hymns

1. As we start our day, dear God, we come to you for your blessing. Help us in every way to be the kind of children you would like us to be. *Amen*

2. As we start our day we praise you, O God. Be with us in all our work and in all our play and guide us in everything we say or do. *Amen*

3. At the beginning of our day, dear God, we say thank you for a restful night and a safe awakening. Help us to use our day wisely and well. *Amen*

4. Before we become very busy today, O God, help us, in the quietness of this hall, to meet with you. Guide us in everything we do today and stay with us to its end. *Amen*

5. Dear God, we come to you this morning before we begin our work. Help us now and all through the day to do and be the very best we can. *Amen*

6. Each morning we like to meet here, O God, to say thank you for all you have given us. Thank you for everything. *Amen*

7. Father God, at the beginning of this new day we ask you to bless all that we do. May we do our best in our work and have happy faces all the day. *Amen*

8. For a restful night, this bright new day, and all the blessings of our homes and school, we praise you, God our Father. *Amen*

9. It isn't a very bright morning, dear God, but we have so many things to be thankful for. So help us to sing our songs to you and, in any way we can, to bring our own special brightness to the day. *Amen*

10. O God, we have so many things for which we say thank you. Help us to remember all the things you give us and be thankful. *Amen*

11. O God, you have made our world and everything in it. You have made us and told us to call you our Father. Thank you for our lovely world and for being so good to us. *Amen*

12. On this lovely sunny morning, dear God, we say thank you for the sunshine, the flowers and everything that makes the world so beautiful. Help us today to do nothing that would spoil it. *Amen*

13. Praise to you, dear God, for a bright new morning, for work to do and games to play, and for the fun of being with each other. Please bless us each one. *Amen*

14. Thank you, dear God, for all the good things that are ours to enjoy. As we start our day we praise you and say thank you for everything. *Amen*

15. Thank you, dear God, for bright sunshine, blue skies and a beautiful world. We ask you this morning to help us to enjoy it. *Amen*

16. Thank you for this new day, dear Father God, and thank you for all the blessings I know I shall receive today. Please keep me thankful. *Amen*

17. Thank you, dear God, for giving us this new day. Please help us to make good use of it. *Amen*

18. Thank you, God, for all the blessings we receive:
For food and clothing;
For health and strength;
For family and friends;
For work and play.
For these and all you give us, thank you, God. *Amen*

19. This is a new day, dear God. We thank you for giving it to us and we ask that you will show us how to use it. *Amen*

20. We come to say thank you, God our Father:
    For this lovely new day,
    *Thank you, God our Father;*
    For all we shall be able to do in it,
    *Thank you, God our Father;*
    For all the people who will share it with us,
    *Thank you, God our Father;*
    And for health and strength to enjoy it,
    *Thank you, God our Father. Amen*

21. We like to sing and talk to you, O God, and so we are glad to praise you now. Take our praise and our love, and help us to be the kind of people you would like us to be. *Amen*

22. We praise you this morning, O God:
    We praise you for all you have given us:
    We praise you for our homes and our school:
    We praise you for our families and friends:
    We praise you for our work and our play
    And for so many things to enjoy.
    Please bless us all. *Amen*

23. We thank you, dear God, for keeping us safely through the night and for bringing us here this morning. Help us to use this day well. *Amen*

24. We thank you, Father God, that we are well and strong and able to come to school today. A whole new day is in front of us. Help us to use it well and to do and be the best we can. *Amen*

25. When days are dark and cold, dear Father God, we think of the brightness and warmth of your love for us and we say a big thank you. *Amen*

*Our school*

26. Our school is like a big family, dear God. Please help us all to be loving and kind, helping and caring for each other, so that we become a happy family in every way. *Amen*

27. This is *our* school dear God. Help us to make it a place where everyone can be happy, where we can work and play together, and where we can help each other. Be with us all through this day, please, and help us. *Amen*

28. We say thank you, dear God, for all the people who make our school like it is; our teachers and welfare ladies, caretakers and cleaners, dinner and playground ladies, and all the other boys and girls. May we all try to make this a really happy place. *Amen*

*A fresh start*

29. Thank you, God, for new books, clean pages, pencils, paints and all those things we use day by day. Show us how to use our time in school so that we may do the very best we can—even in those lessons we may not like. *Amen*

*Beginning of the school year*

30. Today, dear God, we begin a new year in school—a whole year for work and play, and with so much to learn and do. We ask you to bless us at this time of new beginnings, so that we may do the very best we can in every way. *Amen*

*Beginning of a new term*

31. Thank you, dear Father, for our holiday. Now, as we come back to work, we ask you to help us to do our best in everything. *Amen*

*Before Half-term*

32. Now we are half-way through this term, O God, we thank you for all we have done. Help us to enjoy a few days' rest and to return fresh to our work. *Amen*

*At the end of term or school year*

33. We come to the end of this term/school year, dear God, with many things to remember. Thank you for lessons learned and for many happy days with our class-mates. We are thankful for all those people who have helped us. Help us to show our thanks by being thoughtful and kind to others. *Amen*

*A school visit*

34. Today, dear God, the children in Class(es) . . . will be going to visit . . . Be with them and keep them in your care. Help them to enjoy the visit and to behave in such a way that others will enjoy having them around. Then, at the end of the day, bring them safely home. *Amen*

*On open day*

35. Today, dear Father God, our school will be open for our parents to come to see our work and talk to our teachers. Thank you for giving us work to do and for helping us to do it; and thank you for all our teachers and parents who have encouraged us to do it well. *Amen*

The first prayers included in this section are concerned mainly with attitudes of the children towards each other and towards people living near the school. Friction inevitably arises from time to time and these prayers may be helpful on such occasions.

*Ourselves and our neighbours*

36. Father God, please bless the people we shall meet today—the people who live next door; the people we shall meet in the street and those who will serve us in the shops; and all those in and around our school. Please make us thoughtful towards them all. *Amen*

37. Dear God, help us to be polite to everyone today. Show us ways of doing things for people that will show them a little of your love. *Amen*

38. There are many people, dear God, who love and care for us. [We think of . . .] We know that you love us too. May we be thankful and try to return some of that love by being thoughtful and kind to others. *Amen*

39. Dear God, some people we meet are rather grumpy and say nasty or unkind things. Help us to feel sorry for them and try not to do or say things that would upset them more. *Amen*

40. Dear God, sometimes we find it hard to like some people, and perhaps they find it hard to like us. Please help us to be kind to everyone and try hard to be nicer people so that the world about us is a happier place. *Amen*

41. O God, we like to play in the park and have fun [on the swings, the slide and . . .] May we act in such a way that everyone can enjoy the fun and not be hurt or upset because *we* are thoughtless or selfish. *Amen*

42. Please forgive us, dear God, when we know we have done wrong and try to pretend that we haven't. It is hard to own up and say we are wrong, but please make us strong to do right. *Amen*

43. Dear Father God, we find it hard to forgive people when they are mean and hurt us. At those times, please help us to remember that *you* love *us,* even when we are mean and hurt others. So help us to learn how to forgive and forget. *Amen*

44. O God, when we play games we are sometimes tempted to cheat, or argue, or quarrel because *we* always want to win or be the best. Help us to learn that winning or being the best is not as important as the way we play and the fun and pleasure we have in playing together. *Amen*

*Our own community*

45. Today, dear God, we think of our own village [*community/ estate/*. . .] and the people who live in it. We are all different and our ideas are not always the same as those of others, but we have to work together if it is to be a happy place. So help us, please, to learn how to get on well with our neighbours so that we can enjoy each other. *Amen*

*Our town*

46. Our town is a very busy place, dear God. There are so many people and they all seem to have such a lot to do. We think of people who work in shops, offices and factories, on buses and trains, in hospitals, schools and in their homes. There are young folk and old, and some who are not well. And we all need each other. Help us to grow up to be good citizens of our town. *Amen*

## Our local council

47. Thank you, O God, for those people who help to run our town [*city/county/. . .*]. We think of the Mayor [*Lord Mayor/Chairman of the Council/Provost/. . .*] and all the Councillors, who give up so much of their time. We think of people in offices, who are responsible for Housing, Parks, Libraries and Schools. Bless them all, and help them to do what is best for us all. *Amen*

## Election day

48. Today [*Tomorrow*], O God, lots of people will be voting to decide who will be Members of Parliament [*Councillors*]. Please help them to choose well, and help those who are chosen to do what is best for us all. *Amen*

## The Queen and Government

49. Dear Father God, please bless our Queen and her family; bless our Prime Minister and all members of the Government; bless all Members of Parliament and those who help rule our land; and help them all to do their duties wisely and well for the good of us all. *Amen*

## Our world

50. Today, dear Lord God, we remember the nations of the world:
Great powerful nations and very small ones;
Well-to-do countries and very poor ones;
Countries where people have plenty to eat,
And others where people starve;
People in lands where there is freedom,
And those who are often afraid.
We pray for those who need help,
And for the rulers of all the nations,
That we may all learn to help each other
And live together in peace. *Amen*

354

PRAYERS FOR SPECIAL OCCASIONS

*A new baby*

51. We thank you, O God, for new babies. We see their tiny toes and hands and we know that they need us to help care for them. We are glad that . . . has a new baby in the family. Please bless them and keep their baby in your loving care. *Amen*

52. Dear God, a new baby has come into . . .'s family. Please bless *his/her* mother and father, brothers and sisters, and may they all be a loving, happy family. *Amen*

*Someone in hospital*

53. Dear God, we hear that . . . is in hospital. Please take care of *him/her,* and help the doctors and nurses to make *him/her* well again soon so that *he/she* can come back to home and school. Please bless all the family. *Amen*

54. Father God, we know that . . .'s *mother/father/grandma/*. . . is in hospital and that the family will be feeling sad. Please help them to remember that you love them and that there are many people working to make the sick people well again. *Amen*

*After an accident*

55. Dear Father God, we have heard that . . . has had an accident [*and is in hospital*]. *He/she* may be uncomfortable and in pain, so we ask that you will watch over *him/her* and make *him/her* well again soon. *Amen*

## A death

56. Dear God, we know that . . . [and . . .] is/are sad because . . . has died. Please take care of all the family. Help them to understand that . . . is now with you, and that you love and care for them all. *Amen*

## People with problems

57. Dear God, we have heard news today of people who are injured [*hungry/homeless/in danger/. . .*] in . . . Help them in their trouble; speak to people so that they will want to help; and show us if there is anything we can do. *Amen*

58. Dear God, there are many people who need help; people who are sad, or lonely, or sick. Help us to think of these people and do what we can to help them. *Amen*

## In difficult times

59. We hear, O God, about people who hurt each other and we hear of bad things happening in the world. These make us sad. But we know that there are many good things too. Help us to remember the good things we hear and to try to be like the good people we know. *Amen*

60. Dear God, when dark days come and we feel very unhappy or frightened, please help us to remember that you are never far away and that you love us. *Amen*

# CLOSING PRAYERS AND BENEDICTIONS

(An asterisk * denotes a traditional blessing or benediction)

---

61. All through today, in our work and our play, be with us, dear Father, and keep us in your care. *Amen*

62. As we go about our work this day, help us to know, dear God, that you are always with us. *Amen*

63. Be with us, dear Lord, and keep us in your care all through this day. *Amen*

64. Bless us, dear God, at the beginning of this new day; and may your blessing go with us throughout the day. *Amen*

65. Dear God, please show us ways of being kind, loving and thoughtful toward others, all through this day. *Amen*

66. For joy and happiness and all good things, praise be to you, O God. *Amen*

67. Go with us now, O God,
    Help us to do and be the best we can,
    And, at the end of the day, give us grateful
    hearts. *Amen*

68. Help us, God our Father, to remember that we do not just please ourselves but work with other people as a team. Teach us to do our fair share and to do it well. *Amen*

69. Help us to think clean thoughts and to live clean lives, so that we may truly be your children. *Amen*

70. May all we do, and think, and say this day be good and pleasing to you, O God. *Amen*

71. May God the Father bless us and all men everywhere and fill our hearts with his peace and goodwill. *Amen*

72. May the blessing of God Almighty, the Father, the Son, and the Holy Spirit, rest upon us and upon all God's people everywhere, now and for ever. *Amen*\*

73. May the Lord grant us his blessing and fill our hearts with the spirit of truth and peace, now and evermore. *Amen*\*

74. May we use our strength today to help and not hurt, nor offend, nor destroy. May all we do be pleasing to you, O God. *Amen*

75. Now may God bless us and keep us: may he give us light to guide us, courage to support us, and love to unite us, this day and for evermore. *Amen*\*

76. Now, O God, we ask your blessing upon all we do today. Help us to work and play fairly. *Amen*

77. O God, come and dwell in our hearts, so that we may be like you in all our ways; and to you be the glory for ever. *Amen*

78. O God, help me to be nice to know—kind, thoughtful, helpful and a good friend to others. Help me to see any faults that I have and show me how to put them right. *Amen*

79. O God our Father, put that kind of love in our hearts which always makes us think more about others than we do about ourselves. *Amen*

80. O God,
Open my ears that I may hear you speaking to me;
Open my eyes so that I may see how to do your will;
And open my heart so that I may think more of you than I do of myself;
For Jesus Christ's sake. *Amen*

81. O God, our Father,
    You have been with us in this service:
    Be with us as we go to our work and our play,
    And keep near us until the end of the day. *Amen*

82. O God, teach us your ways of wisdom, truth and love, so that
    we may grow more like you in all our ways. *Amen*

83. O God, we thank you for looking after us and for hearing our
    prayers. Help us to learn to love you and to trust you. *Amen*

84. O Lord, may others be able to tell that we love you by the things
    we say and do. *Amen*

85. Please, Father God, hold our hands and lead us in the way you
    would have us go. *Amen*

86. Please God, show us how to use our time today, so that we may
    do the best we can and be the best we can, because we are your
    children. *Amen*

87. Take us into your care and keeping, dear God, and keep us safe
    from all harm and danger. *Amen*

88. Take us, O God, into your care; protect us from evil; help us to
    grow good; and receive us into your kingdom. *Amen*

89. Teach us, O God, to share the good things we have and so bring
    happiness to other folk. *Amen*

90. Thank you, Father God, that you are always with us. Help us to
    remember this all through the day, especially when things go
    wrong. *Amen*

91. Thank you, Father God, that you still love us even when we do
    wrong. Help us to be loving and forgiving to others around us
    today. *Amen*

92. Thank you, Lord, for making us like we are. Help us always to be of use to you and of help to others. *Amen*

93. Thank you, O God, for all the people who love us. Help us to love other people and to be helpful and kind towards them. *Amen*

94. Today, O God, we will find some things easy to do but some will be hard. Please help us to do our best in everything. *Amen*

95. We ask your blessing, dear God, today, for people we love who are far away. And please bless us too. *Amen*

96. We know that you love us, dear God: help us to be more like you today and always. *Amen*

97. We thank you, O God, for all your blessings. Help us to share them with others, knowing that as we do so we are serving you; for Jesus Christ's sake. *Amen*

98. When we find anything difficult today, O God, help us to try hard and give us patience. *Amen*

99. You are always near us, dear God. Help us to remember this all through the day. *Amen*

100. You have given us so many good things, dear God. Help us to use all these gifts for your glory. *Amen*

# INDEX OF HYMNS SUGGESTED

The hymns suggested for use with the various themes in this book have been collated from a number of books that are known to teachers of infants and lower juniors and which are easily obtainable. In some instances only one verse may be particularly applicable to the theme.

All hymns to which reference is made elsewhere are listed below. The letters indicate the name of the hymn book and the figures the number of the hymn in that book. The index is not of page numbers but of the numbers of the themes with which the use of the hymn is suggested.

HYMN BOOK REFERENCES

| | |
|---|---|
| CAS | Come and Sing *(Scripture Union)* |
| JHB | Junior Hymn Book *(Nelson)* |
| MC | Morning Cockerel *(Hart-Davis)* |
| MHB | Morning has broken *(Schofield & Sims)* |
| NCS | New Child Songs *(NCEC)* |
| NO | New Orbit *(Galliard)* |
| S&S | S & S Hymn Book *(Schofield & Sims)* |
| SH | Sing Hosanna *(Holmes McDougall)* |
| SLSL | Sing Life Sing Love *(Holmes McDougall)* |
| SM | Sing it in the Morning *(Nelson)* |
| SP | Songs of Praise (Oxford) |
| SSL | Someone's Singing, Lord *(Black)* |
| SSP | Sunday School Praise *(NCEC)* |
| WCV | With Cheerful Voice *(Black)* |

# INDEX OF PRAYER SUBJECTS

368

370

# GENERAL INDEX

Numbers in brackets refer to activity sections

376

**NOTES**